WORLD
★WAR II★
ON THE AIR

ALSO BY MARK BERNSTEIN

Grand Eccentrics
New Bremen
Gentleman Amateurs

ALSO BY ALEX LUBERTOZZI

The Complete War of the Worlds (with Brian Holmsten)

WORLD ★WAR II★ ON THE AIR

EDWARD R. MURROW AND THE BROADCASTS THAT RIVETED A NATION

Mark Bernstein & Alex Lubertozzi

CD NARRATED BY
DAN RATHER

An Imprint of Sourcebooks Inc.®
Naperville, Illinois

Published by Sourcebooks, Inc.
P.O. Box 4410, Naperville, Illinois 60567-4410
(630) 961-3900
FAX: (630) 961-2168
www.sourcebooks.com

Library of Congress Cataloging-in-Publication Data
Bernstein, Mark.
World War II on the air : Edward R. Murrow and the broadcasts that riveted a
nation / by Mark Bernstein and Alex Lubertozzi.
        p. cm.
    Includes bibliographical references and index.
    ISBN 1-4022-0026-9 (hardcover : alk. paper)
    1. Murrow, Edward R. 2. Journalists—United States—Biography. 3. World
War, 1939–1945—Personal narratives, American. I. Lubertozzi, Alex. II. Title.

PN4874.M89B47 2003
070.92'273—dc21

                                                                2003000842

                Printed and bound in the United States of America
                    LB   10   9   8   7   6   5   4   3   2   1

*To the foreign correspondents
who put their lives on the line to
shed light on one of the darkest
chapters in human history*

Contents

CD Track List

(CD) *This symbol throughout the book denotes text that corresponds to audio on the CD.*

1. **Introduction**

2. **Anschluss**
   Edward R. Murrow (Vienna)—
   March 13, 1938

3. **Eve of War**
   Edward R. Murrow (London) / William
   L. Shirer (Berlin)—August 28, 1939

4. **War Is Declared**
   Edward R. Murrow (London)—
   September 3, 1939

5. **A Peace of Sorts**
   William L. Shirer (Berlin)—
   September 29, 1939

6. **The "Phony War"**
   Edward R. Murrow and William L.
   Shirer (Amsterdam)—January 18, 1940

7. **Hitler's Return**
   Mary Marvin Breckinridge (Berlin)—
   January 30, 1940

8. **Netherlands, Luxembourg, and Belgium Invaded**
   William L. Shirer (Berlin) / Thomas
   Grandin (Paris)—May 10, 1940

9. **Chamberlain Resigns**
   Edward R. Murrow (London)—
   May 10, 1940

10. **German Bombing of Paris**
    Eric Sevareid (Paris)—June 3, 1940

11. **Italy to Enter War**
    Cecil Brown (Rome)—June 4, 1940

12. **Dunkirk / Churchill: "We Shall Never Surrender"**
    Edward R. Murrow (London)—
    June 4, 1940

13. **German Troops Enter Paris**
    William L. Shirer (Berlin)—
    June 14, 1940

14. **France Surrenders at Compiègne Forest**
    William L. Shirer (Compiègne, France)—June 21–22, 1940

15. **London After Dark**
    Edward R. Murrow / Eric Sevareid
    (London)—August 24, 1940

16. **Bombs Over Berlin**
    William L. Shirer (Berlin)—
    August 25, 1940

17. **London Is Burning**
    Edward R. Murrow (London)—
    September 8, 1940

18. **A Few German Pilots**
    Edward R. Murrow (London)—
    September 10, 1940

19. **Rooftop Air Raid**
    Edward R. Murrow (London)—
    September 20, 1940

20. **Christmas / "So Long and Good Luck"**
    Edward R. Murrow (London)—
    December 24, 1940

21. **"The Bombing Has Been Heavy"**
    Edward R. Murrow (London)—
    April 16, 1941

22. **Big Ben Bombed**
    Larry LeSueur (London)—
    May 11, 1941

23. **Japanese Embassy**
    Eric Sevareid (Washington, D.C.)—
    December 7, 1941

Freedom is not to be bought
in the bargain basement—
nor for a lump sum—it must be
paid for and argued about by
each succeeding generation.
—*Edward R. Murrow*

Preface

THIS BOOK, WHICH was conceived aboard an island hopper somewhere over the Caribbean, came into being for the want of two things: an audio compilation of the actual broadcasts of Edward R. Murrow, and a project to take the place of the one I'd just finished.

Having recently completed a book on Orson Welles' infamous panic broadcast, I was searching for something to fill the void left by finishing that lengthy, all-consuming project. In that book, I had noted that the panic created by the "War of the Worlds" broadcast was helped in no small part by the innovative brand of live radio broadcasts that were then interrupting programs to warn listeners of news in Europe. I had been focused for over a year on those prewar radio days—in particular, 1938. It was the year of the Anschluss and the Munich Pact. It was also the year that Edward R. Murrow made his first news broadcast from Vienna—covering the entry of Hitler and Nazi troops into Austria.

Murrow and a man who is today thought of mainly as a great historian, William L. Shirer, quickly became the top broadcast journalists in Europe. They had a keen sense for news and, more important, for seeking out the truth. They also understood, far better than most in America and even Europe, the looming significance of those events and of Hitler's continuing grabs for more and more power. Soon, Murrow would recruit a remarkable group of reporters to cover the war.

So, in short, here were the men and women making the broadcasts of actual attacks, invasions, and conquests—from rooftops, street corners, and battlefields—not simply creating hysteria through the imagined exploits of creatures from Mars. They covered the entire war, from its buildup to its aftermath, all over the globe. It's an unbelievable story surrounding the central event of the twentieth century. It's also a story that has to be heard to be understood.

Others had told specific aspects of this story before, and told them well. What was missing was a book that told the story of the Second World War through their experiences, their eyes, and their voices. And it needed to be told in concert with the broadcasts themselves. It seemed to me then that this was one hell of a story, and one hell of a way to tell it. Mark Bernstein, my collaborator, enthusiastically agreed, and with the help and cooperation of CBS, we began to put it together.

World War II is a massive, daunting subject. Focusing on the reporting of the Murrow Boys allowed us to tell the story of the war in a more cohesive, straightforward way. It also meant that much of the story would necessarily be left out. The war in Asia is touched on—memorably, by Cecil Brown in Singapore and Eric Sevareid in China—but not in great detail. It's not that the war with Japan was not covered on the radio, or by CBS. But it does reflect that coverage in the Pacific was for the most part limited to reports far from the action—a result of the technical constraints at the time of covering island warfare. Despite the limitations of the technology, Murrow and his band managed to cover the conflict live from London, Berlin, Paris, Rome, Amsterdam, Belgrade, Ankara, Singapore, the Soviet Union, China, Australia, and North Africa, and pioneered the use of recordings from the beaches at Normandy, a C-47 flying over Holland, and house-to-house fighting in Aachen, Germany.

For my coauthor and I, the central task of this book was researching and gathering the archival audio. Listening to more than a hundred hours of wartime broadcasts enabled us to construct a framework for the narrative and to assemble the audio excerpts that would illustrate the story on the CD. We chose the broadcasts to include with a great deal of consideration and deliberation. With such a wealth of great reporting on events both large and small, deciding which broadcasts not to include was an agonizing process— akin to having to choose which pinky you could live without. The broadcasts were scrupulously edited for time, so as not to alter in any way their meaning or impact. In a few cases, archival restoration was performed to improve the clarity of the recording, but for the most part, the broadcasts sound exactly as they did when they first aired. The narration, which was written during the audio-editing stage, serves to introduce and provide context for the broadcasts and the broadcasters. We were extremely fortunate to have Dan Rather narrate the CD, as he brought a wealth of knowledge and understanding to the audio component.

You will notice, throughout the book, markers (**CD**) alerting you to the CD tracks that correspond to the passage you're reading. But the book and audio CD are not meant to be used in any one way. Some of you will want to listen to the audio first; some may want to read the book all the way through before hearing the broadcasts; and others will want to go back and forth between the page and the CD player. The idea is to allow you to experience the story in more than one way. The audio component of this book also allows you to share the experience, whether as teacher to student, parent to child, or simply as great drama.

As history, the Second World War represents an endless source of inspiration for writers—it provides conflict on a gigantic scale (both physical and philosophical), and it offers a glimpse into the best and worst of humanity. The story of the Murrow Boys and the war matters. Their story deserves to be told and retold not simply because they bore witness to the best and the worst, but because they represented the best themselves.

Alex Lubertozzi

WORLD
★WAR II★
ON THE AIR

PROLOGUE

AUGUST 1940

For a few brief years a few men attempted to do an honest job of reporting under difficult and sometimes hazardous conditions and they did not altogether fail.
—*Edward R. Murrow*

TRACKS: 15–16

Previous page: Edward R. Murrow in Piccadilly Circus, London

London After Dark

LATE ON SATURDAY night, August 24, 1940, Edward Roscoe Murrow stood at St. Martin-in-the-Fields at the northeast corner of London's Trafalgar Square. Murrow was the chief European correspondent for the Columbia Broadcasting System. Tonight, he was broadcasting from a city at war. Air-raid sirens sounded. As Murrow spoke, Londoners, singly and in clumps, moved silently past him in the dark down the stairs of St. Martin's to the makeshift bomb shelter in its crypt.

Murrow described the scene: "Here comes one of those big buses around the corner...just a few lights on the top deck. In this blackness, it looks very much like a ship that's passing in the night....More searchlights come into action. You see them reach straight up into the sky and occasionally they catch a cloud and seem to splash on the bottom of it." **CD** London is a low, TRACK 15 sprawling city rich in history and tradition; St. Martin's, where Murrow stood, is the traditional parish church of the British monarch. On the night of the broadcast, London was the stage on which the world's most important history was being played out. With the surrender of France two months before, England stood alone, the last nation resisting Nazi domination of the Old World. Adolf Hitler boasted that he would "wring England's neck like a chicken," a boast many thought could be made good. Hitler's instrument of conquest was the Luftwaffe, whose Messerschmitts and Henkels came nightly by the hundreds into England's late summer skies.

As Murrow delivered his broadcast, the Luftwaffe's planes began arriving over London, the sound of their engines clear to Murrow on the ground and to his listeners in America. To the sound of aircraft overhead, Murrow added

TRACK 15

a second. He lowered his microphone to pavement level, so listeners could hear the unhurried steps of Londoners passing by. With London in blackout, faces and bodies obscured, Murrow reached for a telling phrase to describe the sound of footsteps—"walking along the street, like ghosts shod with steel shoes." CD His next sentence underscored the city's calm: "A taxi draws up in front and stops, just waiting for the red light to change as the sirens holler."

This was characteristic Murrow reporting. He was not taking the facts to his listeners as much as he was bringing his listeners to the scene, painting a picture that those in living rooms thousands of miles distant could see in their imaginations. This style was Murrow's own. He did not transfer it from experience with newspaper reporting; Murrow had never worked as a reporter, nor been trained as one. It was not standard to radio—live, on-the-scene news reporting was so recent, no real standards existed. Indeed, it could hardly be said to be the child of experience, as Murrow, at thirty-two, was not greatly experienced at anything. The Second World War brought many, in uniform and government, to broad attention. Murrow became, arguably, the war's most important civilian. He was tall, slender, and earnest, but what millions in America knew best of him was his voice, a resonant baritone that—as on this night—was taking a war far from the nation's thoughts and making it something palpable, nearby, and real.

Murrow's talk from St. Martin's was one segment of a larger production; that night, he was orchestrating "London After Dark," with broadcasts from reporters scattered throughout the city. From Murrow near Trafalgar Square, the broadcast carried to the posh Savoy Hotel, where François Latry, the hotel's famed chef, bid a heavily accented greeting to "his friends in America" and assured them that "the war has not affected my cooking." Whatever privations wartime brought others, the Savoy's diners that evening were choosing from caviar and seven other hors d'oeuvres, as well as eight meat dishes, including fresh game.

Next, the broadcast swung to an antiaircraft battery, where the correspondent reported that the cannon was being "brought around to the direction in which the enemy is expected. I can now hear...the distant drone of the airplanes." From there, the report shifted to an Air Raid Precautions station set up in a London apartment complex. The station, CBS's correspondent

Larry LeSueur reported, received warnings of approaching aircraft from spotters on the coast, then used colors to indicate status. Yellow meant: "Be on your guard." Red meant: "Start up first-aid cars and ambulances." LeSueur heard and passed along the words: "Stretcher party, one ambulance, one car to 114 High Street. Sector 220. Messenger, don't forget your helmet."

The correspondents' voices traveled to an underground bunker at Broadcasting House, the large and unattractive headquarters of the British Broadcasting Corporation. The sound was then relayed by shortwave to Long Island, New York, from there to the host CBS studio in New York City, and on to the 115 affiliated CBS stations and their listeners. Often, sunspots or atmospheric static played havoc with the signal, reducing it to a metallic echo; this night's report came through clear.

THE WAR'S MOST IMPORTANT CIVILIAN

Edward R. Murrow, the most trusted voice on the radio, took his microphone to the streets of London in August 1940.

Those reports included one from Eric Sevareid, hired by Murrow the previous year. At 11:45 P.M., Sevareid was at the huge Hammersmith Palais dance hall, London's largest. "Few spots are busier on a Saturday night," he said, "air-raid warning or not." The orchestra leader had just "told the crowd he was willing to play on past the midnight wartime closing hour." Of those snatching a bit of gaiety in wartime, Sevareid said, "I don't expect more than half a dozen people have left." ⓒⒹ The broadcast conveyed the city's size and variety, moving to correspondent Vincent Sheean, who spoke of the silent streets at Piccadilly Circus and on to London's cavernous Euston Station for some words with British railway workers.

TRACK 15

The program ended at Whitehall Court, a remnant of Whitehall Castle and perhaps England's most famous spot. Here, Henry VIII had secretly married Anne Boleyn; here, their daughter Elizabeth had plotted England's rise. Now, speaking for CBS, British critic and novelist J.B. Priestley spoke of war's dreadful cost. Looking out the window, Priestley said, he could see the Cenotaph, England's tribute to its one million war dead of 1914 to 1918, "many of them friends of mine, boys that I played with as a boy, men that might have been leaders now." Priestley then tied history and war to the urgent present. England was under attack; Europe was under barbarism. The current struggle, Priestley said, made Whitehall "the very center of the hopes of free men everywhere. It's the heart of this great rock that's defying the dark tide of invasion that has destroyed freedom all over western Europe."

The broadcast closed. The correspondents, with the adrenaline rush of performance, remained awake. Murrow and Vincent Sheean walked through the city to London Bridge. Bombs had set oil dumps along the Thames ablaze. The pair watched from the bridge as flames spread along the river.

MURROW AND HIS correspondents had not known at what moment the German bombers would strike. Their arrival lent a chilling immediacy to the CBS broadcast. From the standpoint of the war, however, that night's attack had a greater significance. In August 1940, England feared invasion. If the German Messerschmitts could drive Britain's Spitfires and Hurricanes from the skies, the British fleet would, for lack of air cover, be forced from the English Channel. With the fleet withdrawn, invasion could proceed. The night of the broadcast, the Luftwaffe focused its attacks on Britain's military airfields. The airfields were military targets; thus far, the Luftwaffe had avoided residential London. On August 24, however—and possibly the night before—bombs fell on London's populous East End. The Germans insisted this had been by mistake. Nonetheless, British Prime Minister Winston Churchill ordered retaliation. Eighty RAF bombers were sent to Berlin the following night.

Our Man in Berlin

IN AUGUST 1940, bombs fell on the just and the unjust alike. The bombs from Churchill's "retaliatory" raid on Berlin landed near William L. Shirer, CBS's chief correspondent in Berlin, whom Murrow had signed on in 1938. Churchill's retaliatory bombers reached Berlin just as Shirer was leaving the censor's office, ready to walk the two hundred yards to the broadcast facility for his regular one A.M. broadcast. As he stepped outside, the antiaircraft guns protecting the radio station began firing. Shirer heard a sound "like hail falling on a tin roof....It was shrapnel from the antiaircraft guns." Two days before, he had reported on the potato crop and the urgings of a tennis journal that the game be played in German: *hochball* rather than "lob." Now, somebody was dropping bombs on him. Berliners had been assured by Göring that British bombers could never penetrate the city's defenses. The five million shocked citizens of Berlin, rushing madly to their shelters, were now learning different. Shirer dashed to the studio and reached the door, where an SS guard told him he was "crazy," then asked to see his pass. In the studio, the engineer directed Shirer to speak near the microphone, presumably, Shirer thought, so that his American listeners would not hear the sound of Berlin under attack. 🄲🄳

TRACK 16

OUR MAN IN BERLIN

William L. Shirer made more than two hundred broadcasts
from Nazi Germany—most after the war began.

This was a minor manipulation. In this instance, it failed. In New York, CBS announcer Elmer Davis called listeners' attention to the sounds of bombing. Manipulation was a constant in war coverage. Those who reported on the conflict were always subject to governments that hoped to manage the flow of information to their own advantage. Governments lied, or were simply wrong. Of the raids of August 24, the official German claim was that sixty-four British planes had been shot down; the total later established was twenty-two. Governments censored. The night following the attack, Shirer intended to report: "Almost everyone I ran into today could produce a handful of shrapnel picked up in the streets or in the gardens after the raid." The German censor crossed that sentence out.

Censorship was an obstacle; war was a hazard. On most evenings, Murrow broadcast from Broadcasting House, entering a building latticed with sandbags and descending three flights of stairs to an underground studio. Four times, CBS was bombed out of its tiny London office. Once, just after Murrow, LeSueur, and Sevareid had exited Broadcast House for the street, Murrow darted into a doorway. LeSueur and Sevareid followed suit. At that moment, the shredded casing of an antiaircraft shell crashed where they had been standing.

Faced with the hazards of war and the fogging of governments, Murrow, Shirer, Sevareid, and others reported through a still-new medium on the largest event of the twentieth century. They made thousands of broadcasts.

COLLECTIVELY, THEY BECAME known as the Murrow Boys, though, indeed, not all were male. Individually, they comprised an eclectic group—including several Rhodes Scholars, the great-granddaughter of a U.S. vice president, and a Soviet spy. Through Murrow's inspiration and example, they made broadcast history, creating the forms and fashions of broadcast journalism and giving their employer, the Columbia Broadcasting System, paramount standing in the field. From 1939 to 1941, they reported the Nazi war machine's devastation and occupation of most of Europe, Hitler's shockingly quick defeat of France, the German air force's Blitz of London, and England's steadfast resolve to resist the overwhelming force against it. In so doing, they brought that war, its events, issues, and inevitable consequences, to Americans at home to consider, engage, and choose their own course.

1

THE GATHERING STORM

I sensed that the crowd this time had a definite objective—and it had. In a few minutes, it had poured into the small square opposite the Fatherland-front headquarters. A few ringleaders quickly tore down the government election posters and the Fatherland-front banners, and hoisted the Nazi hooked-cross amid deafening cheers from their followers.

—*William L. Shirer*
report on the Anschluss, March 12, 1938

TRACKS: 1–2

Radio Days

THE STORY OF Edward R. Murrow falls at the intersection of two larger events: the rise of radio and the descent of Europe into war. In the former, Murrow found his character; in the latter, his stage. Without those larger events, his story would have occurred much differently. Without some under-standing of those events, Murrow's achievement cannot be appreciated.

Of Murrow and radio, Murrow was the elder. He was born on April 24, 1908, as Egbert Roscoe Murrow, in his parents' eighteenth-century log cabin, beside Polecat Creek in the Piedmont of North Carolina. The first commer-cial radio station, Pittsburgh's KDKA, didn't begin broadcasting until 1920.

Today, to be "plugged in" might mean an Internet connection and a cell phone. By the late 1920s, the important plug was the one that ran from the wall outlet to the Philco. Demand was huge. In 1928, Americans spent an astonishing $650 million on radios; within a decade, most American homes had one.

The early airwaves were cluttered and disordered. Innumerable small stations sought breathing space on the bandwidth. As is often the case, sig-nificant development came from a man with a better understanding of radio's commercial possibilities than of the new technology itself. Enter David Sarnoff. In 1926, Sarnoff organized the country's first national radio network: the National Broadcasting Corporation. Soon, hundreds of small stations were connected to the two networks he operated—NBC Red and NBC Blue (which was sold in 1943, becoming the basis for the ABC network). A year later, a rival emerged, the Columbia Phonograph Broadcasting Sys-tem—later, simply the Columbia Broadcasting System, or CBS.

One early CBS advertiser was the Congress Cigar Company. Its owners, Samuel and Jacob Paley, credited radio advertising with a boom in sales of their La Palina cigars. Samuel's son, William, an executive with Congress, had supervised the radio program they sponsored, "The La Palina Smoker." William's interest in radio and his overriding ambition, combined with a $1 million windfall from his family's sale of Congress stock, led to his purchase of a majority stake in the Columbia Broadcasting System in 1928. At the age of twenty-six, William S. Paley became the head of CBS.

Paley, more than any other individual, built CBS into the network it would become. In the late 1920s, he won over a large number of new affiliates (he started with only twenty-two) and brought in a great deal more in advertising revenues. He did it in an innovative way. While NBC paid its affiliates for carrying sponsored programming, it charged them for unsponsored, or "sustaining," programs. Paley made an offer to his affiliates: free sustaining programs and an overall increase in network programming from ten to twenty hours per week. In exchange, affiliates would only get paid for sponsored programming in excess of five hours per week and would have to agree to run sponsored programs at the times the network set. At first, the affiliates made no money on the deal, but they received ten additional hours of much-needed programming. Plus, they were guaranteed not to lose money. Advertisers, meanwhile, were drawn by the promise that their ads would run at the same time across the entire network—something NBC couldn't deliver.

Paley also had an ear for what the public liked to hear. He made stars of two little-known singers, Bing Crosby and Kate Smith. He raided NBC's talent, signing George Burns and Gracie Allen, Fred Allen, and others. Radio was then largely light fare: concerts, vaudeville stars like Jack Benny and Al Jolson, and continuing serials such as *Little Orphan Annie* and *Buck Rogers in the Year 2433*.

Radio brought Benny, Crosby, and Little Orphan Annie, but it brought very little in the way of news. A medium with an unparalleled capacity to bring the day's events quickly to millions had no great inclination to do so. In part, this reflected the idea that Depression-era audiences wanted escape. In part, it was because news broadcasts rarely drew advertisers. And in part, it was because news coverage cost money. Some stations sidestepped the

William S. Paley
1901–1990
b. Chicago, Illinois

William S. Paley was born September 28, 1901, in a cramped apartment behind his father's cigar shop, in a poor Jewish neighborhood on Chicago's West Side. His humble beginnings would soon change. William's father, Samuel, had emigrated from Russia as a child, and with his brother Jacob, built the Congress Cigar Company into the basis of the Paley family fortune.

A poor student as a child, Paley was helped in elementary school by a teacher who mistook his dozing behind an open book for reading. He graduated at seventeen from the Western Military Academy in Alton, Illinois, and moved on to the University of Chicago. In 1919, the family and business moved to Philadelphia.

Paley entered the University of Pennsylvania's Wharton School of Business. But his real learning occurred at Congress Cigar, under his father and uncle, who steadily expanded the business. In 1926, the Paleys sold 200,000 of their 350,000 shares for almost $14 million. Paley made $1 million on the sale and was promoted to vice president, making $20,000 a year. But Paley yearned for something more glamorous. The success they achieved in advertising one of their leading cigars on radio led to the pivotal decision of young William's life.

The future godfather of American broadcasting had never even heard a radio broadcast until 1925, when he listened to a primitive crystal set at a friend's apartment. At first, Paley could not believe that music was actually flying through the air. "I was very dubious," he said. "I thought my friend was playing a trick on me." Once convinced, he was hooked. He had a set made and spent night after night trying to pick up signals from as far away as Chicago and Kansas City.

Although Paley later claimed that it was he who had seen the potential of radio, it was initially his father and uncle who convinced *him* of radio's merits. When Paley purchased CBS, it was a minor affiliation of stations with a smattering of programs—a pipsqueak competitor next to the already established NBC, led by David Sarnoff. But the Paleys knew that CBS had the potential to become a much larger enterprise

continued

than Congress Cigar. Even if it didn't pan out, Paley's father reasoned, it would at least bring his son valuable management experience. Paley focused on its grander potential.

Paley followed his father's advice to "hire smart people and then have the good sense to listen to them." In 1929, he brought to CBS Edward L. Bernays, the nephew of Sigmund Freud and the father of modern public relations, who became an integral advisor to Paley in almost every aspect of the business. He hired Ed Klauber, a former editor for the *New York Times*, on Bernays's recommendation (Klauber later fired Bernays, deeming him unnecessary). Klauber would become indispensable to Paley. He helped Paley to see that a strong news division could reap benefits for CBS beyond ratings. It was this, as much as bringing on board such talent as George Burns and Gracie Allen, Bing Crosby, Kate Smith, and Will Rogers, that led CBS to both a more elevated image and higher profits than its larger rival, NBC.

Another influence on Paley at the time was his wife, Dorothy Hart Hearst, whom he married in 1932. Her style and intellect would greatly impact his views while building the network.

When America entered the war, Paley served as the supervisor of the Office of War Information (OWI), setting up Allied radio stations in North Africa and Italy. He joined Eisenhower's staff in London in 1944, as a colonel in OWI's Psychological Warfare Division. After V-E Day, he was in charge of the de-Nazification of all German media.

In 1947, he divorced Dorothy, with whom he had adopted two children, and wed Barbara (Babe) Cushing. Together, they had two children and were prominent figures in New York's social life. The two would stay together until her death in 1978.

After the war, Paley turned his attention to television. He introduced such stars as Lucille Ball and Ed Sullivan to TV and lured away Jack Benny and Jackie Gleason from other networks. By 1950, CBS was the leader among the three TV networks, a lead it held until the mid-1970s. Paley had uncanny programming instincts, supporting such programs as *M*A*S*H* and *All in the Family* over the objection of network executives.

As chairman and CEO, Paley exercised firm control over most areas of the business, which grew to include recording, publishing, and children's toys. He waived the mandatory retirement age in 1966 so that he could remain as CBS's head. He reluctantly retired as CEO in 1977, but remained as chairman until 1983. Unhappy with CBS's performance, Paley returned to the post in 1987. He died from a heart attack on October 26, 1990.

possibility of offending advertisers by letting the advertisers write the news. For a time, the daily NBC news roundup was written by the public relations department of Sun Oil. Many stations cut costs by cadging news from the Associated Press, United Press, or International News Service.

In the place of serious news, the networks presented commentary. NBC had Lowell Thomas, who was a gifted storyteller, but not much of a newsman. CBS offered the public H.V. Kaltenborn, a serious journalist with a clipped, autocratic delivery; and, at one time America's most popular commentator, the absurd figure of Boake Carter. Carter was a figment of his own imagination. Born in Baku, Azerbaijan, this son of an Irish oil executive claimed to be the child of a British diplomat and a graduate of Cambridge. He postured as an English squire, with pipe, tweeds, and an upper-crust accent, through which "by jingo" and "cheerio" added spice to his views. Those views were of uncertain origin. CBS's announcer Robert Trout stated, "Nobody ever had the faintest idea what he was doing, where he got his news." Trying to keep their commentator at least vaguely in touch with the news of the world, CBS ran a special teletype machine to Carter's country estate near Philadelphia. Future Murrow Boy Larry LeSueur manned the machine in New York, giving frequent explanations of the significance of the day's news to Carter. Frequently, however, Carter just made it up. His opinions started out on the conservative side and drifted steadily to the right; eventually, he would declare that President Roosevelt, not Hitler, was the greatest threat to world peace—a point of view that would eventually ease his departure.

There was little news reporting from Europe. In London, CBS maintained a one-man bureau; the man was Cesar Saerchinger, who had sold the network on the idea of "radio talks" by the notable and newsworthy. Saerchinger arranged talks by George Bernard Shaw, Pope Pius XI, H.G. Wells, Leon Trotsky, and hundreds of others. Further afield, he went to Austria to broadcast music festivals, to France to put the nation's Bastille Day celebrations on the air, and to Kent, in England, where he secured the performance of a nightingale, for which he won the award for "most interesting broadcast of 1932." Securing the nightingale's performance was not easy, since CBS required that it be presented live.

Circumstances would soon push CBS into the business of serious news. For years, many stations simply rewrote and broadcast news accounts delivered by the day's wire services. Understandably, the nation's newspapers resented this. Radio had been steadily draining off its advertising revenues, and now it was stealing its thunder as the country's purveyor of news. In 1933, the wire services—under newspaper pressure—cut off the flow. Associated Press announced it would "not allow any news distributed by the Associated Press, regardless of source, to be given to any radio chain or chains." Other wire services followed suit.

As a result, CBS initiated its own news operation. It was principally the work of two men: Ed Klauber, Paley's executive vice president (who essentially ran the network), a former *New York Times* editor with high standards and a strong ego, and Paul White, a former United Press editor, who was then CBS's director of news. CBS set up bureaus in New York, Washington, Chicago, and Los Angeles, adding part-time correspondents in many other cities. The CBS effort broke the lockout, and the networks and the wire services came to terms. By those terms, the wire services agreed to supply a limited quantity of news, and the networks agreed to hold their news broadcasts until after the morning and afternoon newspapers had hit the streets.

The agreement ignored technical reality. Radio was simply too fluid and flexible. To get out the news, a newspaper had to cast a story in lead, clamp it to a rotary press, chop and fold the printed newspapers, and toss them by the pile to waiting newsboys, who would make a street corner resound with cries of "Extra! Extra!" In contrast, all radio had to do was announce: "We interrupt this broadcast..." Still, by the mid-1930s, radio's power to inform lay largely unrealized.

In September 1935, a tall, dark, young man with piercing eyes arrived at 485 Madison Avenue (CBS headquarters in Manhattan) for an interview with Klauber. The young man presented well: he was intelligent, articulate, organized, and quite mature for the thirty-two years he claimed and the twenty-seven he actually was. Klauber offered him the post of "director of talks"—that is, scheduler of live radio presentations—in New York, reporting to Klauber. The young man was Edward R. Murrow.

A Man in the World's New Fashion

A man in the world's new fashion planted
that hath a mint of phrases in his brain.
—*William Shakespeare*, Love's Labour's Lost

ED MURROW, HAVING moved with his family at the age of five from the
Piedmont of North Carolina to the Pacific Northwest logging town of Blan-
chard, Washington, had dropped "Egbert," a named he loathed, by the time
he was in high school. The valedictorian of his graduating class, Murrow
would have to work a full year before earning the money needed to attend
modest Washington State College. Never well-off (the Murrows' first home
in Washington was a tent pitched on relatives' land), Murrow went to work
as an axman on a logging crew in the Olympic forests. He had taken the
name "Ed" while working the Pacific Northwest woods, a name with a more
grown-up ring to it and, as he later explained, one that saved him from having to fight every lumberjack on the West Coast. From this experience, Murrow gained a greater appreciation of the lives of working men, as well as a
lumberjack's capacity to drink and swear.

Once at WSC, Murrow continued to work part-time and initially majored
in business administration. He managed to earn Bs in economics courses his
first semester, despite barely studying. But it was during his second semester
that he found his calling in an instructor who would help change the course of
his studies and his life. Her name was Ida Lou Anderson. A fellow southern
transplant (from Tennessee), she had been deformed by childhood polio. With
the double curvature of her spine, she stood not quite five feet tall. But the
stooped, twenty-six-year-old instructor towered in the minds and hearts of
many of her students. "She was cruelly dwarfed, twisted, and hunched," one
of her students later remarked, "but to [us] she was a fount, a flaming spirit."

One of Murrow's friends spoke of Anderson's profound impact on him,
and recommended he take her "Fundamentals of Freshman Speech" during
his second semester. An accomplished debater in high school, Murrow lobbied Anderson successfully to take the advanced "Intermediate Public

Speaking" concurrently with the freshman course. A remarkable teacher, Anderson eschewed traditional lectures, textbooks, and examinations. She worked her students hard, encouraging them to find and project the essence of the written word. And she recognized talent when she found it. She quickly took a special interest in Murrow, tutoring him privately in her home, and introducing him to the philosophical prose of Marcus Aurelius's *The Meditations* and to the romantic poets she adored, such as John Masefield and Christina Rossetti.

"A MINT OF PHRASES IN HIS BRAIN."

The foundations for Ed Murrow's career in broadcasting were laid in college.

Anderson and her star pupil became devoted friends. He would continue their relationship after college and would seek her advice as his career as a broadcaster blossomed, until the end of her life in September 1941.

Under Anderson's tutelage, Murrow thrived at WSC, going on to become president of the student government, star in student plays, and even become cadet colonel of the ROTC. Eventually, his burgeoning leadership potential took him beyond Washington State. In his senior year, he was elected president of the Pacific Student Presidents Association and attended the convention of the National Student Federation of America (NSFA) at Stanford University in Palo Alto, California. The focus of the convention, and of the organization's delegates, was the prevention of another devastating world war. Perhaps ironically for the ROTC cadet colonel, Murrow delivered an antiwar speech of such poise, tenor, and passion that the delegates' choice for NSFA president was plain.

This student office led to Murrow's first job after graduation. Elected to a second term as president, the NSFA executive committee offered him $25 a week living expenses to run the national office in New York. In 1930, with banks failing, factories closing, bread lines forming, and job prospects looking grim for most, it was the kind of opportunity a young Ed Murrow couldn't afford to pass up.

Murrow did audition for a job as an announcer with NBC while in New York, and he was offered a position. However, he chose the promise of foreign travel with the NSFA over the lure of radio.

His first trip abroad would be to represent the United States to the Confederation Internationale des Etudiants (CIE) at its conference in Belgium. First staying over in London, his initial impression of England was colored by two straight weeks of rain. Upon arriving in Brussels, Murrow's eyes would be opened to the petty bickering and open hostility of the various student factions representing Poles and Germans, Italians and Austrians, Serbs and Croats, and the former allies and enemies from the Great War. German delegates, while permitted to attend programs, were barred from CIE membership by the student delegates from Britain, France, and Belgium, a situation Murrow deplored. Murrow himself was enthusiastically received by his European counterparts, who wished to elect him president of the CIE. Murrow refused to accept the position as long as the Germans were denied membership—a concession Germany's former enemies were ultimately unwilling to make.

During his tenure with the NSFA, Murrow managed to increase the number of black member colleges and integrate black students into NSFA's annual convention in segregated Atlanta, a feat of remarkable integrity, courage, and political acumen for one just twenty-one years of age. He also set up an NSFA-sponsored program on CBS, *University of the Air*. Its first guest speaker, arranged by Murrow, was Albert Einstein. Murrow subsequently helped to deliver other speakers for the series, such as Rabindranath Tagore, Mohandas K. Gandhi, German President von Hindenburg, and British Prime Minister Ramsay MacDonald.

In 1932, after two years' running the NSFA in New York, Murrow was lured away by Professor Stephen Duggan, the founder and director of the Institute of International Education (IIE). Duggan, a professor emeritus at the College of the City of New York and founder of its political science and education departments, was an imposing figure. A close friend of Franklin Roosevelt, the sixty-seven-year-old Duggan was a reform-minded pioneer in international educational exchange—the focus of the IIE. Seeing the chance to advance his career and take on a more prominent role in international education, Murrow jumped at the opportunity. Hired as Duggan's assistant, Murrow ran the day-to-day operation of the IIE, while Duggan formulated policy.

Murrow's last function with the NSFA would be an important one personally, if not professionally. On the train to the 1932 NSFA Convention in New Orleans, he met Janet Huntington Brewster, who was also on her way to the convention, representing Mount Holyoke College in Massachusetts. When they arrived, he asked her to breakfast, and they subsequently began a correspondence and courtship upon returning east.

IN MARCH 1933, Hitler was elected chancellor of Germany, and Nazis dominated the Reichstag. As Hitler proceeded to purge German institutions of his political opponents and all non-Aryans, and as student mobs burned "subversive" books in Berlin, Duggan and the IIE led a coalition of twenty-one American college heads to form the Emergency Committee in Aid of

"TO US, SHE WAS A FOUNT, A FLAMING SPIRIT."
Ida Lou Anderson, who had been crippled by childhood polio,
was Murrow's mentor at Washington State College and beyond.

Displaced German Scholars. The committee's purpose was to place academics targeted by the Nazis in American universities; Murrow would be responsible for implementing its mission. As assistant secretary for the Emergency Committee, Murrow's participation in helping some of the best minds in Europe escape Nazi Germany proved to be one of the most difficult, and rewarding, chapters of his life. He would, over two years, help to bring 335 scholars to American universities, including novelist Thomas Mann, physicist James Franck, political scientist Karl Loewenstein, philosopher Herbert Marcuse, and theologian Martin Buber. Accomplishing this feat was a political and logistical nightmare—Murrow had to fight red tape and conflicting interests abroad, as well as apathy and outright anti-Semitism at home. The more than three hundred scholars, scientists, mathematicians, and philosophers he aided were the fortunate ones from a group of more than six thousand applicants.

In the midst of this drama, Murrow married Janet Brewster on October 27, 1934. Duggan gave the exhausted Murrow a two-month leave to enjoy his honeymoon. As much as Murrow enjoyed his work with the IIE and the Emergency Committee, it was in its way a dead end for the ambitious young man. Frustration with the committee increased, and Murrow would always be number two to Duggan, who limited Murrow's influence to administrative concerns. Murrow's connection to radio, CBS in particular, had lain dormant since the NSFA's *University of the Air*. When Duggan launched an educational series on Columbia's American School of the Air, its educational network, Murrow was thrown into that world again. He coordinated these broadcasts—lectures by Duggan on foreign affairs—with CBS and became reacquainted with Fred Willis, William Paley's assistant, who had worked with Murrow on the NSFA series.

Duggan's talks were, in some ways, a precursor to the kind of reporting Murrow would perfect later on—objective, informed, aimed at a broad audience, but presenting facts from a distinct point of view. The series was a success. Fred Willis, who knew well Murrow's abilities, arranged the meeting for Murrow with Ed Klauber. It was an opportunity for something new, something riskier to be sure (who knew what the future of radio would be?), but a challenge that captured the imagination of the ambitious twenty-seven-year-old. Besides, radio was bound to be less draining than the Emergency Committee. Klauber offered Murrow the job, "director of talks to coordinate broadcasts on current issues," or "director of talks," for short. He accepted.

THE POSITION KEPT Murrow busy. In 1936, Murrow coordinated 311 broadcasts. A company publicity release said of his efforts: "It is Murrow whose work has caused him to telephone Rome at one A.M. of a day early in December and arrange for a speaker to go on CBS at 9:15 the same morning with a report of ailing Pope Pius XI's condition....He it is who watches as Congress goes into session, ready to place on the air speakers representing both sides of a legislative development as it comes out of committee."

The job came with a price. CBS was a corporation on the move, and among those hoping to move up within it was Paul White, director of public affairs and special events. White pegged Murrow as a rival. White, talented in his own right, had an additional talent for spotting and exploiting the vulnerabilities in others. In Murrow's case, curiously, this included his looks. Murrow's CBS secretary, Helen Sioussat, said upon meeting him: "I had never seen such a handsome man in my life." White dismissed Murrow as a "pretty boy" and a "ladies' man"—to the irritation of his recently married and somewhat prudish rival. White considered the capacity to consume alcohol to be a suitable test of manhood. By one account, Murrow, challenged by White, drank him under the table.

In February 1937, Klauber offered Murrow the post then held by Cesar Saerchinger in London. In America, CBS was holding its own against NBC; in Europe, it trailed badly. Klauber thought Murrow might close that gap. For Murrow, the offer was a mixed blessing. It offered far greater scope than his post in New York, but it would make him a subordinate to White. After a good deal of deliberation with Janet, the opportunity proved irresistible. Murrow signed on.

Foreign Correspondent

WAR WAS JUST over the horizon when Ed and Janet Murrow sailed from New York on April 1, 1937, bound for London on the *Manhattan*. They gave the appearance of being a sophisticated couple. This was more natural in her case than in his. Janet Brewster was a Connecticut native who could trace her heritage back to the *Mayflower*. Ed Murrow was from a place called "Polecat Creek," and migrated to the Pacific Northwest, where he was raised amidst loggers and railway workers. She graduated from Mount Holyoke. He attended the nearby "cow college," Washington State. When the couple had married in 1934, Janet set aside a possible acting career to make the match.

Shipboard, the Murrows ran into an American photographer and documentary filmmaker, Mary Marvin Breckinridge. She and Murrow had an odd tie: she was a founder of the NSFA. (Their paths would cross again; in 1939, Murrow signed Breckinridge on as a CBS correspondent.)

BOUND FOR LONDON

By 1937, when he was sent to London as CBS's European
director of operations, Murrow had traveled extensively in Europe.

The Murrows' 1937 crossing came during a decade that was perhaps the century's dreariest. The Depression draped the 1930s. While in America the decade brought on the New Deal, the years saw Stalinism in the Soviet Union, fascism in Italy, civil war in Spain, befuddlement in Britain and France, imperialistic conquest and subjugation in Asia by Japan, and the rise of Nazism in Germany. Europe lived in the shadow of the First World War, remembered for the hideous stalemate and slaughter of the trenches. Few imagined that any might wish war to return. Britain's prime minister, Neville Chamberlain, stated this faith: "Human nature, which is the same all the world over, must reject the nightmare [of war] with all its might." In making that claim, Chamberlain neglected to account for a disgruntled Austrian ex-corporal who would tap the hopelessness and anger of his countrymen and bring the desire for revenge and a return of Germany's glory to a boil. Murrow was, more than most Americans (and many Europeans, for that matter), aware of the danger Hitler presented.

Besides her ties to Murrow, Breckinridge had connections of her own. She was descended from both B.F. Goodrich and U.S. Vice President John Breckinridge. She was en route to England to attend the coronation of George VI. His predecessor, Edward VIII, had abdicated so he could marry the American divorcée Wallis Simpson. The tale of a king surrendering his throne to be with the woman he loved made some of the decade's largest headlines. Murrow was in London for the coronation. Though he and Janet watched the royal procession from a spot near London's Hyde Park Corner, he made no report of the event over CBS. The crowning of a king was news, but in 1937 covering hard news was not what CBS's principal European correspondent did. Murrow would change that.

In London, the Murrows eventually settled at 84 Hallam Street, not far from Broadcasting House. Murrow began acquiring the stylish English clothes that, with his intelligence, his manners, and his understatement, made him welcome to his British hosts. He acquired as well the secretary, Kathryn (Kay) Campbell, who would remain with him most of his professional career. And he began introducing a somewhat more democratic tone to CBS broadcasts from England. He introduced Americans to an opinionated Cockney figure, Herbert Hodge, and broadcast an evening of darts and song from the Spread Eagle pub in Little Barfield, Essex, to which he would return in wartime.

The America the Murrows left was strongly isolationist. The previous fall, Franklin Delano Roosevelt had won a landslide reelection in a campaign that turned almost entirely on domestic concerns—his New Deal—and in which foreign policy was little debated. The Murrows were strongly New Deal in their politics. In Europe, however, concerns were different. There, the decade's central story was the rise of the Nazi Party in Germany. Faced with the restlessness of fascism, Britain and France tried to calm, conciliate, and appease. Geoffrey Dawson, the influential editor of the *Times*, stated, "I do my utmost, night after night, to keep out of the paper anything that might hurt their [Germany's] susceptibilities." Believing that reasonable men could find reasonable solutions, Britain's rulers ruled out the possibility that Hitler might actually be unreasonable. Thus, Prime Minister Neville Chamberlain's remarkable assessment of Hitler upon meeting him: "I got the impression that here was a man who could be relied upon when he had given his word."

Other impressions differed. A young American Rhodes Scholar, traveling in Germany, came within thirty yards of Hitler at an opera. Hitler, he wrote, was a "comical looking man [whose eyes] were beady little black dots with timid circles under them." Nonetheless, the visitor noted, Hitler had built a political party, taken control of a nation, and created the world's strongest army. Back in England, however, when he described the gathering menace, the American found himself declared "a harmless and annoying zealot." The American—future CBS correspondent Howard K. Smith—took his views to No. 10 Downing Street, the prime minister's residence, which he picketed wearing a sandwich board urging the "rascals" be thrown out.

There was little protest from the streets; less inside the House of Commons. There, Winston Churchill stood almost alone, sounding his warnings. On one occasion, Churchill told the Commons that Britain's government was "decided only to be undecided, resolved to be irresolute, adamant for drift, solid for fluidity, all powerful to be impotent. So we go preparing more years—precious, perhaps vital, to the greatness of Britain—for the locusts to eat."

•   •   •

SOME SOUGHT TO avoid knowing; a few wanted the story first. In 1934, William L. Shirer, a journalist working in Paris, confided in his diary, "Wish I could get a post in Berlin. That's the story I'd like to cover." Shirer was born in Chicago and raised in Iowa, which he found culturally narrow and Prohibition-era dry. In 1925, he had headed to Europe where, he said, "a man could drink a glass of wine or a stein of beer without breaking the law." In Europe, Shirer became a noteworthy foreign correspondent; he knew Europe's politics, spoke its major languages, and wrote with insight.

In 1934, the Universal Service news agency posted Shirer to Berlin. Soon, Shirer was nostalgic for the warmer Berlin he recalled from earlier visits. He saw firsthand the hatred that was producing the refugees, whose escape from Europe Murrow was facilitating. Shirer reported that prior to the 1936 Winter Olympics in Garmisch, the Germans removed all anti-Jewish posters from the premises. Shortly thereafter, his wife Tess turned on the radio and heard Shirer attacked as "a dirty Jew [who] was trying to torpedo" the games.

With the Depression, newspapers cut their budgets. Foreign reporting was a low priority. In August 1937, Universal Service closed up shop; almost immediately, International News Service—for which Shirer did occasional work—let him go. He was three thousand miles from home, unemployed, and his wife was pregnant. Almost simultaneous with the news of his dismissal, Shirer had received another wire, this one from Salzburg. He opened it:

CAN YOU MEET ME ADLON 8/27 FOR DINNER...

The wire was signed, "Murrow, Columbia Broadcasting." Shirer wired back, "Delighted."

At dinner, Shirer was initially put off by Murrow's good looks, recording in his diary: "Just what you would expect from radio, I thought." Murrow, however, meant business. CBS wanted to open a news bureau on the continent. Did Shirer want the job? Shirer had had a single previous brush with radio journalism. After the German airship *Hindenberg* crashed in Lakehurst, New Jersey, in 1937, CBS called, asking Shirer to secure comments. During the broadcast, he was so nervous that "my voice skipped up and down the scale and my lips and throat grew parched. Fear I will never make a broadcaster." Now, Murrow was offering just that.

There was, however, a catch. Later, CBS News Director Paul White would claim that in hiring correspondents, "little thought is given to voice quality since it is obvious that in these days of such important news, the emphasis should be upon content." Not so. For Shirer to be hired, he had to audition. When Shirer arrived at the Berlin studio for his audition, he discovered the microphone was tightly fixed at a level well over his head. It would not lower. When he talked up to it, his vocal chords constricted and squeaks emerged. With sixty seconds to airtime, Shirer directed that some packing cases be moved near the microphone. He scrambled onto them, auditioning with legs dangling. New York company executives thought Shirer's voice was terrible. Murrow, however, insisted, and on September 13, Shirer got the job. The seasoned foreign correspondent thrilled at the prospects the new medium offered:

> Murrow had fired me with a feeling that we might go places in this new-fangled radio-broadcasting business.... We might find a new dimension for reporting the news. Instantaneous transmission of news from the reporter to the listener, in his living room, of the event itself so that the listener could follow it just as it happened...was utterly new. There was no time lag, no editing or rewriting, as in a newspaper. A listener got straight from a reporter, and instantly, what was taking place. The sound of a riot in Paris, of the pope bestowing an Easter blessing in Rome, or of Hitler and Mussolini haranguing their storm troopers might tell you more than all the written descriptions a newspaper reporter could devise.

Murrow at this point was skipping about Europe, going after the stories he wanted or the ones CBS wanted him to get. Shirer's own early work was mixed: he went to Rome to be on hand for the death of Pope Pius XI, who declined to die. He was in Brussels for a nine-nation conference on the Japanese–Chinese conflict, which declined to do anything.

William L. Shirer
1904–1993
b. Chicago, Illinois

William Lawrence Shirer was born February 23, 1904, the son of Bess and Seward Shirer, a prominent attorney. Shirer spent the first nine years of his life in Chicago, surrounded by such notables as Clarence Darrow. When his father died in 1913 of peritonitis resulting from a burst appendix, Shirer moved with his mother, brother, and sister to Cedar Rapids, Iowa. Missing his father and the life they led in Chicago, Shirer felt confined by the "cultural poverty of the Midwest small town." He grew to manhood in a small white-frame Victorian house, across the street from the local struggling artist, Grant Wood.

As his family was unable to afford a more prestigious school, Shirer attended local Coe College and majored in history. Upon graduating in 1925, Shirer headed to Paris, working his way across the Atlantic on a cattle boat. He fell in love with Paris, and dreaded the prospect of having to return home. Packed and ready to go, he discovered a note in his apartment offering him a job at the *Paris Tribune*. He worked there until 1927, when he was promoted to foreign correspondent for the *Chicago Tribune*, reporting from Paris, London, Rome, and Vienna. Shirer befriended a number of famous expatriates in Europe, including Isadora Duncan, F. Scott Fitzgerald, Sinclair Lewis, and James Thurber. He covered Lindbergh's solo flight across the Atlantic and the League of Nations meetings in Geneva.

In 1930, the *Tribune* sent Shirer to India to cover the Indian revolution that was being led by a small Hindu man in a loin cloth, Mohandas K. Gandhi. Shirer's two years with Gandhi marked one of the most inspiring periods of his life, and led to the later publication of Shirer's *Gandhi: A Memoir* (1979). During this time, Shirer also traveled through the Khyber Pass to Kabul, where he scored a world scoop on the coronation of Afghanistan's crown prince, Nadir Khan. In January 1931, he married his Austrian sweetheart, Tess Stiberitz, but soon returned to India after Gandhi was released from prison. Having contracted both malaria and dysentery, Shirer returned to Tess and Vienna.

continued

TRACKS: 3, 5, 6, 8, 13, 14, 16, 45

In late 1932, he was let go by the *Tribune*, amid massive layoffs throughout the company. Unemployed in 1933, as America's depression hit Europe, Shirer and his wife took a year-long sojourn in Spain. They shared a house with Andrés Segovia in Lloret de Mar, living cheaply off their meager savings—the "happiest, most uneventful year we have ever lived," Shirer wrote in his diary. In 1934, as the Shirers' pesetas were dwindling, Shirer got an offer from the *Paris Herald*, and set off with Tess to Paris.

The world had changed much in the year Shirer took off—especially Germany, where Hitler was now chancellor. After a little over six months in Paris, Shirer took a job as correspondent with Universal Service in Berlin. The Berlin they returned to was unrecognizable. It was also *the* story to cover for Shirer. He spent the next three years reporting events in Nazi Germany, trying to alert his apathetic countrymen to the danger. On August 24, 1937, with Tess pregnant with their first child, Inga, Universal let Shirer go. He received a cable from Murrow the same day.

In helping to form CBS's European news operation, Shirer and Murrow became close friends. Shirer's broadcasts from Berlin, and his scoop broadcast on the fall of France from Compiègne, established him as a star in his own right. Upon returning to America in 1941, he published his first book, *Berlin Diary*, which became a bestseller and confirmed what many in America were beginning to realize too late. He became a columnist for the *New York Herald Tribune*, but continued to broadcast for CBS until he was forced out in 1947.

Shirer felt that his firing was based on his liberal political views, and blamed Murrow, then a vice president at CBS, for not supporting him. He broadcast for the Mutual network until 1949. Shirer was blacklisted from broadcasting after his name appeared in the anti-Communist publication *Red Channels* in the early 1950s. He devoted the rest of his life to writing books of history, memoirs, and novels. He is perhaps best known for the classic work on Nazi Germany, *The Rise and Fall of the Third Reich* (1961), for which he won the National Book Award. Among his other books were the second volume of his memoirs, commonly known as *The Nightmare Years* (1984); *End of a Berlin Diary* (1947); *The Sinking of the Bismarck* (1962); and his noted history of France between the wars, *The Collapse of the Third Republic* (1969).

He and Tess divorced in 1970. He remarried for a short time after, and a third time to Irina Alexandrovna Lugovskaya in 1988.

continued

The friendship between Shirer and Murrow had been profound, which is what made its irreconcilable dissolution so baffling to friends and family. In 1965, toward the end of his life, Murrow reached out to Shirer, who was civil, but unwilling to heal the rift between them. Shortly before Shirer died on December 28, 1993, he still refused to discuss it with his daughter Inga.

He had witnessed the best of humanity in Gandhi, the worst in Hitler, and had watched as the country of his ancestors lost its soul and its conscience. As his daughter later wrote, "What had happened, and why, was the question he asked over and over and spent the rest of his life trying to answer."

Anschluss

ON MARCH 10, 1938, Ed Murrow and Bill Shirer were running schoolboy errands. Murrow was in Warsaw to broadcast a chorus of schoolchildren; Shirer was in Yugoslavia to air a chorus of miners' children. Shakespeare wrote that there is a tide in the affairs of men that, "taken at its full, leads on to greatness." When Shirer returned to Vienna on March 11, that tide was running strongly. He and Murrow would seize it.

Vienna was in turmoil. In two days, Shirer learned, Austria would hold a plebiscite on whether to remain independent or be amalgamated into Hitler's Third Reich. While Shirer was in Yugoslavia, conflict between Germany and Austria came to a head. Hitler, an Austrian native, had long wished to add Austria to his Reich, a step known as *Anschluss*. Austrian Chancellor Kurt von Schuschnigg, resisting, ordered the plebiscite.

In Vienna, local newsmen assured Shirer that the plebiscite would sustain independence. Midday, he went to visit his wife in the hospital, where she was recovering from a difficult childbirth. En route, he ran into a crowd of Nazi sympathizers. It was, he wrote later, "a bit comical. One lone policeman was yelling and gesticulating to them. And they were giving ground!"

Two hours later, Shirer emerged from the hospital to be swept along by an exultant pro-Nazi crowd. Independent Austria no longer existed. Hitler had summoned Schuschnigg to Germany, demanded that the plebiscite be canceled, that Schuschnigg resign, and that his government yield. Schuschnigg capitulated. Within hours, German troops entered Vienna and the Nazi flag was raised at the Chancellery.

The story had all but thrown itself at Shirer's feet. For the moment, he had an exclusive—no other American radio correspondent was in Vienna that day. And to his mounting frustration, he had no way to get his story told. At the state broadcasting facility, he "argued, pleaded, fought" for four hours, but the Nazi officials who had taken control refused to let him on the air. At three A.M., he was ushered out of the building at bayonet point. Shirer then tried to reach Murrow in Warsaw, to no avail.

Murrow returned Shirer's call at five A.M. Shirer stated, "The opposing team has just crossed the goal line." This was code, meaning the German army

INDEPENDENT AUSTRIA NO LONGER EXISTED
Hitler accepts an ovation from the Reichstag on March 13, 1938,
after announcing the annexation of Austria—the Anschluss.

had crossed into Austria. Murrow asked if Shirer was sure. Moved perhaps by exhausted frustration, Shirer replied with low melodrama, "I'm paid to be sure." Murrow suggested that Shirer fly to London and report from England. Murrow would fly to Vienna to continue coverage from there. Shirer reached London by way of Berlin; Murrow reached Vienna, also via Berlin, where he spent one thousand dollars to charter a twenty-seven-seat aircraft and fly in as its only passenger. Shirer made his broadcast; New York wanted more.

Later, CBS President William Paley claimed it was his idea; announcer Robert Trout said it came from News Director Paul White. The idea, in any case, was to go on the air with a single thirty-minute broadcast presenting reports from the major capitals of Europe, switching from city to city at the push of a button. Radio had never done—nor even tried—anything similar. CBS in Europe had no broadcast facilities of its own; it would need access to state-run shortwave transmitters, each with its own rules, regulations, and frequencies. Further, it would need to find newsmen on the scene to make reports and coordinate the jumps from one city to another while broadcasting live. Plus, it was Sunday.

White phoned Shirer and asked if he and Murrow could do it. Shirer said, "Yes," and hung up, though he later acknowledged that he hadn't had any idea how. Murrow did. There were shortwave transmitters available for use in London, Berlin, and possibly Rome. Their frequencies were cabled to New York for pickup. Newsmen on the scene in Paris, Rome, and Berlin were lined up as commentators. New York called to give the schedule: the moment at which it would cut from one transmitter to another. At six P.M., CBS in New York announced the broadcast.

Behind the scenes it was patchwork, but the thirty-minute broadcast at eight P.M. on March 13, 1938, appeared seamless to the listener. Announcer Robert Trout opened, his baritone voice pushing the close of each phrase for emphasis: "A program of St. Louis blues originally scheduled at this time has been cancelled." The reason was Austria. Trout stated, "The world trembles, torn by conflicting forces, while the outside world, gravely shaken, moves cautiously through a maze of perils....Columbia now presents a special broadcast."

From London, Shirer spoke of the relative calm with which Britons had taken the news. Protesters had gathered at the German embassy, he said, but "after the delirious mobs I saw in Vienna on Friday night, today's demonstrations here in London looked pretty tame." Providing comment, Labor Member of Parliament Ellen Wilkinson gave little suggestion that England would act. "People are asking in America," she said, "why doesn't Britain do something? Well put. No one in Britain wants war." She quoted a speaker who asked, "Who will be pacifists in the coming war?" only to hear from the crowd the rejoinder, "The men who fought in the last war." She noted, with uncertain geography, "the situation here does not seem so clear as it does six thousand miles away in America."

Newsmen Edgar Mowrer and Pierre Huss reported, respectively, from Paris and Berlin. For Italy—where the transmitter proved unavailable—the report was cabled to Shirer, who read it from London.

Murrow's own broadcast from Vienna carried a haunted quality. In Vienna, he said, it was 2:30 A.M.; the city was awaiting the arrival of Adolf Hitler the following morning. Many were in a holiday mood: young stormtroopers were in the streets, "riding about in trucks and vehicles of all sorts, singing and tossing oranges out to the crowd." Already, in Murrow's first turn as radio correspondent, one could hear the signature clipped delivery, the focus on the seemingly mundane detail that brings a faraway event and place to life. He closed on a note of uncertainty: "No one seems to know just when [Hitler] will get here. But most people expect him sometime after ten o'clock tomorrow morning. It's of course obvious after one glance at Vienna that a tremendous reception is being prepared." CD

TRACK 2

In his lead-in, Trout announced that France was taking a strong line, "moving at full speed to bolster the Czechs and tighten its alliances with Russians." England, he added, was "prepared to go a very long way." Actually, no one was going anywhere. A new French government under Leon Blum had come to power just that day; when Chamberlain spoke to the House of Commons, he stated that the Anschluss deserved "the severest condemnation." And he let it go at that. The show carried an American perspective, from U.S. Senator Lewis Schwellenbach, who voiced caution. Clearly, he said, Austrians had lost their freedoms; likely, Hitler would push on to Czechoslovakia, Romania, and elsewhere. Hitler, he said, "is today Europe's leader." The Democrat added, "We will be importuned again to send our resources, in a futile effort to correct conditions in Europe," an importuning he felt America should resist.

The program came off cleanly. Thrilled, New York ordered a repeat for the following night. It included Murrow's sobering report from Vienna: "It was called a bloodless conquest and in some ways it was—but I'd like to be able to forget the haunted looks on the faces of those long lines of people outside the banks and travel offices. People trying to get away." To call attention to an upsurge in anti-Semitism, he added: "I'd like to forget the sound of the smashing glasses as the Jewish shop streets were raided, the hoots and jeers at those forced to scrub the sidewalk."

Whatever its outcome, Shirer believed the Anschluss was the "birth of the 'radio foreign correspondent,' so to speak." They continued reporting on the scene. In April, Murrow broadcast from the underground Maginot Line, the huge defensive works France believed would protect it from Germany. That same month, Shirer interviewed Czech President Eduard Benes. The broadcast signal ran through Berlin. When Shirer asked Benes about the German threat, the signal unaccountably failed. Murrow and Shirer believed Czechoslovakia would be the next scene of conflict. To protect the flow of news, CBS engineers and their Czech counterparts completed a shortwave system powerful enough to reach the United States.

In Germany, a correspondent's lot was becoming a less happy one. As Shirer was crossing the border between Nazi Austria and Italy, guards seized his money, discussed arresting him, then let him through. In June, William and Tess Shirer were to fly to Geneva for a holiday; at the airport, Tess, bandaged from surgery, was hauled off and strip-searched. A great deal more unpleasantness lay ahead.

Munich

THE ANSCHLUSS IN March was an episode; the Munich crisis that September was a siege. At issue was Hitler's insistence that the Sudetenland, a largely German-speaking area of Czechoslovakia adjacent to Germany, be added to the Third Reich. Most Czech border defenses were in the Sudetenland; its loss would leave the country indefensible. Hitler threatened war to gain his object. Treaties bound Britain and France to fight for Czechoslovakia if it was invaded. For them, the issue was their treaty commitments versus their fear of war.

Britain wished to avoid conflict. Early in the crisis, on September 7, the *Times* editorially urged the Czechs to cede the disputed territory. Four days later, CBS approved Shirer's request for daily five-minute broadcasts from Prague, the Czech capital. The time was granted on the condition that Shirer yield it on any day that not much was happening. There were no such days. Hitler ratcheted up the pressure. Nazi-inspired rioting followed in the disputed territory; German newspapers carried reports—Shirer, on the scene, called them nonsense—of "Women and Children Mowed Down by Czech Armored Cars" and "Extortion, Plundering, Shooting." This was news, but the heavens conspired against Shirer: for three straight days his broadcasts were blotted out by atmospheric interference.

To coordinate coverage, CBS revived the "round-up" format. Murrow, in London, had the hardest task. In the three weeks of the crisis, he made thirty-five broadcasts and arranged for 116 more. He interviewed Jan Masaryk, the Czech foreign minister. Masaryk was prepared for a fight: "I tell you Americans," he said in an interview, "our powder is dry." Murrow orchestrated reports from Rome, Paris, and the other capitals of Europe. It was makeshift and improvisational, all under the pressure of rapidly changing events and the demands of a broadcast schedule. A contemporary journalist wrote, "Under the most urgent kind of need Murrow learned what he could and could not do. He learned what newspapermen could be relied on to do a good job and a fast job, before the microphone….Murrow had to be prepared at a moment's notice to step into any breach. He was general understudy of the fourth estate."

On September 17, Chamberlain headed to Berchtesgaden, Hitler's Bavarian mountain retreat, to confer with the German dictator. From London, Murrow reported that the view of Britain's man-in-the-street was, "Well, the only way to settle this business is man to man, and the prime minister has gone out and had a try at it." Chamberlain agreed to pressure the French—and, more important, the Czechs—to accept cession. From Dresden, Shirer reported the rapturous response this news brought from Sudeten Germans: "It was simply a terrific mass hysteria," he said. "The yelling in a big stadium at a homecoming when your side makes the winning touchdown would be nothing to what we heard tonight."

On September 22, Shirer went to Godesberg, a spa on the Rhine where Hitler and Chamberlain were to renew discussion. Tension was high. Quoting a local brochure, Shirer described the local springs, said to be of value "in nervous cases." He added that this might prove handy. Walking near the Rhine, Shirer encountered Hitler: "Every few steps he cocked his right shoulder nervously, his left leg snapping up as he did so....He had ugly patches under his eyes. I think this man is on the edge of a nervous breakdown." From London, Murrow reported the expectation "that Herr Hitler will, in the vernacular, raise the ante." Herr Hitler did. Chamberlain had sold the French on the agreement. The Czechs—told their allies would not fight for them—saw themselves as being sold out. At Godesberg, Hitler declared events were not moving fast enough. He wanted the Sudetenland within a week. The alternative was war.

From Berlin, Shirer opened his September 24 broadcast by saying simply: "We have six days of peace ahead of us." Shirer was startled, however, by the entire absence of war fever in Germany's capital. He walked past the Czech legation expecting to see angry crowds; instead, there was "not a soul outside, not even a policeman." On what might prove to be the last Sunday of peace, Shirer told his listeners, Berliners were heading to the city's woods, lakes, and swimming pools. Those peaceful scenes, Shirer added, clashed with the tone of an address Hitler delivered in the Berlin Sportpalast: "No one in that vast hall—or none of the millions upon millions of Germans who gathered tonight in every town and village of Germany to hear the speech broadcast through community loudspeakers, or who sat quietly in their homes listening—had any doubts." It was cession or war.

The crisis claimed America's attention. In all, CBS broadcast five hundred reports and announcements in three weeks; CBS's commentator H.V. Kaltenborn made 102 presentations. Once, a live broadcast of a horse race was interrupted by a prayer for peace from the Archbishop of Canterbury, leaving race fans uncertain of its outcome. Kaltenborn wrote of seeing clumps of people gathered around parked taxicabs, following the news on their radios.

For those listening in America, Murrow was the spoke in the wheel. On September 28, he reported, "Throughout most of last night, trucks loaded with sandbags and gas masks were to be seen....The surface calm of London remains, but I think I noticed a change in people's faces. There seems to be a tight strained look about the eyes." There was certainly a strained look in Murrow's. He was working himself into exhaustion. After making his own broadcast, Murrow introduced correspondent Thomas Grandin from Paris, introduced a member of parliament, connected with William Shirer in Berlin and Vincent Sheean in Prague, and coordinated two other speakers.

Hitler had one more card to play. In England, his ultimatum had briefly stiffened the government; the minister of war urged mobilization. Then, as Chamberlain was addressing the House of Commons, he was passed a diplomatic note. Peace could still be secured, Hitler said, if the leaders of England, France, and Italy would meet with him at Munich. The Czechs were not invited. The move deflated England's brief resistance. When Chamberlain announced the news, virtually the entire house "rose to its feet in a gesture of ill-judged relief and sent Chamberlain off in a splurge of goodwill."

Briefly, Murrow shared that relief. For some weeks, he broadcast, Europe had been like a man in a dark room, searching for light: "Last night it appeared that at last a faint of light and hope has been found." At Munich, that light quickly dimmed, at least for the Czechs. Murrow spent the evening of September 30 with Jan Masaryk, the Czech foreign minister and a personal friend. Masaryk was awaiting contact from the conference. None came. Those at Munich agreed the Czechs must yield immediately. Murrow got the news from a Munich radio station, to which he was listening with an interpreter. His report on the settlement was a clear scoop, the first to reach America.

Shirer considered Munich a sellout. In his diary, he recorded, "The French say [Premier Edouard Daladier] fears to return to Paris; thinks a hostile mob will get him. Can only hope they're right." In France and Britain, however, peace proved more important than principle. Eric Sevareid, then a newspaperman in France, was present for Daladier's return: "I watched him in the almost hysterical, praying crowd on the Champs-Elysées—a dumpy,

"PEACE IN OUR TIME."

British Prime Minister Neville Chamberlain proudly waves the Munich Pact signed with
Hitler, which dismembered Czechoslovakia and staved off war—for a time.

bent little man carrying his black hat in one hand, looking bewildered and uncertain." Chamberlain's reception was similar. British newspapers, Murrow reported, were advocating a knighthood for Chamberlain—perhaps the Nobel Peace Prize. Murrow added dryly: "International experts in London agree that Herr Hitler has scored one of the greatest diplomatic triumphs in modern history."

On October 2, Shirer rode with the German army into the Sudetenland and a rapturous reception. Shirer broadcast: "A bushel of flowers must have fallen into my own lap, though I brought up the rear." For Shirer, the day had one sour note. During late afternoon, a soldier flung his body in front of the car in which the reporter was riding—the driver had come within five feet of an unexploded mine. By Shirer's account, the German officers riding with him found the incident amusing—had the bomb exploded, one said, "they never would have found a piece of us or this car." Shirer was not amused.

Mostly, he was depressed. He and Murrow met in Paris to drown their sorrows, without success. Shirer wrote, "We try to get it out of our systems by talking all night and popping champagne bottles and tramping the streets, but it will take more time, I guess." A few weeks later, the non-athletic Shirer—seeking distraction—took up golf.

There were compensations. In America, Munich and its coverage made Murrow a minor celebrity, whose name and voice were recognizable to most. That coverage had been expensive—between them, CBS and NBC spent $190,000 covering the crisis, a huge sum for the time. Agreement was general that CBS's coverage was superior; in the words of Erik Barnouw, it "stole the radio spotlight. It was the greatest show yet heard on American radio." And Murrow was its ringmaster. Laudatory press accounts followed, including a perceptive one in *Scribner's*. Writer Robert Landry accepted Murrow's then best estimate of his age—thirty-three (he was actually thirty)—and described Murrow as "tall without being lanky, darkish without being swarthy, young without being boyish, dignified without being uncomfortable," adding that he was a "stout chap" who had never done anything outlandish. Apparently, no one had told the writer of the time Murrow, inebriated, drove a car up the steps of the U.S. Capitol in Washington.

But Landry caught a close take on Murrow's task: "He must deal with the nations of a tense and hate-pocked continent, retaining his freedom of action and speech without forgetting that there will be other days and new needs for cooperation." A year later, *Newsweek* would claim that "the scattering bits of wireless news and comment" from radio had generated interest in broader analysis "furnished only by the daily and weekly press." Landry was closer to the truth. Murrow, he wrote, was more influential than a shipful of newspapermen. With the power of radio, Murrow could beat newspaper coverage by hours and reach large stretches of the country where the provincial press gave only cursory accounts of foreign events. Interestingly, the third advantage Landry cited was that "he writes his own headlines"—Murrow's accounts came through unedited, framed as he wished them framed.

NAZIS MARCH INTO SUDETENLAND

*German troops are welcomed with Nazi salutes from ethnic
Germans in the Sudeten region of Czechoslovakia, October 1, 1938.*

With Munich, Europe stepped back from the edge of war. The general
judgment of history, however, was that Munich made war more likely, and
at worse odds. The settlement effectively swept the thirty-five-division
Czech army from the side of those ranged against Germany. England's position was weak: it had fought the First World War allied with Italy, Russia,
and France. Now, Italy was siding with Germany, Russia was neutral, and
France was in confusion. Post-Munich, Winston Churchill confronted two
British cabinet members and, all but calling them cowards, described the
settlement as "sordid, squalid, sub-human, and suicidal."

·   ·   ·

MUNICH BROUGHT PEACE, but not peace of mind. Once the rush of relief had passed, commentators in England noted a sense of shame creeping across the country.

Such anxiety was felt in America as well. While Murrow was home for the first time in eighteen months, a twenty-three-year-old boy wonder used the medium of radio to throw more than one million listeners across the country into a panic. On October 30, 1938—a month after Munich—Orson Welles and his *Mercury Theatre on the Air* used a series of on-the-scene news reports—the kind that Murrow and Shirer had innovated earlier in the year—in their adaptation of H.G. Wells' *The War of the Worlds*. Broadcast on CBS, the drama featured actors playing the roles of correspondents, reporting from the scene of a Martian invasion in Grovers Mill, New Jersey, from military command posts, and even from the roof of the broadcasting building in Manhattan, as the Martians decimated the city. The reports, which interrupted the fictional program of dance music by "Ramón Raquello and his orchestra," achieved the sort of realism Welles could only have hoped for in his wildest dreams. The panic revealed not only the visceral power of radio, but also the tenor of the times. Several of those who panicked that night later told interviewers they thought that the Martians being described on the radio were actually Germans launching an attack on America. The "panic broadcast" could be laughed away by most, but the course of world events was not about to change.

The Munich crisis was past, but the future looked no brighter. In London, the BBC began constructing an underground broadcast facility, a safe haven in the event of bombing. Murrow's own view was that Europe might not prove sufficient to the challenge. While still in the United States late in 1938, he told a Buffalo, New York, audience, "Whether we like it or not, the answer to Europe's problems will be found, not in Europe, but right here in the United States."

2

WAR IN EUROPE

Getting off the plane and meeting people who had stayed in America was a strange experience, because they hardly seemed to know that anything was wrong....

It was like the dream in which you yell at people and they don't hear you.

—*A.J. Liebling*
upon returning to the U.S. in 1941

TRACKS: 3–14

Previous page: German troops march to the Polish front, September 13, 1939.

Poland

IN JULY 1939, Paul White, the beefy, hard-nosed, and hard-drinking news director for CBS, headed for Europe to assess the chances of war and the preparations his network should make to cover it. White, in many ways similar to Murrow, was in many other way the complete opposite—where Murrow was soft-spoken and elegant, White had the build and disposition of a linebacker, with the "center-parted, lacquered-down look of an oversize Dink Stover." They would both be instrumental in creating a news organization that could cover a worldwide war.

In America, few believed that war was coming. In Europe, Murrow, Shirer, and correspondent Thomas Grandin thought war all but certain. In London, they presented White with a plan for the means of sending the news via shortwave transmitters and transmission lines, and for an expanded corps of American correspondents to cover it. White had his doubts. Back in New York, he dictated a memo on the plans, adding parenthetically, "I don't think it will work either." While White did not think war was certain, he approved hiring an additional correspondent.

Murrow wanted a young American, a tall brooding newspaperman named Eric Sevareid. Sevareid had grown up in Velva, North Dakota, a small town in a sea of wheat. As a college student, Sevareid led an effort to abolish compulsory ROTC at the University of Minnesota (whereas Murrow had been cadet colonel of the ROTC at Washington State College). In 1937, Sevareid and his wife Lois headed for Europe to be near the war they believed was brewing. In London, Sevareid wrote, he met "a tall thin man with a boyish grin [and] extraordinary dark eyes....He seemed to possess that rare thing, an instinctive, intuitive recognition of truth." The man was Ed Murrow.

Sevareid landed a newspaper position in Paris. Murrow followed his work. When White approved the additional correspondent, Murrow offered Sevareid the post. In Sevareid's recollection, Murrow said: "I don't know very much about your experience, but I like the way you write and I like your ideas." Sevareid, in fact, knew nothing about radio broadcasting. There was, of course, an audition. CBS in New York had balked at Shirer; they balked harder at Sevareid. Shirer was a dull monotone; Sevareid, apparently, was a mumbler. Murrow was unruffled. He told Sevareid he would "fix" New York, adding, "Quit your other jobs anyway and don't worry about it." Sevareid's appointment letter, dated August 16, set his salary at $250 and noted, "Incidentally, the matter of terms of employment and the salary paid are normally matters of strict confidence, even between colleagues." The CBS press release announcing the hiring said that Sevareid's credentials were impressive in one "only twenty-nine years old." Actually, Sevareid was twenty-six. A penciled note on that announcement stated, "Ed [Murrow] said he had to be at least twenty-nine; so far as CBS is concerned, he is."

As a reinforcement, Sevareid arrived just in time. While Murrow and CBS skirmished over Sevareid's hiring, Hitler was readying to do battle with Poland. The settlement following the First World War had left a part of Germany, East Prussia, separated from the German "mainland." A strip of land, the Polish Corridor, ran between it to the Baltic Sea. Hitler's territorial claims started with the corridor. Two political facts were paramount: following Munich, Britain and France gave military guarantees to Poland. More startling, on August 22, Hitler signed a nonaggression pact with Germany's longstanding ideological rival, the Soviet Union. That pact isolated the Poles.

Tensions mounted. On August 23, star CBS commentator H.V. Kaltenborn was refused entry into Germany. Kaltenborn, in a speech given in Kansas City, had sharply criticized Hitler. Somehow, word had filtered back to Germany. Now, he was informed, "Your presence in Germany is not desired." Adding injury to insult, the German secret police confiscated the pipe tobacco Kaltenborn was bringing to William Shirer.

Eric Sevareid
1912–1992
b. Velva, North Dakota

Arnold Eric Sevareid was born November 26, 1912, in Velva, North Dakota. His father was a bank president, and young "Arnie" grew up in a cold, stern household that left him insecure and wanting affection. When he was twelve, his father lost everything when the wheat market collapsed. The family went from middle class to poor overnight. Not surprisingly, Sevareid yearned to escape from his stilted, unsatisfying home.

The family moved to Minneapolis, where his father got a job as a cashier in a local bank. Sevareid became editor of his high school paper in his senior year, but nothing could prepare him for the adventure he was about to take. At seventeen, urged on by an older friend, Sevareid set out with his companion to canoe the Mississippi River up through Canada to the Hudson Bay on the Atlantic Ocean, a 2,200-mile trek over many uncharted lakes and rivers. It almost killed them, ill-prepared as they were. But six weeks into their journey, they spied the white buildings of the Hudson's Bay Company as they rowed into a wide expanse of water. They had reached the Atlantic. Sevareid sold a series of articles to the *Minneapolis Star* on their exploits; five years later, he published an account of the adventure as a children's book, *Canoeing with the Cree*.

Sevareid soon after took a job with the *Minneapolis Journal* and started taking night courses at the University of Minnesota. After another journey in 1931—this time west to work the gold fields of California's High Sierra—Sevareid returned to the university full-time and worked on the school paper, the *Minnesota Daily*. He and his fellows at the university were pacifists—they campaigned successfully to eliminate compulsory ROTC drills and signed the Oxford Oath not to fight for God and country. Sevareid was like many in the early 1930s—disgusted by the senseless carnage of World War I, disillusioned by the government's inability to stem the Great Depression, and drawn to the leftist doctrine of the time.

continued

TRACKS: 10, 15, 23, 30

He met and married another college activist, Lois Finger, a law student, in 1934. Upon graduation, he returned to the *Journal* and worked as a reporter there for two years. When he was fired in 1937—essentially for backing the paper's union—he and Lois decided to go to Europe, where Sevareid could cover the most important story of the time. In Paris, he took to being called "Eric," and was hired as a reporter and city editor for the *Paris Herald*, later also as the night editor for United Press. Murrow hired him in 1939, in time to cover the start of war and France's fall. After escaping France and the advancing German army with Lois and their newborn twin sons, Sevareid joined Murrow in London, covering the Blitz. He returned to America in late 1940 to report from Washington, D.C., and remained there until 1943, when he was asked to cover the war and civil unrest in China. After parachuting out of a damaged plane over Burma and surviving several weeks among local headhunters, Sevareid returned to work, broadcasting from Chungking. He later covered the Italian invasion, the liberation of Rome, the post D-Day landings in southern France, and the Allied crossing of the Rhine.

After the war, Sevareid became a national correspondent for CBS, and later gave nightly commentaries alongside Walter Cronkite on the *CBS Evening News*, until his retirement in 1977.

Sevareid wrote several books after the war, including *Not So Wild a Dream* (1946), *In One Ear: 107 Snapshots of Men and Events* (1952), *Small Sounds in the Night* (1956), *This Is Eric Sevareid* (1964), *Politics and the Press* (1967), and *Edward R. Murrow* (1979).

As Lois's manic depression worsened during the 1950s, their marriage dissolved. They divorced, and he remarried twice, first to Belèn Marshall, a singer, and then to Suzanne St. Pierre, with whom he stayed until his death on July 9, 1992. More than four hundred people attended the memorial service held for him at the National Press Club in Washington. He was described by Daniel Schorr as the "dean" of CBS.

"We were like a young band of brothers in those early radio days with Murrow," Sevareid said in his last broadcast for CBS on November 20, 1977. Always the best writer of the bunch, he distilled what it meant for him to be a journalist: "Mine has been here an unelected, unlicensed, uncodified office and function. The rules are

continued

self-imposed. These were a few: not to underestimate the intelligence of the audience and not to overestimate its information. To elucidate, when one can, more than to advocate....To retain the courage of one's doubts as well as one's convictions, in this world of dangerously passionate certainties."

Beyond his books and brilliant World War II reporting, Sevareid's commentary and analysis on the civil rights movement, Vietnam, urban riots, the youth rebellion, and Watergate established him as, in many ways, the conscience of the nation during those tumultuous decades.

In New York, CBS was hardly keeping pace with events. For August 25, White wanted a show named "Europe Dances," with reports from famed European ballrooms. While New York danced, Murrow and Shirer fumed, demanding the show's cancellation. On August 28, Shirer reported from Berlin: "The entire press...maintains that Germany cannot and will not compromise...the Reich will not budge an inch from its demands on Poland for the return of Danzig and the corridor." **CD**

TRACK 3

Back in New York on August 30, Kaltenborn told a reporter "the odds [are] still seven-to-five in favor of more appeasement." In London, Murrow doubted this. The "man on the street," who during Munich had said, "I hope Mr. Chamberlain can find a way out," was now, Murrow reported, saying, "If this is peace, give me a good war." From Paris, Sevareid reported that the Greek and Roman statues in the Louvre museum were being moved to safety, "carted out in wheelbarrows." Elsewhere in the city, he added, Parisians were buying up candles, flashlights, and batteries.

Germany invaded Poland early on September 1, 1939. The British and French responded with ultimatums, demanding German withdrawal. Hitler ignored them. On September 3, speaking by radio, Prime Minister Chamberlain announced, "I have to tell you that we are now at war with Germany." Fifteen minutes later, London's air-raid sirens sounded. Murrow told America, "It wasn't a pleasant sound." **CD** He—and the city—began moving for the air-raid shelters. Out on Bond Street, he reported, "One man began to run—after he'd run about half a block, he looked around, saw that no one else was running, and stopped, with perhaps the British desire not to be

TRACK 4

conspicuous." (Shortly before, Howard K. Smith had walked into the United Press office on London's Fleet Street seeking employment in the event of war. A UP official told Smith to take a desk; war had just been declared.)

In Paris, Eric Sevareid had an exclusive on France's declaration of war. His script had cleared censorship. At the broadcast studio, however, he learned that his allotted time slot had been reassigned. For thirty minutes, a frantic Sevareid, shouting orders at the studio engineer, tried to get back on the air. Suddenly, the engineer ordered him out. The engineer, Sevareid

NAZIS INVADE POLAND
On September 1, 1939, German ground and air forces launched an all-out assault on Poland, triggering World War II.

wrote, had served four years in the First World War, one of them in a German prison camp, and had been wounded three times. He had received his call-up papers that morning. What difference was Sevareid's scoop to him? Sevareid adjourned to a sidewalk café, with the same sense of imposition he had when, working for a Minneapolis newspaper, he "had gone to demand photographs in families where a death had occurred."

War's outbreak meant a whirl of activity. Sevareid wrote, "Apparently all America was sitting beside the radio; New York could not get its fill. Tom Grandin and I were on a relentless treadmill for the first two or three days. I would rise at two or three in the morning, never having removed my clothes, stumble into the car, and go to the studio. When I returned, he would repeat my performance." Grandin reported on French offensives. The Germans, he said, had "abandoned and destroyed certain of [their] own villages while withdrawing." Other journalists reported huge battles at sea, water pouring through the Belgian dikes, and aerial dogfights over England. None of these—including the fighting reported by Grandin—actually occurred. In the war's early days, Britain and France clamped on a censorship so severe that almost nothing escaped the front except rumors, which expanded as they traveled.

The real fighting was in the east. The Poles fought with courage; the Germans, with tanks, dive bombers, and heavy artillery. By September 3— the day Britain and France declared war—the Poles were retreating. CBS did not have a correspondent in Warsaw; for the Polish side of the story, it relied on reports forwarded through Budapest. From the German side, all news was good. On September 8, William Shirer announced that the German army was nearing the Polish capital.

For CBS, however, that day's most important development came from New York. Its rivals, NBC and Mutual Broadcasting, were suspending all European news broadcasts. The networks were concerned that by broadcasting in wartime, they might somehow run afoul of the Neutrality Act (a Congressional mandate established in 1935 aimed at preventing the U.S. from becoming involved in another European conflict). Until their rivals reconsidered, CBS had a broadcast monopoly on the day's central story.

On September 16, CBS broadcast from New York an optimistic report on Poland's standing. The Polish army, it said, was intact "and in a very strong position. The Germans are furiously upset over the length and determination of the Polish resistance." Shirer, closer to the action, was closer to the truth. That same day, he reported, "The Polish war is over…at least so far as the German Army is concerned." The following day, the Soviet Union sealed Poland's destruction by invading from the east.

German officials allowed Shirer a single trip to the battle zone. He had imagined battle as long lines of men, moving back and forth across a field of conflict. What he saw was a great deal less. "I'll be frank," he told listeners. "We heard an awful lot. But in modern warfare you don't see very much….Only when the German infantry, led by tanks, advanced could we see how the battle was going. Even then it was difficult, because the infantry constantly took cover, and a camouflaged tank at two miles, when it's not moving, looks like a bush." What Shirer saw clearly, however, were the bitter faces of women in a nearby town. He thought it was "grotesque" that he was standing there "watching the killing as though it was a football game" within easy sight of the civilians whose lives were being destroyed. He closed, "Well, it was your job, but that gave you little comfort."

The Phony War

ON SEPTEMBER 28, 1939—after Poland's formal surrender—William Shirer went on the air with a coup. He had been permitted to talk with Herbert Schultze, the German commander whose submarine had sunk the British merchantman the *Royal Sceptre*. Britain claimed the attack came without warning and that sixty sailors had perished. Schultze gave a different version. He told Shirer he waited until the British crew had boarded its lifeboats: "I sank the *Royal Sceptre* only after I saw the smoke of a ship on the horizon," Schultze said. He wired the second ship, the *Browning*, directing it to collect the crew. Schultze also told Shirer that, earlier, after sinking the *Firby*, he sent a radio message to Winston Churchill telling him where

PARIS FRONT

*Thomas Grandin, Ed Murrow, and William Shirer have drinks at a café
in Paris before a joint broadcast in the weeks leading up to the war.*

the ship had been sunk and adding, "Save the crew, if you please." Shirer asked to see the telegram. The commander said it was in his logbook back in Kiel. As the story developed, Shirer said, "One good break followed another." Between the time he first talked with Schultze and the time of the broadcast, the radio message was located, confirming Schultze's version. And, more important, a wire service reported that the *Browning* had reached port in Brazil with the crew of the *Royal Sceptre* on board.

Shirer's interview was the last good "war story" CBS broadcast for some while. For seven months, an all but silent stalemate hung over the western front. No war and no peace meant less news. Led by Murrow, the CBS correspondents broadened their reporting to their twenty-two million listeners to include the human stories behind the conflict. On November 12, Murrow described the war's impact on an English village. He began with a sentence that could have opened a novel: "Here is a story of an English village of 168 souls." He sketched the scene: "a twisting gray country road runs through the center of Little Barfield, Essex. There is a green cricket pitch, an old Norman church, and a pub, the Spread Eagle." He conveyed its isolation: "only three telephones; very few electric lights, [where] many had never seen a movie, half had never been to London and they had no desire to go." War meant an influx of women and children evacuated from London, whose arrival created a language problem. The local accent and the newcomers' nasal Cockney "provides a contrast that could only be retold by moving half of a Vermont village into a town in the Mississippi delta." He closed, "There isn't much talk of the war in Little Barfield....They think they know what Britain is fighting against, and that's enough for them. One man said, 'This fellow Hitler just went too far. Something had to be done about it.'"

Eric Sevareid delivered a similar report from France. Sevareid spoke about a village down river from Paris, a place where people could "swim and row, and in the evening sit in front of the river inn and see the boys and girls dancing," as Sevareid himself had done in the last week of peace. Sevareid described the village memorial to its dead from the First World War. The first to die in that conflict, he said, was Emil Dary; the first to be called up for this one, he added, was Emil Dary Jr. Refugees had tripled the town's population, and the mayor was kept busy tending to their needs. "He took me into the town hall where the coal stove is burning. Two women were waiting for him. Their husbands were fighting and they wanted their daily allowance of fifty-five francs." The town's most sought-after individual, however, was not the mayor but the postman, who carried letters from the front. "As soon as they spot him coming up the street, twenty women and girls will be out on him and take the mail right out of his bag."

These reports reflected Murrow's emphasis on telling the "human side" of the conflict. They had the additional advantage—though this may not have figured in Murrow's calculations—of being noncontroversial. Fearing the controversy of war, NBC and Mutual had closed up operations a week into the Polish invasion. CBS was still in the field, but CBS in New York was not about to give its correspondents in that field a totally free hand in how they covered it. CBS chief William Paley took a consistently strong line against editorializing. That line was laid down in a four-page memo on editorial standards issued September 5, 1939, by company vice president Ed Klauber. As news analysts, he wrote, Murrow and the others were entitled to "elucidate and illuminate the news out of common knowledge possessed by them or made available to them by this organization through its news sources. They should point out the facts on both sides, show contradictions with the known record, and so on. They should bear in mind that in a democracy it is important that people not only should know but should understand, and their function is to help the listener understand, to weigh, and to judge. But not do the judging for them."

In practice, Murrow's conflict with this directive was slimmest. His first impressions of England, formed during his 1930 visit, had not been wholly favorable. He later told an English audience, "I thought your streets narrow and mean, your tailors over-advertised, your climate unbearable, your class-consciousness offensive. You couldn't cook." As war came, Murrow's view of the British changed. When the Germans invaded Poland, he had been one of the few correspondents of any nation to predict that England would fight, not fold. He developed a view of the English as sturdy, quaint, unruffled, and determined to see the conflict through. This view allowed Murrow, without "editorializing," to present the British in a way that would appeal to American sympathy for the underdog.

Severeid's circumstance was more complicated; or, at least, he made it so. The one-time pacifist now strongly believed that fascism must not be allowed to defeat democracy. He believed America should join the war on France and Britain's side. And he tried to follow a path that would let him push those beliefs without incurring CBS's wrath. The path was a narrow one, and the following year it would bring him into sharp conflict with Paul White.

The unhappiest was Shirer. He could barely hide his deep distaste for things German. With the war's outbreak on September 1, 1939, air-raid sirens had sounded over Berlin; Shirer wrote that he hoped "they bomb the hell out of this town without getting me." His disdain extended, ungallantly, to Berlin's women, who "are certainly the least attractive in Europe. They have no ankles. They dress worse than English women used to." Only rarely did his attitude soften, as when he witnessed Berliners in a park feeding their rationed bread to ducks.

On the surface, a reporter's life in Germany was a soft one. The foreign press received the same larger rations as "heavy laborers." They were issued special passes that "worked like a magic wand in getting taxis [and] at smoothing over minor infringements of law." This mattered little to Shirer. To him, a reporter's job was to confer with officials off the record and sample the opinions of people on the street. But German officials did not talk "off the record," and people on the street shied from foreigners asking questions. It was a closed society. Germans were, for example, forbidden to listen to foreign radio broadcasts. At the time, the BBC tried to lure German listeners to its broadcasts by announcing during each show the names of German pilots and seamen who were safe in British hands. Shirer planned to broadcast about one incident: eight listeners wrote a German woman that they had heard her son was alive in England. The woman denounced the eight to the police; all were arrested. The German censor refused to let Shirer broadcast the story. American listeners, the censor said, would not understand that the woman who denounced her friends was a hero.

Shirer took advantage of a brief vacation in Switzerland to vent his frustration in a letter to Ed Klauber. "I note that you, White, and Murrow still think I am doing a useful job in Berlin, though personally I sometimes doubt it." There was, he said, no real way to report the news. "We are not only rarely told anything truthful, but are prevented from getting news ourselves. For instance, we cannot go to Poland to check up on the reports we get from there of German sadism, murder, repression."

Through the fall of 1939, CBS added correspondents. By year's end, their number reached fourteen. The new recruits included William L. White in Helsinki, Betty Wason in Stockholm, Larry LeSueur in France, Cecil Brown in Rome, and others. Murrow, working with Paul White in New York, selected the staff. In hiring, Murrow put his faith in people rather than in credentials.

One new hire was Mary Marvin Breckinridge. Though an established photographer, her journalistic credentials were weak, and she had never broadcast. (Almost forty years later, in 1976, Breckinridge spoke at Boston University and began by noting that her visit that day marked the first time she had set foot in a school of journalism.) In July 1939, she sailed for Europe, intending a six-week visit and "equipped with a dressing-case, two suitcases (one full of riding and evening clothes), hatbox, typewriters, and Rolleiflex camera." War engulfed her. She landed in Europe the day the German–Soviet nonaggression pact was signed. She rode through France on a train that was collecting French reservists. During her first morning in England, the waiter at the Savoy Hotel brought her tea, a menu, and news that Britain had declared war. Breckinridge decided to remain in England, and gained a few freelance assignments. In mid-November, she had dinner with Ed and Janet Murrow, telling them about a story she was doing on evacuated children. Murrow suggested she tell it on CBS. Breckinridge agreed, "partly because I knew that my parents in California would be pleased to hear their daughter's voice."

Breckinridge made the report. Murrow wished to sign her on as a regular correspondent. CBS New York was adamant: no female reporters in a war zone. Murrow was more adamant, and Breckinridge was hired. In the next six months, she made fifty broadcasts from seven countries.

DECEMBER 25, 1939, marked the war's first Christmas. Murrow, Sevareid, and Shirer reported on how the belligerent nations observed their shared holiday. Shirer, at the German naval base in Kiel, told listeners, "I am speaking to you on this Christmas night from the pitch-dark, lonely deck of a German warship." On shipboard, he said, the crew's quarters shone with candles from Christmas trees. Decorations were elaborate, including an intricate replica of the Hamburg Christmas carnival, complete with working merry-go-rounds and roller coasters. His segment closed with German sailors singing "Stille Nacht."

Sevareid broadcast singing from France's underground Maginot Line on Christmas Eve. He wrote, "the men sang with moving effect," and he thought that "all America must have been deeply stirred by this vivid voice picture of front-line life." Soon after, correspondent Tom Grandin called from Paris to tell Sevareid that, due to a scheduling misunderstanding, none of the broadcast had actually been aired. (In its stead, CBS aired a report from William L. White, its correspondent in Finland. That report prompted Robert Sherwood's play *There Shall Be No Light*. Sevareid commented on his lost broadcast, "so perhaps it was just as well.")

From London, Murrow reported on the king's Christmas message. George VI told a fable about a man who sought a light from his king so "that I might tread safely into the unknown." The king of the fable replied, "Go out into the darkness and put your hand into the hand of God. And that shall be to you better than light, and safer than a known way." It was, Murrow suggested, the British monarch's way of telling his subjects to trust themselves. Characteristically, Murrow went further. He was curious: where did this story come from? "The king doesn't know," he told listeners. "Court circles can't say. Even the poet laureate can't say. The keeper of manuscripts at the British Museum [doesn't know]. It's a first-class literary mystery, which I will clear up in just a moment." The rest of the story, Murrow said, was this: the words were from a book, *The Desert*, written by an elderly woman, one M.L. Haskins. "As an author, she is unknown," Murrow closed, but the king was making her words famous.

Set by Murrow, the style was something new, a combination of news and "color" presented as a spoken essay. In consequence, Sevareid wrote, "familiar, very American voices now brought faraway scenes and issues into millions of American living-rooms at regular hours in precise succession." For many who listened, the reports at first were "news from nowhere"— accounts of things happening in the world at first gave them little reason for concern. With time, the skill of the reporting would help drive home the magnitude of the events.

Breckinridge was posted to Amsterdam, where on January 18, 1940, she played host to a joint broadcast by Murrow and Shirer. The pair had not seen each other in four months. The Netherlands was neutral, so unlike London and Berlin, Amsterdam was not subject to blackout. Murrow told listeners he was startled to see "street lights, automobiles with real headlights, and light pouring out of windows…it's a shock." Knowing their broadcast would be heard by censors in their host countries, Murrow and Shirer presented carefully crafted scripts.

Mary Marvin Breckinridge
1905–2002
b. New York, New York

Born on October 2, 1905, in New York, the foundations for Mary Marvin Breckinridge's pioneering career in radio journalism were laid at an early age. Known by all as "Marvin," she hailed from a family that included tire mogul B.F. Goodrich and former vice president John Breckinridge. As a child, she attended a total of twelve schools in a variety of different countries. She returned to the U.S. in 1924 to attend Vassar College, where she once convinced a friend to join her in swimming across the icy Hudson River. They both nearly froze. She found another, safer outlet for her energy by cofounding and presiding over the National Student Federation of America, which brought her into contact with Edward R. Murrow for the first time. She graduated in 1927 with a degree in modern history and languages.

Breckinridge learned to fly after college and became the first woman in the state of Maine to obtain a pilot's license. Shortly thereafter, she spent time in Kentucky, where she worked as a horseback courier for the Frontier Nursing Service, an organization founded by her cousin, which was responsible for reducing the maternal death rate in rural Kentucky by two-thirds. In 1930, her cousin encouraged her to take lessons in the still blooming field of motion-picture photography. After a year of private lessons, she wrote, directed, and filmed a documentary about the FNS. Breckinridge liked the experience so much that she began to explore the world of still photography, and for the first time felt she had a real calling in life. She would become a photojournalist.

In 1937, she renewed her friendship with Ed Murrow on her way to George VI's coronation in England. She returned to Europe in 1939 as a reporter for *Town and Country*, *Life*, and the *New York Times*. When war broke out in September, she thought about returning home, but in a letter to her mother wrote that it would be foolish "to run away from the most interesting thing that I could be doing on earth right now." When Murrow asked her to broadcast a story she was doing on evacuated children, and she followed that with a report on an all-woman night shift in a

continued

TRACK: 7

London firehouse, he was impressed. She had a strong voice, knew how to translate complex issues into human terms, and was unflinchable on air. Over the objections of management, Murrow made her the first female correspondent at CBS. He assigned her to cover neutral Scandinavia and the Low Countries.

She worked for six months, broadcasting from Amsterdam and filling in for William Shirer for a time, before leaving on June 20, 1940, to marry U.S. diplomat Jefferson Patterson, who was stationed in Berlin. Having left broadcasting, she had hoped to resume her career as a photojournalist. But the State Department barred her from publishing, as it feared her reporting might compromise her husband's job. She thereafter devoted herself to being a diplomatic spouse.

She and Jefferson had two children, and bounced from one Foreign Service assignment to another, which included an ambassadorship to Uruguay in 1956. Since Mr. Patterson's death in 1977, Mrs. Patterson continued to live in their Washington, D.C., home up until her death on December 11, 2002.

As the only Murrow Boy who was a woman, Mary Marvin Breckinridge Patterson claims a unique distinction in broadcasting history.

For his part, Murrow said, "The British think they're doing pretty well with things just as they are....[They] think their blockade is squeezing the Germans pretty hard...[A] considerable number of people have some sort of vague idea that, if they just keep the pressure on the Germans, the Germans will finally crack without any major military action." The Germans, Shirer responded, see "only two alternatives. Either to win the war, in which case they have a bright future. Or to lose the war, in which case their present leaders assure them that there will be such a peace as will make Versailles [the 1918 World War I settlement] look like an ideal instrument of justice and fair dealing. Don't underestimate the sacrifices the average German would make to avoid another Versailles." **CD**

TRACK 6

Post-broadcast, Murrow, Shirer, and Breckinridge returned to their hotel. It was one A.M. A heavy snow was falling, and feeling the freedom of a neutral city, they had a snowball fight.

Shirer wanted to take a vacation. Murrow asked Breckinridge to cover for him. In his diary, Shirer wrote, somewhat patronizingly, "I've invited Marvin

JOINT BROADCAST

Murrow and Shirer, who had become close friends by the time
war broke out, made very few broadcasts together, but they did
broadcast from neutral Amsterdam on January 18, 1940.

to come…do the 'women's angle.'" Shirer and Breckinridge went to Berlin, where he introduced her to broadcast personnel. She went to the Berlitz School "to learn the correct words for arms of various kinds, aircraft carrier, cruiser, destroyers, etc." Murrow went on to Paris to meet with Sevareid and Grandin. Paris was bitterly cold. Murrow had been nursing a "cold." At the Paris airport waiting for his flight out, he was coughing so badly that Sevareid insisted he get medical attention. Murrow ended up hospitalized with a strep infection and pneumonia, ailments brought on, or at least worsened, by over-work and smoking.

In Berlin's broadcast facility, Breckinridge wrote, "I sat at one desk and a technician sat at another with a copy of my script and his finger on the button to cut me off if I departed from it in any way." Initially, she covered "women's stories." She reported that Berlin nightclub orchestras were forbidden to play swing music. She reported on a "Brides' School," where young women intending to marry members of the SS learned how to be "useful wives and mothers, and good Nazis." And at a cocktail party during the winter coal shortage, she listened as young women talked about "the right color nail polish to wear when your hands are purple with cold."

In Paris, Sevareid also fell victim to CBS's desire to aim broadcasts at women. His February 5, 1940, broadcast opened, "While France is at war, one of the great peacetime arts goes on—the art of fashion." With Carmel Snow, editor of *Harper's Bazaar*, Sevareid was cohosting a fashion show. As Sevareid made small talk, Snow reported, "I feel modesty has great sex appeal. Not the fashion to be dramatic in one's dressing....Waists are, if anything, shorter...." Sevareid later wrote that the show was an appalling thing to do in wartime.

Meanwhile, Breckinridge was getting meatier stories: on January 30, she covered Hitler's first public appearance since the attempt on his life in a Munich beer cellar the previous November—a speech at the Berlin Sportpalast. ⓒⓓ She also reported on the German press. German newspapers, she wrote, "allow no exchange of ideas and leave little to the reader's judgment." That comment was censored. She discussed the German Winter Relief effort, adding that some believed money raised went not to the unfortunate but for armaments. That comment was censored. She described the success of the *Völkischer Beobachter*, adding that the newspaper was published by a firm "in which Hitler and other government leaders have large interests." That was censored. She closed with the comment, "The motto of this important official paper is 'Freedom and Bread.' There is still bread." The German censors, apparently unable to recognize irony, let that comment slip through.

TRACK 7

NEUTRAL AMSTERDAM
*Murrow, Mary Marvin Breckinridge, and Shirer
enjoy some time at a skating rink—and away
from the war—in Amsterdam on January 19, 1940.*

Scandinavia

BRECKINRIDGE'S MOST NOTABLE report came a few days later. On February 16, the German ship *Altmark* was intercepted by a British destroyer in Norwegian territorial waters. The destroyer, *Cossack*, rescued 303 British merchant seamen who had been prisoners aboard the *Altmark*. There was shooting—six German sailors were killed. The German government, with some justification, expressed outrage over the incident. CBS sent Breckinridge from Holland to Norway. There, she reported on the funeral for the dead sailors, and interviewed the German commander. The following day, Breckinridge flew to Stavenger, where the *Altmark* had been run aground, to talk to the crew and tour the ship. She got the full tour. "Under the gangway along the middle deck," she reported, "I saw a line of frozen blood and a lump of flesh which fell through the slats...where a German sailor was fatally shot." She returned from Stavenger by car, an eighty-mile trip that took twenty-five hours in a blizzard. The only trouble, she cabled CBS in New York, "was cold feet. Physical, not psychological." She had been the only woman on the scene and the only reporter allowed to talk with and photograph the crew.

Despite *Altmark*, relative peace lingered. The last week of March 1940 brought stories characteristic of their countries. In Germany, private automobiles had already been ordered from the roads. Now, Shirer reported, in an effort to scavenge metals, car owners were ordered to turn in their batteries. They would be compensated, he said, "from thirty-five cents to three dollars, depending on the condition of the batteries." From Holland, Breckinridge reported on the country's plans to defend itself by flooding fields. From London, Murrow reported on an incident of labor–management strife. A carpenter had taken overlong with his tea—reprimanded, he swore at his boss and was fired. Five hundred carpenters went on strike, and, two months later, were still holding out. "During wartime," Murrow commented, "over a cup of tea."

Altmark had a delayed effect. Hitler considered the seizure an insult; now, he bowed to his navy's wish to seize Norway. The navy wanted Norway to protect the flow of iron ore from Sweden, and as a base to use against England.

On April 9, the Germans invaded Denmark—a "land bridge" to Norway—and landed troops at scattered points along the Norwegian coast.

That night, Shirer reported the German viewpoint. Germany had, he said, "taken over the protection of Denmark and Norway for the duration of the war. That is to say, at dawn this morning the Nazi army invaded the two neutral states of Denmark and Norway. The reason given—and we correspondents were given an explanation by the German foreign minister himself this morning—is that Norway and Denmark were unable to protect

INVASION OF DENMARK AND NORWAY

German soldiers move heavy artillery to battle lines in Norway. Germany invaded Denmark and Norway, according to Nazi officials, to protect them from the Allies.

themselves from an approaching invasion by Allied troops." Denmark did not resist. Shirer reported that "Danes on the street [were] amazed to find German soldiers attacking the castle." Shirer's broadcast was part of a CBS special presentation on the Scandinavian situation, preempting the broadcast of "Americans at Work." From Paris, Eric Sevareid predicted a strong reaction: "The atmosphere in government circles today was electric. Certainly the French will strike as hard as time and geography permit. If they should not, public reaction against the government would be violent."

The German move was a surprise. On April 10, Shirer reported, "Neutral naval attachés were scratching their heads at the news." How had the Germans managed to move troops up the Norwegian coast under the noses of the British Navy? Four days later, Shirer had a scoop: the Germans had moved troops and supplies up the coast in the cargo ships normally used to move iron ore. He added, "It has even been reported that these German transports were escorted to their secret destinations by Norwegian warships in order to protect them from the British."

The French Invasion

FIGHTING FLICKERED ON in Norway; in France, all was quiet. On April 29, 1940, William Shirer reported the scene along the Rhine River where it ran between the French and Germany armies: "Not two hundred yards from the river and in full sight of a French blockhouse, some German soldiers were frolicking about kicking an old football....Not a shot was fired." But Shirer was picking up signs. On May 4, new gasoline restrictions were ordered. Were supplies low? Shirer wondered. Or were stores being accumulated for some new military movement? Rumors were flowing. On May 9, CBS New York broadcast a report from Germany that rail travel might be restricted on the coming weekend. Travel was restricted because the German army was on the move.

On May 10, Shirer broadcast from Berlin, "The decisive battle of the war has begun." Germany launched simultaneous invasions of France, Belgium, Luxembourg, and the Netherlands. That same day, Neville Chamberlain resigned as Britain's prime minister. From London, Murrow reported, "history has been made too fast over here today." Winston Churchill was forming a new government. Churchill, Murrow said, had for years been "a rather lonesome and often bellicose figure" in Parliament, sounding unheeded warnings against Nazism. Now, at sixty-five, Churchill—"plump, bald with massive round shoulders"—was England's chief.

TRACK 8

TRACK 9

While the combined French, British, and Belgian armies outnumbered the Germans, all other advantages were with the invaders. The French were dispirited. A British general watching a French column observed "men unshaven, horses ungroomed, clothes and saddlery that did not fit, vehicles dirty, and [a] complete lack of pride." German morale was high; its tactics revolutionary. The Dutch believed their flooded fields would thwart invaders; German Junker 52 transport planes flew over the water and landed troops on dry land. The Belgians thought their Eben Emael fortress would prevent the Germans from crossing the Meuse River; the Germans dropped paratroops on its roof and captured the fortress in hours. With that fortress captured, German tanks pierced the Allied line in Belgium, north of the Maginot Line. The first tanks to cross the Meuse were commanded by a German general named Erwin Rommel.

In France, a scheduled tour of the front by reporters was cancelled; Eric Sevareid took that as a bad sign. Returning to Paris from Cambrai, Sevareid heard the sounds of battle. A companion noted the flashes of artillery, then counted the seconds until the sound of explosions—as one might to estimate the distance of lightning. He concluded that France's border defenses had been breached. From Paris, Sevareid sent a coded message to New York; the message sat for several hours before anyone remembered about the code. CBS's Elmer Davis then went on the air and, referring to Sevareid as "a usually well-informed source," announced that the Germans had broken through.

The advance in the north continued, almost too rapidly to be reported. On May 15, Shirer reported, "Last night, for instance, we had a hard time keeping up with the High Command communiqués." He was about to

GERMANS BREAK THROUGH

German troops hurry through the streets of a small, bombed-out French town.

announce an assault on Rotterdam, when news came that the city had surrendered. He was preparing a report on how the Dutch would defend Amsterdam and Utrecht, "when the High Command informed us laconically that the Dutch army had capitulated."

On May 16, Tom Grandin reported that the Germans were "not far from Paris according to the American sense of distance." That same day, Sevareid reported from a French village, where bombs intended for the rail yard had killed seventeen children. The bombs "landed in a row on the streets and on private homes which exploded like blown-up paper bags." He described a "grimy Belgian factory town" and "the old men in little groups and the women holding their children, standing in the doorways and always looking up....The sky is alive—for them an invasion like from the strange creatures of Mars."

From London, Murrow speculated upon Hitler's objective—was it Paris or London? Hitler would have to make a choice—"the whole history of German strategy seems to prove that he will concentrate upon a single objective"—and Murrow predicted that the target was Paris. In London, he added, official attitudes were hardening. Parliament voted the government extraordinary powers over British life. Murrow opened his report with the sentence, "The British Parliament in one hundred and sixty-three minutes yesterday swept away the freedom acquired in the last thousand years." The public mood was becoming harsher. *Peace News*, Murrow reported, "a publication of the pacifists, has gone out of business—the printers did not want to print it." When twenty-two German airmen were landed at a southeast coast port, an angry crowd, including many women, shouted, "Shoot the murdering swine!" The British, Murrow said, believed their country "could hold out as long as the Navy is afloat and ships continue to arrive." He added, "Increased help from America is hoped for and expected."

However the battle in France might be faring, CBS News Director Paul White wired from New York his praise for his troops' performance. He reiterated the need to put news ahead of feature, to avoid editorializing, and to steer clear of atrocity stories unless "you have absolute confidence in the source." Sensibly, he added, the reporting of atrocities "frequently results in similar acts on the other side, and thus the stories, if not true at first, lamentably do become all too accurate."

War's chaos and censors' commands made it difficult for reporters to get a clear picture of events. Still, there were conclusions some perhaps wished to avoid. From Paris, Breckinridge quoted French military authorities' assertion that German losses were triple those of the Allies. From Berlin, Shirer reported that while the Germans had won the "first round," there was as yet no knockout. The figures were faulty—after-battle reports actually revealed that French casualties were triple those of German losses. And if there had as yet been no knockout, then France was certainly down for the count. Sevareid, walking in Paris one day, concluded that the French were beaten. He had been reluctant to acknowledge this, he later wrote, because if he did, he would need to report it and the secret would be out.

Paul White
1902–1955
b. Pittsburgh, Kansas

Paul White was born June 9, 1902, in Pittsburgh, Kansas, where his father worked as a stone contractor. He displayed an affinity for language at an early age, taking part in both debate and journalism in high school. He attended Columbia University, earning a degree in journalism. After college, he worked for a number of small papers around the Midwest, including a six-year stint with United Press. Later, he would work for the *New York Evening Bulletin* before becoming news editor for CBS in December 1930.

The combination of his blue-collar background and Ivy League education provided White with a uniquely hard-nosed, yet intellectual, approach to journalism. Even as a young reporter, he was known for his aggressive style and uncanny ability to scoop fellow journalists. It was for this reason that he was recruited by CBS, where he would turn his attention to surpassing NBC as the leader in radio news. White flourished in this highly competitive environment, and was a key player in CBS's rise to prominence in the years preceding World War II. White soon began looking beyond his role as news editor and set his sights on vice president, although he often feared that the same tough style that had won him so much success as a reporter would prevent him from succeeding as an executive.

After his initial success at CBS, White's war years were fraught with tension and frustration. During the war, Murrow and White were engaged in a power struggle over how CBS should be reporting the news. For White, it was a losing battle. With the ever-growing popularity of Murrow and his team, White saw his own role as policy maker at CBS decline. Although White won a Peabody in 1945, Murrow was promoted to vice president, placing White in the role of Murrow's subordinate. Never a teetotaler, he began drinking more heavily. He finally lost control one day in 1946 when, after insisting he introduce a new program Murrow was producing, he went on the air drunk. Murrow heard the broadcast and fired White on the spot.

continued

After leaving CBS, Paul and his wife moved to San Diego, where he secured a position as news editor with CBS affiliate KFMB. White set to work on a book about his life in radio entitled *News on the Air.* Out of the shadow of Murrow, White once again seemed to flourish and redefine himself. He continued broadcasting until succumbing to emphysema and heart disease at the age of fifty-three.

With the distance of an entire country separating them, White and Murrow put their differences behind them and developed a close friendship, which lasted until White's death on July 9, 1955. White is remembered through the Paul White Award, the highest honor of the Radio-Television News Directors Association, whose recipients have included Ed Bradley, Charles Kuralt, Jane Pauley, Bernard Shaw, and Dan Rather.

•   •   •

AS IN POLAND, William Shirer was trying to get to the scene of the action. On May 21, he was permitted to observe fighting on the German side near Aachen, close to the Belgian border. "Before we start, the army officer in charge warns of the danger. Warns that we must follow his orders promptly. Explains how to dive for a nearby field and lie flat on your belly if the Allied planes come over or the French artillery open fire."

Still, he saw little. Two days later, Shirer broadcast on the fighting, "I, at least, found it difficult to observe the varying fortune of the infantry. For one thing, they were operating in wooded country near the banks of the river. For another, dense smoke from the artillery barrages laid down by both sides often hid what was going on." He gauged the flow of battle by how the German artillery changed targets: "When the German artillery advanced its barrages and peppered the roads in the rear of the Allies, this meant that the German infantry, led by tanks, was going forward." Progress seemed slow. "When we left at dusk, the German artillery, I noticed, was moving forward to new positions, so their advance here, though slow, seemed to be going on."

North of the main German tank thrust, the British, French, and Belgian armies were in retreat. On May 25, Shirer reported, "The Germans now believe [that these forces] cannot escape." Three days later, Belgium's

Leopold II ordered his armies to surrender. From Paris, Mary Marvin Breck- inridge reported French Prime Minister Paul Reynaud's "disappointment and disillusionment that a king who had called France to help his country eighteen days ago should give up suddenly without telling the men who tried to come to its aid—and he calls it 'unprecedented in history.'" Quoting Rey- naud further, Breckinridge said, "'Dark days have come,' he said, 'but our faith in victory is intact.'"

Dark days, indeed. France might face a new opponent. From Rome, CBS correspondent Cecil Brown reported a bellicose speech by Benito Mussolini, Italy's fascist dictator. Brown described the speech as "in the Mussolini tradi- tion—curt, precise, and commanding." His CBS colleague, Elmer Davis, reported an address to Italian troops by that country's leading soldier, Marshall Rodolfo Graziano. The Italian army, Graziano said, "is ready to go wherever the king wishes and wherever the Duce leads." Likely, it would go to France.

The Belgian surrender hastened the collapse in the north. Already, British and French troops were retreating rapidly to the coast, at Dunkirk. There, over a third of one million soldiers crammed into a pocket just thirty miles wide and six miles deep. Beginning May 27, the British Navy and hun- dreds of other craft that were volunteered for service removed 335,000 men from the beaches in the next week.

Murrow, typically, found the personal angle to the story. The evacuation took 224 naval vessels and 665 "other" craft—"yachts, riverboats, pleasure steamers, trawlers, fishing craft, surely the strangest armada ever assem- bled." In a June 3 broadcast, Murrow focused on a single ship, the *Blackburn Rovers*, a trawler earlier pressed into service as a minesweeper. Murrow had ridden on it and reported on its work. Now, he was reporting on its death— the ship had been sunk in the evacuation: "She was a dirty, rusty, weather- beaten little vessel. One of her crew told me he hoped to go back and tend his cabbage when the war was over—another wanted to continue a philoso- phy course at night school. The cook of the *Blackburn Rovers* confessed that he generally fed his tough, hard-faced crew on Irish stew, three times a day. She wasn't much of a ship, but the men on her were brave men. I saw them sweeping mines and I know."

England's mood, Murrow reported, was somber. He reported, "I saw more grave, solemn faces today than I have ever seen in London before. Fashionable tearooms were almost deserted; the shops in Bond Street were doing very little business; people read their newspapers as they walked slowly down the streets....I saw one woman standing in line waiting for a bus begin to cry, very quietly. She didn't even bother to wipe the tears away."

The Fall of France

ON JUNE 4, 1940, the forty thousand Allied troops remaining at Dunkirk surrendered. William Shirer reported from Berlin, "Church bells have been ringing and millions of flags flying throughout Germany today." One man told Shirer, "Perhaps the English and French now wish they'd had less butter and more cannon." In Rome, Cecil Brown described the steps Italy was taking to enter the war on the side of the Germans. 🆑 In London, Murrow reported on the military disaster at Dunkirk. He reported how Winston Churchill used that defeat to rally the nation in one of his most stirring speeches: "We shall go on to the end," he said. "We shall fight on the beaches...we shall fight in the fields and in the streets. We shall never surrender." It was a prophetic speech, and Murrow recognized its significance: "I have heard Mr. Churchill in the House of Commons in intervals over the last ten years. Today, he was different. He spoke the language of Shakespeare with the direct urgency such as I have never before heard in that house." 🆑 In retreat, Britain was beginning to show its stubborn resolve.

The previous day, German bombers appeared over Paris. Their target, the Citroën factory, was not far from the restaurant in which CBS correspondent Eric Sevareid was having a late lunch. Sevareid was sitting near an American student studying for his examinations—one on international law, the other on German philosophy. Now, some hybrid of German philosophy crossed with international lawlessness was about to wreak havoc. Paris had had air-raid warnings before. Sevareid said, "Everyone in the room had an uncanny conviction immediately that this time it would really come." He

TRACK 11

TRACK 12

reported the sounds of running feet and doors and shutters slamming, then an ominous silence, soon broken: "First, the explosion of antiaircraft, and then the drumming of distant motors, which grew louder and louder. Just when the bombs began falling we couldn't tell—all the sounds started to melt and mingle together…like an approaching thunderstorm, it was constant and unrelieved." **CD** After the attack, Sevareid went out into the street to discover block after block of shattered windows.

"WE SHALL NEVER SURRENDER."

As prime minister of Great Britain, Winston Churchill inspired his countrymen with his words and his iron resolve to defeat Hitler and Nazism.

TRACK 13

North of Paris, the remaining French armies attempted a stand, but were steadily pressed back. The country was unraveling. A fighting army is a collective; chaos is individual. As France disintegrated, individual desperation followed. From the second week of conflict, Mary Marvin Breckinridge reported on the masses of refugees fleeing the fighting. These, she said, were lugging carpetbags "stuffed with treasures," baby carriages filled with quilts, and boxes tied with bits of string. She told listeners of a boy of seventeen, who, upon learning that the Germans were ten kilometers from his village, "simply ran, without even being able to find his mother to say good-bye." She gathered a group of refugees for a photograph. An air raid sounded, and one young boy said, "We must lie down." No one moved, however, until the picture had been taken and the proof of their misery recorded.

Along with all the others, chaos was engulfing the CBS correspondents. Lois Sevareid, after a difficult delivery, gave birth to twins two weeks before the invasion. She was recuperating in a Paris clinic. When Sevareid visited, he discovered that the medical personnel had fled. Sevareid managed to round up a Danish nurse for his wife and the infants and an ambulance to carry them to a private home outside Paris. Safety seemed available only in America. The Sevareids returned to Paris in a train that passed streams of refugees, who, Lois Sevareid wrote, "seemed to move forward with strange unseeing eyes and set faces." Sevareid's personal appeal to the head of a shipping line brought his wife and their twins passage from Genoa on the *Manhattan*—the same ship that had carried the Murrows and Mary Marvin Breckinridge to Europe in 1937.

Breckinridge was managing to stay just in front of the German advance. She had reached Paris from Amsterdam by way of Brussels on the last train to pass safely through the Belgian capital. Her ultimate destination, curiously, was Berlin. In Germany earlier in the year, she had renewed acquaintance with an American diplomat, Jefferson Patterson. The couple planned to marry. Uncertain how to get that news through censorship, Breckinridge informed Murrow that she was "going to follow Tom's example"—correspondent Tom Grandin had recently married. Murrow's response was "Whee." Breckinridge wrote, "And I said it was an all-American affair (I didn't want him to think I was marrying a Nazi)." As a precaution, Breckinridge in Paris purchased a bicycle; whatever the Germans did, she wanted a means out. In the end, she left Paris on June 8 by train for Genoa, then to Berlin, where she was married on June 20, wearing a deliberately patriotic ensemble of red, white, and blue.

With her marriage, Breckinridge's broadcasting career ended. CBS wished her to continue, but the U.S. Department of State ruled that for the spouse of a diplomat, broadcasting was a conflict of interest. That effectively ended participation by women as CBS war correspondents. Betty Wason, who made a dozen broadcasts from Scandinavia, was replaced that same spring by Winston Burdett. The replacement was done because she was a woman. CBS policy was now firm: no women near the war. Later, when Murrow tried to hire renowned *New York Tribune* columnist Dorothy Thompson, CBS New York vetoed the proposal.

EVACUATION OF DUNKIRK

British soldiers return home from the French seaport of Dunkirk, having escaped siege by German forces.

As the fighting neared Paris, Sevareid and Grandin's job became increasingly difficult. Sevareid later wrote, "We talked to everyone we could find who returned from a sector of the atomized 'front.' No two stories, no two conclusions or predictions were alike. Accurate, consistent reporting of developments was an impossibility." The city he loved was collapsing around him. Sevareid later wrote, "Paris was dying, like a beautiful woman in a coma, not knowing or asking why." On June 10, he learned that the city's transmitter would be closed down that night. He wrote his script, delicately phrasing the situation by saying that any further broadcast from Paris "would be under jurisdiction other than the French." The censor, who "had no heart to delete anything," allowed the comment to pass. All news was bad for France. On June 11, Mussolini declared war on the French, and a new battlefront opened.

Sevareid was now on the lam. His instructions were to quit Paris and follow the French government, which had relocated southwest to Bordeaux on the Bay of Biscay on the Atlantic coast. He located a still functioning short-wave transmitter about an hour from that city, with a broadcast studio in a former perfume factory. Sevareid's days as a broadcaster in France were running out. Every few hours, he wrote, "the transmitter crew phoned in to Bordeaux to report the enemy position and to ask how long they should remain on duty. They were told to remain at their posts until the Germans walked in; and they did not desert."

Larry LeSueur, one of the correspondents recently recruited by Murrow to cover France, was also attempting to stay ahead of the advancing German army. He had been with British troops in Belgium, who had then fled to the beaches of Dunkirk. LeSueur walked and hitchhiked the 150 miles from the Belgian border to Paris, arriving just in time to join the exodus out of that city. LeSueur managed to make it to Tours in a hired car. There, he hoped to join Sevareid in covering the invasion of France. Sevareid, however, according to LeSueur, did not want any help. He offered LeSueur the 2:30 A.M. broadcast slot and refused to share his hotel room. Discouraged, LeSueur traveled west to Nantes, where he hoped to catch a British troop ship out of France. Desperate for sleep, the only accommodations he managed to find were in a prostitute's hotel room. The next day, he made his way to the ship, started up the gangplank, but was stopped before he could board. Informed that the transport was full, LeSueur had to make other plans. After hitching a ride with a British army truck on its way to Brest and another ship, he watched in horror as a German bomber made a direct hit on the troop ship he had just attempted to board. The bomb ripped through the engine room, exploding and killing thousands of soldiers. Several days later, LeSueur would be back, unscathed, in London.

Sevareid, however, had one more important story to broadcast. France had formed a new cabinet. A rival correspondent—noting the number of generals who had been appointed—informed America that it was a government determined to fight on. Sevareid, with a better knowledge of French political figures, rightly concluded the reverse. He informed New York, "Regardless of what you may have heard, this is not a cabinet designed to carry on the war." Having broadcast, Sevareid was startled to realize that he had, in effect, announced that France was quitting the war without getting a censor's clearance for the statement. He reasoned that, since the position of minister of information in the new government was still vacant, he could claim there had been no one officially responsible for clearing his statement. (A further wrinkle: as first reported, Sevareid's statement that it "is *not* a cabinet designed" to continue the war was reported as "is *now* a cabinet designed." CBS carried the corrected version a few hours later.)

Sevareid's other colleague, Tom Grandin, was also in the soup. His plan was to take his wife, Natalia, to Bordeaux, put her on a ship for America, and return to the action. He discovered, however, that since his wife was not an American citizen, she would likely not be allowed to disembark in New York unless he traveled with her. Faced with this prospect, Grandin sailed. Murrow later called his departure "entirely justifiable under the circumstances," but it put an end to his days as a CBS correspondent as, in the eyes of Paul White, Grandin had abandoned his post.

On June 14, the German army entered Paris. Three days later, William Shirer followed. He had first come to Paris as a journalist in 1925; now, with the city conquered, "I had an ache in the pit of my stomach and I wished I had not come." Two-fifths of the city's five million residents had fled. The rest, Shirer told listeners, "are still dazed. They were dazed when the unbelievable happened, when the gray-clad German troops entered their capital last Friday morning." They had reason. In the First World War, France had fought for four years. Now, she had been overrun in six weeks.

REPORTING THE FALL OF PARIS

*Eric Sevareid (left) and Tom Grandin report the imminent collapse
of French forces in June 1940 from a CBS studio in Paris.*

Shirer was present when worse news came on June 17. France was seeking an armistice. He reported, "I stood in a throng of French men and women on the Place de la Concorde when the news first came over. They were almost struck dead." Shirer pointed out an irony—the crowd was near the Hotel Crillon, where President Woodrow Wilson had stayed during the Versailles Conference following World War I. The hotel was now German army headquarters.

Thomas Grandin
1907–1977
b. Cleveland, Ohio

Thomas Grandin was born on July 19, 1907, in Cleveland, Ohio. He graduated from Yale in 1930, and went on to study international law at L'Ecole des Sciences Politiques in Paris and the University of Berlin. The mild-mannered and scholarly Grandin had no experience in journalism prior to being the second correspondent hired by Murrow, but his expertise in international issues and his capacity for languages were assets that few journalists could claim. He worked in the International Chamber of Commerce in Paris from 1933–34, and in 1939, he was among the first foreign correspondents to cover Europe on the brink of war. As the war continued to escalate, Grandin became increasingly valuable to Murrow and became known as his "man in Paris." However, Grandin's broadcasting abilities remained rough around the edges, which was a constant source of tension between Murrow and CBS News Director Paul White. Despite White's repeated efforts to force Grandin to resign, Murrow supported him throughout.

In 1940, when the front collapsed and chaos reigned throughout France, Grandin returned to America with his Romanian wife, Natalia, whom he'd met the previous winter at a Balkans foreign ministers' conference in Belgrade. Grandin learned that Natalia, lacking a U.S. passport, would not have been let into the country without him. Though some, including Paul White and William Shirer, thought he deserted his post, Murrow supported him and recommended him for a job with the FCC in Washington. While there, Grandin served as chief editor of the FCC's Foreign Broadcast Intelligence Service. He later worked for the government on a variety of confidential assignments throughout Europe, Africa, and India. In 1944, he signed on with ABC to cover the war, and that June, he accompanied the first wave of troops to land at the heavily defended Omaha Beach on D-Day.

Grandin retired from broadcasting after the war to pursue a career as a sales executive. He and Natalia had three children and retired to a ranch in Arizona, where they lived until Grandin's death on October 19, 1977.

GERMAN TROOPS ENTER PARIS

*On June 14, 1940, the advancing German army captured Paris—conquering
German troops march on the Champs-Elysées under the Arche de Triomphe.*

For Sevareid and Shirer, the story of France's fall was not yet complete.
Sevareid faced the dangerous necessity of getting out of France, presumably
to England. Shirer was still to make his most famous broadcast, that of the
French surrender. On June 19, 1940, Shirer reported that the Germans had
demanded the French surrender in the Forest of Compiègne, about forty-five
miles north of Paris. They were being unsparing of French pride. The site
chosen was the identical site on which Germany had sued for peace in 1918.

That same day, Shirer reached Compiègne, where preparations for the surrender were being made. As much as he disliked the Germans, he was impressed by the efficiency of their technical support: "By a super-human effort, army communications engineers had laid down in a couple of days a radio-cable line from Brussels to the Compiègne Forest." His broadcasts, when they were made, came through "clear as a bell." He was startled to discover "German army engineers feverishly engaged in tearing out the wall" of the museum housing the railway car that had been the site of the signing of the 1918 Armistice (so that the car could be used again). Same site, same railway car, and—as it turned out—even the same desk.

On June 21, the Germans presented their terms. Shirer made a joint broadcast with a part-time NBC correspondent, William C. Kerker. "Everything," Shirer said, "everything that we've been seeing here this afternoon in Compiègne Forest has been so reversed. The last time, the representatives of France sat in that car dictating the terms of the Armistice. This afternoon, we peered through the windows of the car and saw Adolf Hitler laying down the terms." **CD** Hitler was sitting, Shirer noted, in the same chair that in 1918 had been used by Allied commander Marshal Foch.

TRACK 14

After the terms had been presented, Shirer watched Hitler stroll past the granite block that proclaimed Germany's 1918 surrender. Its inscription read:

HERE ON THE ELEVENTH OF NOVEMBER 1918
SUCCUMBED THE CRIMINAL PRIDE OF THE GERMAN EMPIRE...
VANQUISHED BY THE FREE PEOPLES WHICH IT TRIED TO ENSLAVE.

Shirer watched Hitler through opera glasses. "I have seen that face many times at the great moments of his life. But today! It is afire with scorn, anger, hate, revenge, triumph....He glances back at [the monument], contemptuous, angry—angry, you almost feel, because he cannot wipe out the awful, provoking lettering with one sweep of his high Prussian boot."

The signing itself took but a few minutes on June 22. Afterward, the Germans bundled most of the press back to Berlin to await the official communiqué that would be issued once Hitler had approved its wording. Shirer and Kerker stayed behind. Shirer managed to persuade German officials who had remained to contact the Berlin shortwave transmitting station and direct

SURRENDER AT COMPIÈGNE FOREST

Shirer prepares his report on the French surrender to Germany on June 21, 1940, in the same spot that Germany surrendered to the Allies in World War I.

it to broadcast a call from Shirer to New York. Shirer's broadcast went out less than ninety minutes after the actual signing. His report was brief, less than four minutes. He was, for Shirer, in good voice. He reported: "At 6:50, the gentlemen in the car started affixing their signatures to Germany's armistice conditions. It was all over in a few moments, the armistice had been signed." 🔘 That he was there at all was remarkable, as all other foreign, as well as German, correspondents had been ordered back to Berlin, where Hitler planned to announce the armistice to the world. Unknown to Shirer (and presumably the German military engineers in Compiègne and censors in Berlin), his broadcast was a world scoop.

TRACK 14

Also unknown to Shirer, he had one unlikely listener. Sevareid, his tenure in France over, was scrambling to find a way out. On a tip from a fellow American, he tracked down a ship's captain, who told him, "I don't care whether you've got passports or visas or any of that red-tape nonsense." The ship, the *Ville de Liége*, was reachable only by ferry. Sevareid was traveling with an American couple. He later wrote, "The grizzled old Frenchman who ran the ferry said he was sorry, but it was against the law to take a woman out. Five hundred francs altered the law." The party reached the ship, which set sail for England. On board, Sevareid was in the captain's quarters when the radio was turned on. The announcer's voice was instantly recognizable. It was William Shirer, announcing the surrender of France.

LONDONERS, ED MURROW reported, were little undone by the undoing of the French. It would be difficult, Murrow broadcast on June 17, to locate "an Englishman who would talk seriously of the possibility of peace with Germany now." Two days later, the British government set down instructions for resisting invasion. Murrow reported them: remain where you are; ignore rumors and report anything suspicious. Food, bicycles, maps, and gasoline were to be denied the invaders. These instructions ended, "Think of your country before you think of yourself." The French surrender drew from George VI this entirely English comment, stated in a letter to his mother: "Personally, I feel happier now that we have no allies to be polite to and to pamper." England had no allies; it stood alone. Among those who would aid England most effectively was Edward R. Murrow.

3

THIS IS LONDON

I first came to England sixteen years ago....I admired your history, doubted your future, and suspected that the historians had merely agreed upon a myth. But always there was something that escaped me. Always there remained in the back of a youthful and undisciplined mind the suspicion that I might be wrong.

—*Edward R. Murrow*
"A Reporter Remembers" broadcast for the BBC (1946)

TRACKS: 17–22

London Is Burning

ERIC SEVAREID MADE it out of war and France with luck and misgivings. Shipboard on the *Ville de Liége*, he wondered if Ed Murrow might regard his fleeing France without orders to be "desertion." When Sevareid landed in Liverpool on July 1, 1940, those misgivings were quickly allayed: Murrow was rightly relieved that his missing reporter had turned up somewhere, and safe. The war Sevareid had left behind, however, had made it to England before him. When Sevareid boarded a train for London, the conductor came through, pulling down the shades. "Air raids, ye know," he said.

England awaited Hitler's next move. On July 9, William Shirer broadcast from Berlin: "The suspense is getting intense. Will it be the Mediterranean or England? And when will it come?" Would Germany strike directly for England, or indirectly by way of the Mediterranean and the vital Suez Canal? Hitler was uncertain. On July 16, he ordered planning of Operation Sea Lion, code name for the invasion of Britain. The German dictator hoped, however, that Britain would seek a negotiated peace. From Berlin, Shirer reported an odd sign that peace was anticipated: "Three hundred Germans have started learning Swahili." Swahili was spoken in East Africa, a colony Germany had lost in 1918. Now, Shirer suggested, Germans thought peace would bring its return. On July 19, Shirer reported Hitler's offer of peace. That offer, Shirer elaborated, was that if Britain accepted German control of Europe, Germany would not dispute British control of the seas. The British quickly turned it down. In Berlin, Shirer reported, that rejection left the populace "depressed." But, he added, Berliners "pin their hopes on a quick victory which will be over by fall and therefore save them from another war winter."

LONDON FIREFIGHTERS

Firemen battle a blaze caused by German incendiaries
in front of a bombed-out building after an air raid.

The war may well have been decided by that winter, though not as the
Berliners to whom Shirer spoke might have wished. In retrospect, Hitler
stood closest to victory that summer, apparently able to launch an irresistible
military force against the under-defended island that was his last standing
opponent. Britain braced for an air attack, an attack that might pave the way
for armed invasion or bomb London into surrender. Britain's key defenders
were its RAF pilots—dubbed "The Few," they never numbered more than
fourteen hundred. On August 1, Hitler ordered the Luftwaffe to "crush

Britain." In Berlin, Shirer took bets offered by two German officials, "First, that the Swastika will be flying over Trafalgar Square by August 15. Second, by September 7."

The battle's key weapons were its fighter aircraft, German Messerschmitt 109s and British Spitfires. Operationally, they were a near equal match; numerically, the Germans maintained a four-to-three advantage through the conflict. Britain, however, had the advantages of defense. Most fighting took place over England—a British pilot forced to bail out might well return to service; his German counterpart likely became a prisoner. And England had a vital early-warning system, the world's only effective web of radar stations.

Air combat began over the British Channel, England's southern ports, and at scattered sites around the country. In mid-August, Shirer visited the airstrips constructed by the Germans in Belgium and France as bases against Britain. They were well camouflaged: "Once in Belgium our German pilot couldn't find his landing field for several minutes because it looked just like all the other farms from the air." Standing with Fred Oeschner of United Press, he watched German aircraft leave for bombing runs over England. Almost surreally, Shirer noted, "Nearby, a French peasant would be sitting behind a team of horses cutting wheat. Cows would be grazing, perfectly oblivious to these roaring air monsters of destruction."

Across the Channel, Murrow felt a similar unreality. By now, he had been granted relative freedom of movement by the British government. He and other correspondents scrambled about England's southeast, trying to track the fighting in the skies. On August 16, he broadcast, "Much of it you can't see, [because] the aircraft are up in the clouds, out of sight." A week later, he added, "Even when the dive bombers come down looking like a duck with both wings broken and you hear the hollow grunt of the bombs, it doesn't seem to have much meaning."

In September 1940, the crisis sharpened. Readying their invasion, the Germans gathered barges, trawlers, and fishing boats in French ports. They readied, as well, in Berlin. During the fighting in France, Shirer said, German press officers used "a gigantic, illuminated map of the western front" to describe the battle. On September 2, he added, "that map has been taken down, and an equally large one substituted. It was a map of England. And it left us all wondering, well, whether one of these days we would be following a new campaign on this excellent map." Two days later, Shirer reported Hitler's teasing of his British foe. At the Berlin Sportpalast, Shirer said, Hitler posed a rhetorical question: "'The English ask: Why doesn't he come?' Hitler stepped back, raised his arms and said, 'Be calm. Be calm. He's coming. One must not be so curious.'" "Whereupon," Shirer closed, "the house exploded with laughter." In Berlin, Shirer recorded in his diary, "Rumor sets invasion for September 15; moon and tides good." In a broadcast of his own, Murrow stated, "The currently favored date for this invasion…is sometime about September 18."

The air battle intensified. The Luftwaffe retained the initiative. Britain offered multiple targets. The Germans could strike at the RAF in the air, at British aircraft factories on the ground, at the RAF's airstrips, or at the radar installations that were its "eyes." Beginning August 24—the night of the "London After Dark" broadcast described in the prologue—the Luftwaffe attacks focused on the military airfields. Defending its fields over the next two weeks, the RAF suffered casualties it could not sustain—290 aircraft downed; 231 pilots killed or injured. The Luftwaffe was gaining the upper hand. In German calculations, however, time pressed. Invasion would become much more difficult with October's tides and fogs. In a key decision, Hitler redirected the Luftwaffe. He would use it to break British will through direct bombing of London.

On September 6, Larry LeSueur broadcast "a typical day in London." As much as anything, his report conveyed wearied boredom. Air-raid sirens waking him for a breakfast of oatmeal, toast, and tea. An elevator operator urging him to stuff cotton in his ears for sounder sleep. A chat on the day's news with Murrow at the small CBS office. A fruitless search for an open post office. Fact-gathering visits to two government ministries. Dinner with Sevareid. Then, an evening drink at the Murrows' where all listened to anti-aircraft fire from east of the city. LeSueur went to bed at one A.M., and "slept fitfully." Likely, it was his best night's sleep for some while.

The following day, wave after wave of German bombers struck London in a twelve-hour attack. Murrow was southeast of the city, trying to get a bead on the action. He spent part of the day near an RAF airbase. "On the airdrome," he broadcast the following day, "ground crews swarmed over

"LONDON IS BURNING."
*A block of flats goes up in flames after
a particularly fierce air raid.*

those British fighters, fitting ammunition belts and pouring in gasoline. As soon as one fighter was ready, it took to the air, and there was no waiting for flight leaders or formation. The Germans were already coming back, down the river, heading for France." He spoke of "the hollow grunt of the bombs, [the] huge pear-shaped bursts of flame." He talked to a pub owner who "told us these raids were bad for the chickens, the dogs, and the horses." And for a time, he simply took cover. As Murrow described it, "Vincent Sheean lay on one side of me and cursed in five languages....Ben Robertson, of *PM*, lay on the other side and kept saying in that slow South Carolina drawl, 'London is

TRACK 17

burning, London is burning.'" ⒸⒹ

London, indeed, was burning. Four hundred were dead, triple that many were injured, and fires blazed throughout the city. From Berlin, Shirer reported the German view: "All this combined to create the impression of a blazing inferno, ghastly beyond human imagination." The government statement continued, "For weeks the British people have been deluded into believing that the German raids on London have been repulsed. In reality no such raids took place. They did not begin until yesterday." And that attack continued, daily for nearly two months. The battle wavered. On September 15, Germany launched its largest yet fleet of bombers over London. Buckingham Palace was damaged in the attack, which was otherwise an expensive German defeat. The *Times* published the exaggerated claim that 185 German planes had been shot down. The actual total was sixty, but many in England regarded the day as a turning point.

From the Streets to the Rooftops

THE BOMBING GOT closer to Murrow. On September 20, a vacant CBS office was hit. A few days later, Larry LeSueur viewed the damage. "It was a sad sight," he broadcast. "The clock had stopped permanently at nine minutes past two in the morning, when the bombs tore the top floor of the building off." The floor was littered with shattered glass, not from its windows—these, as directed, were open—but from the glass office dividers. LeSueur added, "A flood caused by a broken water pipe forced rivulets out of our cracked walls, water dripped from the lighting fixtures, and the carpets were red marshes of mud, broken glass, and chunks of concrete." What was becoming clear, however, was that a city the size of London could absorb considerable punishment. From Berlin, Shirer reported these surprisingly uncensored comments: "I was talking with a German airman the other day who's been making regular flights to London. He said that every night he came over London, he was surprised, after the terrific amount of explosives dropped on it, to see so much of the city still standing. 'It's an awfully big city,' he exclaimed."

And Murrow got closer to the story. He had for weeks been working on the Ministry of Information to get permission to do live regular broadcasts of the air raids from London's rooftops. The Ministry finally relented to Murrow's badgering, on one condition: he would have to make test recordings of his reports for six nights in a row—to, as Murrow later put it, "persuade the censors that I could ad-lib without violating security." Having made and submitted the recordings, the Ministry promptly lost them. So he went back up and did it again for another six nights. This time, the Ministry reviewed the test recordings, heard Murrow report what he saw without giving away vital information to the enemy, and decided to deny his request anyway. After all, who knew what he might say in an actual broadcast, with bombs falling all around him? At this point, Murrow used his considerable connections to get word of his idea to the prime minister. As a former newsman, Churchill knew a great story. As an embattled leader, he believed that broadcasting England's plight would gain American sympathy. Churchill approved the broadcasts. Soon, Murrow was standing on rooftops, mixing his report on the day's news with accounts of the bombing then in progress. 🅒 **TRACK 19**

The British people, Sevareid later wrote, "will probably never know what Murrow did for them in those days." Over one hundred American correspondents were in Britain during the bombing, but Murrow's work ranked an unquestioned first in importance. In part, this reflected the rising importance of radio. About this time, CBS News Director Paul White reported a poll that said 65 percent of Americans ranked radio news and comment as their most important source of information. More, it was from how Murrow used the medium. Murrow, Sevareid said, "was not trying to 'sell' the British cause to America; he was trying to explain the universal human cause of men who were showing a noble face to the world. In so doing, he made the British and their behavior human and thus compelling to his countrymen at home."

ST. PAUL'S CATHEDRAL

The large dome of St. Paul's is wreathed in smoke after a raid. It was one of many London institutions damaged by German bombs during the Battle of Britain.

At year's end, CBS announcer Robert Trout expressed the view that the most famous three words of 1940 were "This is London." This was the signature phrase with which Murrow opened his broadcasts, though, in fact, the phrase was not his own. Cesar Saerchinger, Murrow's predecessor in London, had greeted his audience by saying, "Hello America. This is London calling." For a time, Murrow did likewise. Then he received a letter from his old college mentor, Ida Lou Anderson. She wrote that she thought the Saerchinger opening was stagy. She suggested that Murrow replace it with "This is London," with a slight emphasis on the first word (*"This* is London"). Murrow had begun using the new opening on September 22, 1939.

Initially, the American audience to which he spoke was largely unmindful of Europe's war. The country had not fully emerged from the Depression, and many were more concerned with domestic matters. Many, too, believed the nation had little to gain by becoming embroiled in foreign conflicts. President Roosevelt was reelected to an unprecedented third term in the fall of 1940 on a platform of, among other things, keeping America out of Europe's war. American opinion shifted with time. It shifted, in part, through the tug of presidential leadership and some subtle political manipulation—Roosevelt clearly wanted America to enter the war against Germany. And it shifted through the pressure of events, events that for millions of Americans were reported in the voice of Ed Murrow.

Murrow's reports from London established him as incomparably the day's most skilled broadcaster. He combined the engaging voice of a gifted storyteller with an essayist's ability to make his point clear. Murrow's broadcasts had their characteristics. He wrote for the ear, with a keen sense of how his audience would hear and experience what he said.

Murrow liked understatement. His September 9 broadcast, coming two days after the first big raid on London, began, "I spent the day visiting the bombed areas. The king did the same thing." Broadcasting from a fire station, he said, "I saw a man laboriously copying names in a ledger, the list of firemen killed in action over the last month. There were about one hundred names." He liked irony. On September 11, he reported, "Walking down the street a few minutes, ago, shrapnel stuttered and stammered on the rooftops and from underground came the sound of singing, and the song was 'My Blue Heaven.'" He placed himself, and, thereby, his listener, on the scene. On

December 23, 1940, he began, "This afternoon, I followed my breath down Regent Street. It was cold, plenty of fur coats and heavy tweeds being worn. A few soldiers on leave wearing their Balaclava helmets, but there was a tough-looking Canadian striding along without so much as an overcoat."

Murrow painted pictures and made them vivid with detail. At one bombing site, he described "a row of automobiles, with stretchers racked on the roof like skis, standing outside the bombed buildings." At another, he noted, "Two cans of peaches had been drilled clean through by flying glass and the juice was dripping down onto the floor." Knowing that moonlight made London more visible to attacking aircraft, he referred to one night sky as being brightened by "a bomber's moon."

He was attracted to the *how* of things—for example, London's system for locating fires caused by the bombing. He described how spotters around the city called in the compass readings of blazes they saw. At district headquarters, each spotter was represented by a pin, from which a string dangled. Each string was moved to the degree a spotter indicated. The fire was located where strings crossed. Murrow commented, "Watching that system work gave me one of the strangest sensations of the war. For I have seen a similar system used to find the exact location of forest fires out on the Pacific Coast."

Murrow had an American's appreciation for those who bent the rules in the cause of simple pleasures. When a hotel keeper asked Murrow if he'd like a pork sandwich, Murrow asked about a government order forbidding the killing of hogs. "That's right," the hotel keeper replied, "but sometimes they have accidents." He spoke of Londoners' solidarity in the shelters, but noted that—even there—the rich fared better than the working classes. He spoke of a cluster of "old dowagers and retired colonels" who took refuge at the Mayfair Hotel. There, he noted, the protection was not great, but "you would at least be bombed with the right sort of people."

He was tolerant of simple, unheroic humanity. Early in the air war, he broadcast, "Just as I reached London this afternoon, the air-raid sirens were sounding again, the people were heading for the shelters in an orderly fashion. Only a few of them running. I saw no signs of panic. I did see a woman drive through a red light at about sixty miles an hour, but that may have had nothing to do with the excitement or preoccupation created by the sirens."

And he was admiring of simple, understated courage. From one bombed location, he reported, "The girls in light, cheap dresses were strolling along the streets. There was no bravado, no loud voices, only a quiet acceptance of the situation. To me those people were incredibly brave and calm."

Sevareid considered Murrow a natural, untrained and unpracticed in radio, and "simply born to the new art. It was his and—I sometimes think—his alone, never to be shared." Murrow had a practical advantage. He had never worked as a newspaper journalist. The constricting format of "who-what-where-when-how" that was standard to newspaper writing had not been hard-wired into his outlook. He could appreciate the nature of the new medium, therefore, without the clouding effect of experience with another. Murrow, however, was not untrained. He was self-trained. From his first days at CBS, Murrow sought the advice of Robert Trout, the CBS announcer whose conversational style was most to Murrow's liking. An announcer, Murrow wrote, "will engage the interest of millions if he can discover the essential intimacy of a medium which puts every listener within whispering distance of his lips."

Murrow was influential, perhaps ironically, because he did not seek to persuade. He was deferential to his audience. On September 1, 1939, the day Germany invaded Poland, he reported the speculation about England's next move, then added: "I have an old-fashioned belief that Americans like to make up their own minds on the basis of all available information. The conclusions you draw are your own affair." On another occasion, he said, "What I think of events in Europe is no more important than what you think, but I do have certain opportunities for observation and study." The suggestion was that Murrow, when offering an opinion, was not giving his own view but expressing a conclusion his listeners might well reach if they had access to the same information. He was his listeners' ally, not their instructor. He required of his listener no special insight or insider's knowledge, only a decent curiosity about the events of the day. Still, his sentiments were clear. On September 10, 1940, Murrow broadcast, "We are told today that the Germans believe Londoners, after a while, will rise up and demand a new government, one that will make peace with Germany. It's more probable that they will rise up and murder a few German pilots who come down by parachute." (CD)

TRACK 18

BOMB DAMAGE

*A double-decker bus was thrown end over end into a London building
by the force of a German bomb—note the bomb's crater (bottom left).*

What was defining of Murrow's broadcasts, perhaps, was not their characteristics, but Murrow's character. A number of CBS correspondents—
Shirer, Sevareid, Howard K. Smith among them—were political in outlook.
They regarded ideas and policy debates as important, and were liberal,
sometimes highly so, in their own politics. Murrow admired Franklin Roosevelt, but politics was not at his core. Perhaps reflecting the influence of his
Quaker upbringing, Murrow was not an ideologue, but a moralist. He was
less concerned with advocating ideas than with ascertaining his conception
of truth. He expected a great deal of people, including his reporters and primarily himself.

It did not come easily. The day's most famed broadcaster, Murrow approached the microphone with something approaching dread. The voice might be calm, but the fingers fiddled and the toes worked a jittery tapping. Ernie Pyle, often regarded as the war's outstanding print journalist, wrote an account in which Murrow realizes, mid-broadcast, that his approved script is too long:

> As a nervous censor and thirty million Americans listened, [Murrow] rewrote in his head, wound up the prepared copy and ad-libbed through the remaining minutes, walking a fine line between dead air and uncensored material. His voice betrayed no hint of effort. But when it was over, he sagged back, beads of sweat on his forehead and upper lip. By now, however, even a routine broadcast on any night would produce rivulets of nervous sweating—the result of tension, awareness of responsibility, and, above all, of mike fright.

Nor was Murrow easy on himself. Work took his almost every waking thought. He propelled himself with coffee and a cigarette habit that was climbing past three packs a day. It was difficult on his marriage. Janet Murrow remained in England during the bombing, where she faced comparable danger, a distracted husband, and a great deal less useful work to distract her. Beginning in August 1940, she became an occasional broadcaster on the effects of rationing and other "women's" stories. The following year, she became active in Bundles for Britain, a private program whereby American women acted to aid Britain's war effort.

For both of them, there were hazards more real than stage fright. The Murrows' home on Hallam Street lay in a heavily bombed district. Larry LeSueur was a frequent houseguest. The stress from bombing was considerable. At one point, Murrow woke LeSueur up to tell him that the building was on fire. By one account, "Larry gathered up his clothes and shut himself in the dark and crowded closet to put them on." LeSueur himself reported how he and Murrow "would walk along the paths cleared between the debris. We'd come back from dinner and the sirens would start and the guns went to work. One day you passed a building. The next day it was gone. There was a perverse exhilaration to it all." Murrow went through it with a nonchalance that was part policy, part pose. He refused to set foot in a bomb shelter. The reason, he told LeSueur, was that once you did so, you would lose your nerve. Murrow, LeSueur, and James "Scotty" Reston of the *New York Times* regularly played golf on a nine-hole course on London's fashionable Hempstead Heath. The course was dimpled with unexploded bombs, cordoned off with ropes. By agreement, a ball that rolled under the ropes was judged an unplayable lie.

September, too, saw its first casualties among the CBS staff. One was Sevareid, who was ailing, dispirited, and homesick, and who lacked the nonchalance with which Murrow faced the bombings. He lived not far from the Murrows, several blocks from Broadcasting House. Covering the ground to the broadcast facility at night, Sevareid wrote, "I would shuffle cautiously through the inky blackness....When the shrieking came I would plaster myself against the nearest wall, and, however sternly I lectured myself, I not infrequently found myself doing the last fifty yards at a dead run."

Berlin Blues

IN BERLIN, WILLIAM SHIRER was suffering from the "Berlin Blues," the name correspondents gave to the dreary effect of living in the Nazi state. Further, with heightened censorship, he felt he was doing little worthwhile work. From neutral Switzerland on September 12, Shirer wrote to CBS News Director Paul White to say he wanted to pack it in. His broadcasts, Shirer said, had been "reduced to mouthing absurd Nazi propaganda." An example, which aired later that month, was Shirer's report of the German claim that "the English themselves admit" that all London was a military target. Shirer added, "If the London public suffers, says [German] radio, then the British authorities who allowed the city to become such an armament center are responsible." Shirer realized, he told White, that the next few weeks might resolve the conflict. In that case, CBS would need someone—meaning

Shirer—to tell the story from the side of the German victors. He would remain a while longer. But if stalemate followed, he would leave.

The air war over England was the world's lead story, but not the only one. From Rome on September 20, Cecil Brown reported on meetings between Italian dictator Benito Mussolini and German foreign minister Joachim von Ribbentrop. Brown reported, "The impression in Rome tonight is that the Axis partners have formulated a program for the drive down the homestretch. They expect it to bring them to victory." Brown offered no details, but said the conferees believed that "London and major British cities can be destroyed whenever Germans choose to use their full resources. They have not done so thus far because of the Germans' 'high conception' of humanity."

The meeting was preliminary to the September 27 signing of the Tripartite Pact. This mutually pledged Germany, Italy, and Japan to defend an attack on any one of them from "a power not yet involved" in the European or Japanese–Chinese conflict. In Berlin, Shirer—treading around censorship—reported that the pact specifically excluded the Soviet Union as the "unnamed" power. His implication was that the pact was aimed at the only remaining uninvolved "power," the United States. In his diary, Shirer speculated that Hitler might no longer be expecting a quick end to the war. Otherwise, Shirer wondered, why bother with the pact?

September's most important event, however, was the one that did not occur. On September 17, Hitler postponed Sea Lion. The postponement, Shirer reported from Berlin a few days later, "does not mean [the invasion] has been called off. The army is there, strung along the coast. And it may be well to remember that the last man to land in Britain and conquer it nine hundred years ago, William the Conqueror, did it in the middle of October." A month after Shirer's broadcast, Murrow was reporting on the preparations for invasion. Reconnaissance flights over German-occupied French ports, he said, indicated that "Germany had commandeered every barge of over five hundred tons, and the armies of workmen were busy in the shipyards altering the bows of the vessels so that tanks and guns could be more readily embarked."

For the British, fall 1940 was a close call, twice. They had been pressed hard in the air. In the view of military historian John Keegan, "The victory of 'The Few' was narrow." Many historians believe that had the Luftwaffe focused on a given target—say, the RAF airfields—victory in the air may well have followed. Invasion, too, is a question. In late October, William Shirer wrote he was "very skeptical that a successful invasion could have been launched." Many on the German side agreed. General Wilhelm Keitel, commander of the western front, called invasion "an exceedingly difficult operation." Historian Telford Taylor wrote, "However that might have been, in fact the Germans were never readier to attempt the invasion than they were on the twentieth of September. The basic orders had been distributed, the shipping assemblage was nearing completion and the bulk of the assault troops were ready and willing." In short, the Germans chose not to risk defeat, even though their victory could not be achieved so long as England remained standing.

"REDUCED TO MOUTHING ABSURD NAZI PROPAGANDA."

*By September 1940, Shirer was ready to leave his post in Berlin,
believing that his usefulness there had ended due to Nazi censorship.*

"I Was a Citizen of London"

MURROW, BY NOW, was not just a source, but a destination. His intelligence, his engagement, and his style gave him entrée into all circles of British government and society. He became for many visitors from America a more important "man to see" than the American ambassador. In the view of many, he knew England better and had better access. He was a sought-after interview; in November, for example, he was interviewed by Ralph Ingersoll, the editor of *PM*. Murrow told Ingersoll about standing outdoors with a British pilot while London was being bombed. The pilot had made raids over Germany. A stick of bombs came whistling down across the street, Murrow said, followed by a series of explosions. The British bomber pilot said, "My God! What's that?" Murrow told him they were bombs. The British pilot, Murrow said, turned white as a sheet, and added, "I had no idea they were like that."

When it came time for Sevareid and Shirer to return to America, Murrow, the consummate boss, saw them off personally. Murrow drove Sevareid to London's Waterloo station. From England, Sevareid flew to Lisbon and then on to America. Sevareid left after an October 4, 1940, farewell broadcast in which he talked about the French, who had folded, and the British, who had not and whose struggle had his whole heart. He described the British as "a peaceable people who had gone to war in their aprons and their bowlers, with their old fowling pieces, with their ketchup bottles filled with gasoline and standing ready on the pantry shelves." He ended by quoting the comment that at war's end many would say with pride that they had been a soldier, sailor, or pilot. He added, "others will say with equal pride: 'I was a citizen of London.'"

The week Sevareid departed, Tess Shirer left Berlin for America. Soon thereafter, William Shirer's replacement, Henry Flannery, arrived in Berlin. With Flannery up to speed, Shirer in early December left Germany for Portugal. From there, he would sail for New York. Murrow flew to Portugal to see him off. Their reunion was somewhat spoiled by the news that the London office into which CBS had moved following the September bombing had itself been bombed. Shirer and Murrow had been colleagues since before the

Anschluss. Shipboard, Shirer reflected on their relationship: "We have worked together very closely, Ed and I, during the last three turbulent years over here and a bond grew that was very real, a kind you only make a few times in your life." Their parting was clouded. "We had a presentiment," Shirer wrote, "that the fortunes of war, maybe just a little bomb, would make this union the last."

Having departed, Shirer wrote Paul White to say he thought his usefulness as a reporter in Europe had ended. Censorship was one reason; immobility another. "It's impossible to get around," Shirer wrote. "Chaos of communications, no railroads, or must go through Germany or German-controlled nations like Spain, Hungary, etc. Therefore there is no continent of Europe to go back to for my kind of reporting." Shirer had another reason. Shortly before leaving Berlin, he wrote out an assessment. The British bombing of Germany, he believed, was ineffective. German morale remained high. Germans would fight because they wanted revenge for their defeat in 1918 and because they feared the consequences of defeat. These and hundreds of pages of other thoughts Shirer confided in his diary. He did not wish to return to Europe as a reporter; he wanted to write a book.

As 1940 ended, Murrow, Shirer, and Sevareid shared with listeners their thoughts on the year. Broadcasting from New York, Shirer said, "Most people [in Germany] thought war would be over before the present winter set in. When war didn't end before Christmas, it would be a mistake to think morale greatly shaken. Vast majority is convinced that Germany will win." Also in New York, Eric Sevareid called 1940 "the most tragic year in the history of the French people." He called France's quick defeat that year "perhaps the greatest surprise in the history of the world." He had assumed, he said, that when the challenge came, France would rise to it: "We should have known better."

Murrow, in London, began, "The first year of the famished '40s is ending. All Europe is on short rations." Murrow termed 1940 "Hitler's year." He added, "No one expects the new year to be happy. We shall live hard before it is ended." Britain faced immediate problems, he said—among them, night bombing, submarine warfare, and the need for better underground shelters. The year 1940 might best be summarized, he said, in the words written by poet William Wordsworth in "November 1806," when England stood alone against Napoleon:

Another year!—another deadly blow!
Another mighty Empire overthrown!
And We are left, or shall be left, alone;
The last that dare to struggle with the Foe.

Soon thereafter, Shirer took a leave of absence from CBS to work on a book. The book was *Berlin Diary*. Published that spring, it was an instant bestseller and a rallying point for anti-Hitler sentiment in America. Sevareid also wanted to write, or, at least, do something. Soon after arriving in America, he received a letter from a former British reporter, now serving with the Gordon Highlanders. "I have not the faintest shadow of regret at giving up newspapering for soldiering," it read, "and if America ever comes near the frightful position in which we find ourselves I advise you to do the same." Sevareid did not know what action to take. Americans, he thought, were dangerously indifferent to the fight against Hitler. His mind was made up. Friends, he wrote, "were no longer friends unless they thought as I did about the only things that mattered."

Sevareid wanted to dramatize for Americans the changes he thought the bombing was bringing to English society. Like Murrow, Sevareid believed—and, like Murrow, may have exaggerated—that the stress of war was producing in England a society more democratic and egalitarian. In February, he shared his thoughts in a lengthy letter to playwright Robert Sherwood. "It is not just that the people lying under the streets of London are being brave and are holding up," he wrote. "There has been a release in the soul of the ordinary garden variety of Englishman. He doesn't want to hold up during this siege and then just fall back into his old mold again." He sketched for Sherwood some possible characters, and asked, "Do you think there is a play somewhere in this stuff?" Sherwood did not. Nor did several other playwrights to whom Sevareid took the idea. Somewhat uncomfortably, Sevareid settled in as CBS correspondent in Washington, D.C.

With Shirer and Sevareid back in America, CBS in Europe added two new faces, both handsome, both former Rhodes Scholars. They were Charles Collingwood and Howard K. Smith. A student at Oxford when war broke out, Collingwood wanted to get near the action, and took a London post with the United Press. Smith said of Collingwood, "of all the Charleses I have ever known, he was the least likely to be called Chuck." Collingwood was "silent-film handsome," intelligent, articulate, a skilled writer, and an even more fashionable dresser than Murrow. (Later, when Collingwood was covering the war in North Africa, he was described as the only man on the continent who knew where to get a suit pressed by the following morning.) Murrow's fine eye for talent spotted Collingwood. They lunched at the Savoy. By one account, Murrow "glanced down at the wild expanse of Argyle socks that Collingwood wore" and wondered whether Collingwood was right for CBS. Murrow overlooked the socks. He overlooked, as well, Collingwood's lack of broadcast experience, and hired him for the London office.

BOMB SHELTER IN A TUBE STATION

London Underground stations served as bomb shelters at night during the London Blitz.
Murrow never went into a shelter, fearing that once he did, he would lose his nerve.

Charles Collingwood
1917–1985
b. Three Rivers, Michigan

Charles Cummings Collingwood was born on June 4, 1917, in Three Rivers, Michigan. He was student-body president of his high school and later attended Deep Springs College, a two-year men's school in California, where students worked on the college's 420-acre ranch when they weren't studying. He eventually transferred to and graduated from Cornell University. In 1939, he won a Rhodes Scholarship to attend Oxford, where he studied international law. While at Oxford, he wrote part-time for the United Press wire service, and in 1940 he left Oxford to pursue a full-time job there. He had only worked one year for UP when Edward R. Murrow hired him to cover North Africa. He was known for his attention to clothing and manners, and Murrow nicknamed him "Bonnie Prince Charlie." His coverage of the Allied advance in North Africa won him a Peabody at the age of twenty-six. He would go on to cover the fall of Paris and the end of the war in Europe.

After the war, to the surprise of many of his friends, Collingwood broke with his English girlfriend of seven years, Gracie Blake, to marry Hollywood movie star Louise Allbritton, who some said had swept him off his feet. Collingwood continued to work for CBS radio and television throughout the 1950s and '60s, appearing on *The CBS Morning Show*, *Person to Person*, and *The CBS Evening News*. In 1964, after having lost out to Walter Cronkite as anchor, Collingwood enjoyed international success as a CBS foreign correspondent in Europe, Asia, and the Middle East. He was the first network newsman admitted to North Vietnam, and in 1969, he was awarded the Overseas Press Club award for his reporting there. In 1970, Collingwood published a novel, the Vietnam thriller *The Defector*.

In 1975, Collingwood returned to New York after having resigned as foreign correspondent. Now classified as a CBS "special correspondent," he was in reality little used by the network, and often sat at his desk for days without work. In the era of television, Collingwood, like other early broadcasters, saw respect wane for his ability to seek out, write, and present hard-hitting news stories.

continued

TRACKS: 27, 37

After his wife's death in 1978 and his retirement from CBS in 1982, Collingwood sank into depression and alcoholism. His spirits rallied briefly in 1984, when he married his former Swedish lover, Tatiana Angelina Jolim, who persuaded him to seek treatment for alcoholism.

Collingwood died on October 30, 1985, shortly after having been diagnosed with colon cancer. At his funeral, Charles Kuralt said, "There came those years when Charles was the most honored of all of us, and the most respected, and not on the air very much. He accepted that puzzling turn of events with great dignity, as he accepted everything in life, but not with much happiness."

Howard K. Smith reached CBS without benefit of lunch. Hired by United Press the day England declared war, he was posted to Berlin in 1940 because he was fluent in German. There, he became an occasional source for William Shirer, and continued when Henry Flannery replaced Shirer. Flannery was not Shirer's equal—he knew little German and little of Germany. Paul White urged Flannery to hire an assistant; Flannery hired Smith.

In early 1941, American sentiment—stirred in no small measure by Murrow's reporting from London's rooftops—was shifting slowly toward greater support for Britain. It was being urged in that direction by President Franklin Delano Roosevelt. On January 6, Roosevelt had announced the "Four Freedoms"—broad goals for the world that would underlay American action. These were freedom of speech and expression, freedom of worship, freedom from hunger, and freedom from fear. Roosevelt did not stop at words. The United States undertook joint military talks with Britain, planning against the eventuality that they might one day be allied against Hitler. In March, at Roosevelt's urging, Congress passed the Lend-Lease Act. This allowed Churchill's near-bankrupt government to acquire war supplies from America with payment deferred. (Murrow reported with some amusement Churchill's comments on one piece of aid—the arrival of ten revenue cutters. These, Churchill told the House of Commons, had originally been built to enforce America's Prohibition. In the fight against Hitler, the prime minister—whose fondness for drink was well known—added, "they will now serve an even higher purpose.")

More generally, Murrow reported that England had come through a difficult winter well enough. He said, "The winter that is ending has been hard, but Londoners have many reasons for satisfaction. There have been no serious epidemics. The casualties from air bombardments have been less than expected. And London meets this spring with as much courage, though less complacency, than at this time last year." The British, he reported, no longer feared invasion. Indeed, he said, the populace might welcome the attempt, believing that the invasion would be defeated and the war brought nearer to a close.

While Britain was holding its own at home, Germany was on the offensive elsewhere, in the Balkans and in Greece. CBS accounts of the region came from Cecil Brown in Rome and Winston Burdett in Ankara, Turkey. Brown wrote rather startlingly like a sportswriter. One report began: "According to the not-too-secret signals here in Rome, Hitler is about to toss another pass, a pass to the Greek and Turkish one-yard line, a pass to be caught by two Bulgarian ministers who are to take the ball over for the next Axis touchdown."

Burdett was calmer, his prose better. In April, he described the German dual invasion of Yugoslavia and Greece, and both nations' quick collapse. On April 9, the Germans turned Greece's eastern flank, and, Burdett reported, "the entire Greek army east of Salonika capitulated." That surrender, he said, imperiled Greece's remaining armies and British forces fighting alongside them. As in France, the Germans moved quickly, advancing seventy-five miles in three days. Burdett reported, "German armored troops descending from Salonika have broken through the second Greek line of defense." That news came from German sources, Burdett acknowledged, but added: "Until now German reports on the progress of the Greek war have been remarkably accurate, and in this case, too, I believe them to be true." British forces faced entrapment, Burdett said. He reported their escape through a "second Dunkirk"—a seaborne evacuation the day before German troops raised the Swastika over the Acropolis. (The British fell back on Crete, where they were reinforced, again defeated, with most of the survivors once again evacuated by sea.)

Burdett was to become perhaps the most traveled of CBS correspondents. Beginning in Stockholm in May 1940, he had by war's end made broadcasts from Bucharest, Belgrade, Ankara, New Delhi, Cairo, Algiers, Rome, and Paris. In May 1941, his "beat" included the eastern Mediterranean, North Africa, and the Middle East. In a single broadcast, Burdett reported on the prospects of a pro-British coup in Iraq, German efforts to establish themselves in Syria, the effects of war on Turkish trade, and the escape from Greece of that country's King George. From Berlin, Henry Flannery gave the official German view of the monarch's departure. King George, it said, was "a cowardly and irresponsible royal nincompoop."

In Britain, the fighting in Greece took second place to renewed heavy bombing of London. On April 15, two hundred bombers struck the city. Murrow called it "one of those nights where you wear your best clothes, because you're never sure that when you come home you'll have anything other than the clothes you are wearing." It was always difficult, he said, to judge the severity of a bombing attack. All one knew was what was happening nearby. "Tonight," he reported, "having been thrown against the wall by blasts—which feels like nothing so much as being hit with a feather-covered board—and having lost our third office—which looks like some crazy giant had been operating a eggbeater in its interior—I naturally conclude that the bombing has been heavy." **CD** It had been, in fact, the heaviest bombing thus far in the war.

More bombs were to fall, and to land more closely. One evening, Ed and Janet Murrow were walking to their apartment after dining at a neighborhood restaurant. Murrow wanted to stop at the Devonshire Arms, a pub favored by reporters. His wife objected, so they went home to watch the bombing from their rooftop. By one account, "Then, a tearing, whooshing shriek seemed to be coming down on top of them. They wrapped their arms around their heads to protect their eyes and ears. The blast flung them against the wall. The building shuddered. A column of smoke, shot through with sparks, rose near them, close enough, it seemed to touch." Murrow dashed for the nearby CBS office, where he found secretary Kay Campbell bruised but unbloodied. The bomb had landed directly on the Devonshire Arms. All inside were killed.

The major cost was human, but the damage extended as well to historic London. On May 11, Larry LeSueur broadcast: "Big Ben is solemnly chiming the hours tonight, despite the bomb which last night struck the tower on which the great clock stands." 🔘 The glass had been ripped from the clock face and the surrounding masonry was badly burned. The raid had also damaged "buildings which are a part of the very substance and symbol of England," including the Houses of Parliament, Westminster Abbey, and the British Museum. LeSueur joined the hundreds of Londoners who went to view the damage and reported seeing the "two gaping black holes in the roof of Westminster Hall."

Berlin or Washington

WHILE THE CONFLICT between Germany and England held world attention, the United States remained the great offstage presence. In late May, Franklin Roosevelt moved toward center stage, announcing a major speech on America's position. The speech came as a further shift in American opinion was being registered: a Gallup poll that month reported that 62 percent of Americans believed that if Britain was defeated, Germany would attack the United States within a decade. Previewing Roosevelt's speech, Murrow described for his American audience the phases through which British opinion had passed. Initially, he said, Britain—though grateful for American "moral support"—believed it could win the war unassisted. Later, the British came to feel that victory would require American munitions. Now, Murrow said, the British had come "to admit that British victory, if not British survival, will be made possible only by American action. There are too many Germans, and they have too many factories." Many Britons, Murrow said, now believed "that this world, or what's left of it, will be largely run either from Berlin or from Washington."

President Roosevelt's May 27 address was heard by the largest-ever radio audience. His listeners included sixty-five million in America and, by special hookups, twenty million more in England, Canada, and Latin America. Roosevelt pledged "every possible assistance to Britain and to all who, with

Britain, are resisting Hitlerism." The United States would build more weapons, he said, and more ships in which to transport them. The U.S. Navy would help secure their delivery to Britain. Germany, Roosevelt asserted, had designs on the New World as well. To forestall this, the United States would resist by force any German advance on such "stepping stones" as Iceland, the Azores, or the Cape Verde Islands.

In London, Murrow reported, many arose early to hear the speech live at 4:30 A.M. local time. British reaction, Murrow said, was that it was "a great speech [that] could be one of the hinges of history." He added, "Some were frank enough to wonder if their own government would have gone so far if things had been reversed." Howard K. Smith, still working as a United Press reporter in Berlin, reported the official reaction from Germany. There, he said, the speech was judged "neither new nor convincing." German officials dismissed Roosevelt's claim that Germany might attack the Americas as "empty words." "We should know," a German spokesman added, "because we are supposed to be the threat."

As American aid to Britain increased, attitudes toward Americans in Berlin had hardened. A single newspaper editorial, Smith noted, called President Roosevelt "a 'gangster,' a 'butcher,' a 'cannibal in a white collar,' a 'negroid maniac,' and a 'depraved Jewish scoundrel.'" American reporters found their telephones bugged and themselves followed. Twice, Smith was tossed out of Berlin restaurants for speaking English. In March, Smith had walked into the Berlin office of the United Press to find a Gestapo raid in progress. Smith, by his own account, "was plenty scared." His desk contained notes on the German economy, air raids, and the German army that could be regarded as the fruits of espionage. He wrote, "My heart bobbed up and down in the pit of my stomach while I watched the little foreman of the group diddling unconsciously with the knob of my drawer...but he never opened it."

That same day, United Press reporter Richard C. Hottelet—later with CBS—was arrested for "serious suspicion of espionage." Hottelet was held for two months. Interrogated daily, he was refused all contact except a single visit by the American ambassador. Smith believed the Nazis hoped to place Hottelet on trial as a spy and Roosevelt agent. (In early July, Hottelet was released. He and an American journalist imprisoned in France were exchanged for two Germans held in New York as suspected spies.)

A Citizen of London

British soldier Bill Hewey and Murrow talk during a quiet moment.

All of this left Smith with a profound case of the "Berlin Blues." Planning to leave Germany, he resigned from United Press. Then—anticipating that a major story was about to break—he reversed field and asked to substitute on air for Flannery, who was covering the fighting in Crete. The story Smith anticipated was the German invasion of the Soviet Union. He was picking up signs that the Non-Aggression Pact between the two countries would not hold. One incidental sign was that when Smith tried to buy a volume of Russian short stories in a Berlin bookstore, he was told that all Russian books had been ordered from the shelves. Invasion came on June 22, 1941. CBS had no one in the Soviet Union to cover the story. The previous year, Paul White reported, "The Soviet government alone in Europe has forbidden its shortwave facilities to American broadcasters." For the time being, the war's largest battle was largely Smith's to cover.

In Washington, Sevareid had a good deal less than Smith to complain about. He was complaining anyway. In a July 5 commentary, he suggested that those isolationists who wished America to stay neutral no longer merited "equal time" to present their views. The comments brought a tart rebuke from News Director Paul White. White told Sevareid, "It seems to me that...it is essential to a democracy that anyone and everyone should have his say at all times." By questioning this, White added, Sevareid had "ventured into a dangerous line of territory." Sevareid made a lengthy reply. He was not suggesting, he wrote, that isolationists such as Senator Burton K. Wheeler or aviator Charles Lindbergh should "be silenced or denied access to the means of reaching the public." He believed, however, that "we have a grave problem when we get down to deciding how much space and time to give their statements, which according to a lot of wise men, are confusing and dividing the American people and tending to paralyze its action." White replied tactfully, saying he shared many of Sevareid's concerns. But he added, "I don't believe that you have any more right to discuss your private opinions in the guise of a reporter than I would have to instruct CBS correspondents to plead for a negotiated peace." White's view prevailed. He had the better argument, and he was the boss.

In Berlin, Smith's reporting on the invasion of the Soviet Union consisted largely of passing along German claims of continuing victory. For a time—as the German army advanced four hundred miles in six weeks—those claims were largely true. As autumn brought cooler weather, progress slowed. In October, the Germans made a final push for victory. Smith reported their progress, "On the central front, [the Germans are] advancing on Moscow; on the southern front, the situation of the Soviets is even more precarious. Only in Leningrad is there a ray of hope for the Soviets, according to German reports."

In making that push, German officials announced that Soviet defeat was at hand. Smith wrote that this statement was "generally believed by the foreign press corps. Offers of visits to the front—generally sought after—were declined by journalists who wanted to be in Berlin for the surrender announcement." Even in German accounts, however, it was clear how fiercely Soviet armies were resisting. Near Leningrad, Smith reported, on October 12, Russian forces made five attempts by sea to land behind the German lines. Smith added: "After hours of fighting, the Germans finally gained the upper hand in a bitter fight and drove the Reds into the sea. On the shore lay hundreds of bodies; from past experience the Germans had learned to shoot first and ask questions later. And, sure enough, the bodies [who had been feigning death] sprang to life and the fight proceeded until they were killed."

Smith's 1942 book, *Last Train from Berlin*, argues that the invasion of Russia decimated the German standard of living. With goods redirected to the battlefront, potatoes were rationed in Berlin, clothing was scarce, shoes were unavailable, and the city's few remaining taxi drivers were allotted one half gallon of fuel a day. Germany imposed rationing on its Italian ally. From Rome, CBS's Charles Barbe reported, "Sugar is universally rationed at one pound per month, if you can get it. Coffee doesn't even exist on the rationing list." The allotment of cooking oil, he said, was "about enough to cook one batch of French-fry potatoes, if it was permitted to cook French-fry potatoes, which it isn't."

There were, for Smith, less pleasant consequences than rationing. The atmosphere in Berlin was increasingly hostile. The publication of Shirer's *Berlin Diary* did not help matters for American reporters. A German official told Smith that Shirer was an "ingrate" who had "abused the years of hospitality and cordial cooperation we have offered." In November, a radio script by Smith came back from the censors with two paragraphs added. He was directed to broadcast them. He refused. What came next, Smith said, was "a conversation of the kind one does not easily forget." The censor told him, "You have gotten away with this writing whatever you wish too long. We cannot allow you to use our facilities and our time and effort to make hostile broadcasts. We are fighting for our lives. You Americans think you own the world."

Smith and other American broadcasters were banned from the airwaves. Smith talked with Paul White, who to Smith's great relief offered him a CBS post in Switzerland. Smith still had to get there. In the first week of December, he daily sought an exit visa from Germany. Each day he was refused.

That same week, Ed Murrow was in New York for what one observer called the greatest public tribute paid an American journalist since Henry Morton Stanley returned from Africa, having found Dr. Livingstone. Murrow had returned from London for a much-needed rest and a speaking tour. The occasion in his honor was a formal banquet at Manhattan's Waldorf-Astoria, attended by one thousand guests. The event—titled "In Honor of a Man and an Ideal"—featured talks by Archibald MacLeish, the Librarian of Congress; CBS chief William Paley; and Murrow.

MacLeish's talk emphasized that Murrow's broadcasts from Britain had destroyed "the superstition that what is done beyond three thousand miles of water is not really done to all." Murrow had spoken in London, MacLeish said, but he had been heard "in the back kitchens and the front living rooms and the moving automobiles and the hotdog stands of America." By doing so, Murrow had made "real and urgent" the central event of the day. "You burned the city of London in our houses and we felt the flames that burned it. You laid the dead of London at our doors and we knew the dead were our dead—were all men's dead—were mankind's dead—and ours." Speaking briefly, Paley called attention to the freedom of speech without which Murrow could not have done his work and without which "we would not be meeting here tonight to honor him for the doing of it." He introduced Murrow as "a student, a philosopher, at heart a poet of mankind and, therefore, a great reporter."

Murrow's own talk was a well-crafted plea for American support of Britain. He was self-deprecatory, recalling how one BBC staffer said of a just-completed talk, "That was Murrow's contribution to the confusion of his fellow countrymen." He offered humor, recalling the Scotsman who, after Dunkirk, had said, "If England is forced to give in, it will be a long war." He spoke as a figure of some influence, intent on using that influence to persuade the evening's audience of the need for greater American support for Britain. He had come to believe, he said, "Lend-Lease is not enough, that unless the United States enters this war, Britain may perish or at best secure a stalemate peace." He warned that a defeated Britain might become an avowed enemy of the United States. And he offered a challenge. The question those "thoughtful Englishmen" most often asked, Murrow said, was, "'If America comes in, will she stay in? Does she have any appetite for the greatness that is being thrust upon her? Does she realize that this world or what is left of it will be run from either Berlin or Washington?'" Murrow closed by noting that America would reach its decision by democratic means. "Coming as I do from the creeping blackout of liberty all over Europe," he said, "I am grateful that our decision will be taken in the full light of free and better informed debate and discussion than exists anywhere else in the world. For such is our heritage and may it always be our habit."

That decision was closer than Murrow likely thought. The date of the dinner was December 2, 1941.

AMERICA AT WAR

Japan has…undertaken a surprise offensive extending throughout the Pacific area. The facts of yesterday and today speak for themselves…

No matter how long it may take us to overcome this premeditated invasion, the American people in their righteous might will win through to absolute victory.

—*Franklin D. Roosevelt*
December 8, 1941

TRACKS: 23–34

Previous page: The USS Arizona *sinks into Pearl Harbor after being bombed by Japanese planes on December 7, 1941.*

To Awaken a Sleeping Giant

THE FIRST SATURDAY in December 1941, the German government unexpectedly issued an exit visa to Howard K. Smith, CBS correspondent in Berlin. CBS had announced a replacement for him, who Smith believed would serve as a "hostage" against Smith's future behavior. Smith was greatly relieved. Life in Berlin had gone from unpleasant to menacing. Shortly before, a minor German government official sought Smith out, and said, "My dear Smith, if I were you I would get out of Germany as fast as I could. If you do not leave soon, you will have reason to regret it." The visa arrived late afternoon; it was valid for two days. Smith told fellow staff member Jack Fleischer that he would take the extra day to say proper farewells. Fleischer was having none of it; he was putting Smith on the night train to Switzerland, he said, "by brute force" if necessary. The pair headed to Berlin's Potsdamer Station. Friends arrived for the departure. Homebrew was drunk. "Swanee River" and "Lily Marlene" were sung. Smith, in good spirits, announced he would stay another day. Those present put him on the train. En route to Switzerland, Smith sat with a German who asked if he actually believed Germany would attack America. Smith later wrote, "I said I certainly did believe it." He was right about the attack, wrong about the assailant. In the morning, over the Swiss border, the train made a brief stop, and Smith stepped out on the platform to buy a paper. The paper carried the date December 7, 1941.

· · ·

THAT SAME SUNDAY morning, half a world away, 360 Japanese aircraft operating from a fleet of six carriers struck the U.S. naval base at Pearl Harbor. The
Japanese fleet had arrived by a circuitous route, sailing behind a weather front
whose cloudbanks helped hide its movement. The attack came at 7:55 A.M.
local time, early evening in Berlin. Within two hours, four U.S. battleships—
the *Arizona*, *Oklahoma*, *California*, and *West Virginia*—had been sunk. Nearly
two hundred American aircraft were destroyed on the ground. More than
twenty-four hundred American servicemen and civilians were killed, and
more than a thousand others wounded. In the midst of the general disaster,
individual stories were overlooked, including that of Howard K. Smith. Had
Smith waited the extra day, he may have sat out the war as an enemy internee
in Germany.

ED AND JANET MURROW had gone to Washington, D.C., after the big New
York banquet in Murrow's honor. On Sunday, they took advantage of unsea-
sonably warm weather to play a round of golf at Burning Tree. On the fourth
hole, a messenger arrived reporting the Japanese attack. When Murrow
learned that the report came from Reuters, he was inclined to dismiss it.
Confirmation soon followed.

LESS THAN THREE hours after the attack, the phone rang in the room of
Larry LeSueur, CBS's correspondent in the Soviet Union. It was 1:30 A.M. in
Kuibyshev. LeSueur's roommate, Eddy Gilmore of the Associated Press,
answered. LeSueur heard Gilmore say, "The Japs bombed Pearl Harbor."
Gilmore then stumbled back to bed, and the pair lay silent. Then, LeSueur
later wrote, "in one voice we both said: 'Pearl Harbor! Why, that's America.'"
Someone opened a bottle of Scotch, and they toasted their nation's entry into
the war.

JAPANESE ATTACK AT PEARL HARBOR

Airmen at the Ford Island Naval Air Station watch smoke and flames billow from the USS Shaw which had just been hit by Japanese bombers during the attack on Pearl Harbor.

THE MURROWS HAD a dinner engagement at the White House set for Sunday night. They assumed that with the attack, the dinner would be cancelled. Janet Murrow called to check, and was told that the engagement was still on. The meal was served personally by Eleanor Roosevelt, a gracious hostess but somewhat indifferent to food. Dinner consisted of scrambled eggs, pudding, and milk, eaten as strained government officials came and went. When the Murrows prepared to leave, Ed Murrow was informed that the president wished to speak to him.

Murrow was led into the president's study after midnight. Roosevelt, Murrow said later, looked pale and gray. They made small talk about conditions in England: How would that nation respond to U.S. entry into the war? Then, Roosevelt unburdened himself on the full extent of the disaster that had struck that morning in Hawaii. Murrow was startled, both by the news itself and by the fact that the president was telling him, a newsman, without having gone off the record.

Murrow was uncertain what to do—arguably, it was the story of his life. In the end, he decided to sit on it. On his way out, Murrow stopped by the White House press office, where Eric Sevareid was working. Earlier that evening, Sevareid had broadcast a report of the scene at the Japanese embassy, where guards had left a gate unlocked, and American reporters and photographers came in just in time to witness clerks throwing boxes of embassy documents on a bonfire. "Each box was set afire by a quick action fuse," said Sevareid, "and as Americans started to come in, the Japanese shouted, 'You must not come! You must not come!'" **CD** Sevareid asked Murrow what he knew; Murrow said, simply, "It's pretty bad." The following morning, Murrow was in the press gallery in the House of Representatives as Roosevelt gave his "Day of Infamy" speech, seeking a declaration of war. **CD**

The details of Pearl Harbor reached the public piecemeal. On Monday, a broadcast by Eric Sevareid gave the full story. Author Roger Burlingame wrote that it was Sevareid's broadcast "that really set the wheels turning in American factories." Sevareid, he added, "told the grim truth about Pearl Harbor: that the damage of the American fleet had been disastrous, that it would be impossible to exaggerate it—that indeed the very core of naval defense in the Pacific had been wiped out."

THE NEXT STAGE of the war was set in motion. The United States declared war on Japan, following FDR's impassioned address to Congress, on December 8, 1941. In turn, Japan's Tripartite allies, Germany and Italy, declared war on the United States on December 11.

TRACK 23

TRACK 24

Sinking Ships

AS SEVAREID SPOKE to the nation from Washington, Cecil Brown—CBS's correspondent in Singapore—was aboard the British cruiser *Repulse*, sailing behind the battleship *Prince of Wales* in the South China Sea. The warships had put to sea to register Britain's naval presence in the region. Brown was invited along at the last moment. He wired CBS's Paul White: OUT TOWNING FOUR DAYS SWELL STORY. That seemed likely. As the ships reached the open ocean, Captain William Tennant of the *Repulse* announced over the ship's loudspeaker, "We are off to look for trouble. I expect we shall find it."

Trouble found them first. On the afternoon of Tuesday, December 9 (because Singapore was west of the International Date Line, it was still December 8 in New York), a break in the clouds allowed the ships to be sighted by a Japanese airplane. The next morning, the Japanese moved in to attack. At 11:15 A.M., Brown spotted nine Japanese aircraft "stretched out across the bright blue, cloudless sky like star sapphires of a necklace." The Japanese strafed the British ships. Attack by torpedo bomber followed. At 12:14 P.M., the *Repulse* notified the *Prince of Wales*, "We have dodged nineteen torpedoes thus far, thanks to Providence." Ten more bombers approached. As Brown later described the attack in a broadcast from Singapore:

> From all angles, [the torpedo-carrying bombers] darted straight at us; the flashes were blinding and the roar deafening. The *Repulse* was swerving and zig-zagging at crazy angles to avoid the torpedoes....Nine more torpedo bombers came. Gunners on the pom-poms, machine guns, and the high-altitude guns shot without sighting, so near were the bombers. It was something like a cowboy shooting from the hip. The first torpedo hit us amidships, about twenty yards from my position. A minute later, another torpedo crashed into us. The order came to abandon ship. 🔘

TRACK 25

The *Repulse* and *Prince of Wales* were crippled and sinking. Brown saw an eighteen-year-old sailor dive from the air defense–control tower of the *Repulse* directly into the ocean, 170 feet below, and begin swimming. Brown felt certain he was going to die. Then, he thought, "I cannot lie here and let

Brown was aboard the British
cruiser Repulse on December 10, 1941,
when it and the Prince of Wales were
sunk by Japanese bombers. He was
photographed a half hour after his rescue.

the water come over me without fighting back somehow." He leapt twenty feet into the water, which was coated with oil escaping from the *Repulse*. The oil weighed him down, making it difficult to swim away from the suction of the sinking ship. Around him, five hundred men were bobbing about in the open water. Brown reached a floating table, then managed his way to a raft. Eventually, he was picked up by a destroyer. Of the three thousand sailors aboard the two vessels, nearly seven hundred died. Back in Singapore, Brown learned he was more fortunate than he knew—the floating oil could have ignited but didn't, and it may have been what kept the sharks away.

Brown cabled CBS: "I was aboard the battle cruiser *Repulse* when she and the *Prince of Wales* were sent to the bottom." From CBS New York, Paul White cabled, "Overjoyed about your rescue"—Brown was alive, and, further, had a great story. Everybody wanted it. CBS, of course, got it first. White had instructed Brown to file "voluminously." Brown told his harrowing account on the air December 12. *Newsweek* cabled and ran a full-page, first-person account the same week. Random House publisher Bennett Cerf cabled: "We want to publish your book whenever you write it." (Brown's book, *Suez to Singapore*, came out in 1942.)

Cecil Brown emerged triumphant. For the time being at least, the Americans and British were doing markedly less well. From the abrupt entry of Pearl Harbor, victory for America lay nearly four arduous years away. For the CBS radio correspondents, U.S. entry changed everything. Previously, they had been citizens of a neutral power. However an individual reporter might sympathize with Britain or France, they still stood a step apart. Now, their nation was at war. Narrowly, that meant they were now subject to U.S. censorship. The more difficult task was internal—balancing their citizens' desire to support their nation's war effort with their newsman's urge to get the story.

With the U.S. in the war, CBS greatly expanded its corps of correspondents. The story sprawled with the fighting, across the continents of the world. Much of that story can be told, however, by focusing on a few key reporters in a few key campaigns. Among them, Larry LeSueur in Soviet Russia; Charles Collingwood and Winston Burdett in North Africa; Ed Murrow in a British bomber over Berlin; Burdett and Eric Sevareid in Italy; and Cecil Brown in Singapore.

The Fall of Singapore

FOR THE ALLIES, one more disaster was pending. Cecil Brown would cover it, and, once again, escape. The attack on Pearl Harbor was part of an orchestrated Japanese grab of land and ocean, a grab that included the Malaysian peninsula, five hundred miles long north to south and tipped by the island port of Singapore. While the British army outnumbered the Japanese two to one, it was poorly trained for jungle fighting. Further, it suffered from low morale, and much of the British leadership was imbued with a "colonial" mentality that believed no non-white army could outmatch them. This the Japanese did, advancing four hundred miles down the peninsula in five weeks.

To Brown, a disaster was in the making, one he felt it was his duty to report. Brown had doubts about everyone. About the military skill of the British—as early as December 23, he broadcast, "The fighting thus far has revealed many weaknesses in the British conception of jungle warfare." About the "walking death" attitude of British colonials in Singapore— characterized, he reported, "by an apathy in all affairs, except making money from tin and rubber, having 'stengahs' [stingers] between five and eight, keeping fit, being known as a 'good chap' and getting thoroughly 'plawstered' on Saturday night." And about the local Singapore population of Malays, Chinese, Kamus, and Indians, who seemed indifferent to their peril—on January 3, he broadcast, "To these people it is incredible that their country should be visited by war, and that notion has not yet worn off."

Brown's reporting did not endear him to the local authorities. In early January, they bounced him from the air. The British official in charge of war coverage told Brown, "I have this day sent a signal to the War Office, informing them that you are no longer an accredited war correspondent and asking them to cancel your license." Brown protested, of course, as did Paul White. The protest reached Parliament, where a question was placed to Brendan Bracken, minister of information. Bracken, a great admirer of Ed Murrow, drew the line at Cecil Brown: "Mr. Brown's comments passed the bounds of fair criticism and were a source of danger." For Brown, there was some compensation. On January 13, he received a cable that CBS had sent four weeks earlier after Brown had survived the sinking of *Repulse*. It read: "Columbia

Cecil Brown
1907–1987
b. New Brighton, Pennsylvania

Cecil Brown was born on September 14, 1907, in New Brighton, Pennsylvania. Brown developed an interest in journalism at an early age, and was known for seeking adventures in order to create writing material. At the age of seventeen, he and his brother paddled a canoe four hundred miles down the Ohio River from West Virginia to Cincinnati. After his junior year at Ohio State University, Brown stowed away on a ship bound for South America, which became the basis for a series of articles about the adventure. After graduating from Ohio State in 1929, Brown traveled to Europe where he worked as a seaman in the Mediterranean and Black Seas. He returned to the United States several years later to try his hand at professional journalism, and worked for a number of small papers around the country before returning to Europe in 1937 to work as a freelance journalist.

Brown quickly garnered a reputation as an aggressive and persistent journalist. While working as a CBS correspondent in Rome from 1940–41, he openly criticized Mussolini's policies. In one broadcast, he referred to the mobilization of Italian troops as "a comic-opera army preparing for slaughter under the orders of a Duce with a titanic contempt for his own people." Brown's contempt for Italian authorities resulted in numerous suspensions of his broadcasting license and finally expulsion in 1941. Brown continued to cover the war from Yugoslavia, and then extensively from North Africa.

His narrow escape from the sinking *Repulse* led to fame and the publication of his book, *Suez to Singapore*, in 1942. Booted out of Singapore for criticizing the doomed English military contingent, he landed in Australia, and then returned to New York to do regular commentary for CBS. Brown battled regularly with censors and network brass, which ultimately resulted in his resignation from CBS in late 1942. He covered the remainder of the war, including the D-Day invasion, for the Mutual network stateside. After the war, Brown continued to travel and work as a

continued

TRACKS: 11, 25

correspondent for Mutual, ABC, NBC, and finally as commentator and director of news and public affairs for KCET, the public television station in Los Angeles. He retired from broadcasting in 1967.

Cecil Brown received many of broadcasting's top awards during his career, including the Peabody and the Overseas Press Club's Best Reporter Award. In 1970, Brown began teaching a course in American Civilization at Cal Poly Pomona where he received the Outstanding Professor Award in 1980. He died on October 25, 1987.

[CBS] has told your bank you did one grand job." The message mystified Brown, until a colleague suggested, rightly, that CBS had given Brown a $1,000 bonus.

Expulsion had its advantages. While Brown did not wish to be kicked out, it was better than being captured by the Japanese. By January 31, the British had been forced back into Singapore itself. Two weeks later, 130,000 British soldiers laid down their arms in the largest surrender in British military history.

On February 14, 1942, Charles Collingwood reported from London that the loss of Singapore, "as a strategic setback, ranks with the fall of France." From Sydney, Australia, Brown offered his assessment: "The Japanese are at Singapore and pushing everywhere because they were underestimated by the British." As fighters, he said, they "don't stop to consolidate their positions. Their whole approach is to attack; move on, giving neither themselves nor their adversaries a chance for a second breath." The Allies needed to know, he said, that their enemy was "tough, well-trained, shrewd."

Singapore marked Brown's second expulsion from the airwaves. Earlier, he had been ordered out of Italy for broadcasts regarded as unfriendly to Mussolini's government. The next time Brown was tossed off the air, it would be by CBS.

War in Russia

ON JANUARY 15, 1942, less than a week after Cecil Brown was expelled from Singapore's airwaves, Larry LeSueur was en route to Moscow by train. He obtained hot water from the conductor, and headed to the bathroom to shave. LeSueur lathered and shaved one side of his face. He went to lather the other side, only to discover his shaving brush had frozen solid. Brown had had a warship sunk from under him; later, Eric Sevareid and Richard C. Hottelet would each have to bail out of crippled aircraft. But for sustained frustration and discomfort, Larry LeSueur's assignment to the Soviet Union was unmatched.

Simply getting to the scene was a considerable chore. LeSueur had sailed from Scotland aboard the Lend-Lease freighter *Temple Arch* on October 14, 1941. The trip felt something like a fool's errand—en route, the ship's radio received reports placing the Germans progressively closer to Moscow. LeSueur was no supporter of the Soviet Union. He was, however, curious about the Soviet experiment with socialism, and thought this "might be a last-minute opportunity to see the gigantic Russian 'test-tube' and to examine the Russian experiment before it burst like a bubble in front of the German tanks."

LeSueur reached the near-frozen port of Archangel only to learn that he was being rerouted from Moscow to Kuibyshev, five hundred miles to the east, to which the Soviets had relocated their capital. LeSueur reached that city in fits and lurches by a seventeen-day train voyage. At one point, they passed squads of civilians hand-digging tank traps in the frozen earth. At another, German aircraft strafed the train. Once, when the cars pulled to a halt, many aboard got off to wash in the snow. LeSueur declined—it was fifteen degrees below zero.

LeSueur reached Kuibyshev on November 22, 1941, just as the final German thrusts toward Moscow ground to a halt. LeSueur and other western correspondents heard few details. The Soviet Union was a closed society—when war broke out, all radio sets were confiscated so the populace could not listen to German propaganda. The government had no concept of a free press, officials were deeply suspicious of foreigners, and little information was forthcoming. Philip Knightley wrote, "Marooned in Kuibyshev, the correspondents passed their time playing poker and fighting with the censor and each other, well aware that as the battle for Moscow raged they were missing one of the great stories of the war."

News was hard to get and harder to broadcast. Given the time difference with New York, LeSueur had to give his reports at four A.M. He often missed his broadcast segment. The CBS cables that assigned specific broadcast times were so delayed in transit, they often arrived after the fact. The censorship was absurd—LeSueur was reprimanded because he said "very" when the approved script read "much." And the weather was frightful. LeSueur fell ill. His translator tracked down a doctor who had once been physician to the Shah of Persia. The correspondent was patched back together with a combination of mustard plasters, butter, and honey from a special store for diplomats, and a hard-to-find electric stove to heat his room.

On December 14, western correspondents were flown to Moscow. This, LeSueur decided, meant the battle of Moscow had been won. Otherwise, Soviet officials would not allow reporters anywhere near the city. His efforts to report that news, however, proved "a nightmare." LeSueur was traveling from his lodgings to the studio by government car. Every few hundred yards, LeSueur's car was stopped and "grim-faced Red Army men threw open the door, poked a loaded rifle tipped with a shining bayonet inside, flashed a light in my face and demanded my night pass and my passport." Unfortunately, the Russian spelling of "LeSueur" on his passport did not match that on his press pass, so one patrol hauled him off to talk to the secret police. Released, LeSueur got to the studio, gave his broadcast, and returned to his hotel—being stopped and questioned on his return by the identical sentries he had met on the way in. The next day, he got a cable from CBS: "Broadcast unheard in New York."

Occasionally, LeSueur got through. In a muffled January 9 report from Kuibyshev, LeSueur described how government offices there operated twenty-four hours a day. He added, "The Soviet Union has always been interested in efficiency and efficiency methods for its factory workers; but today—a record for machine-gun efficiency in the Red Army." By government claim, a Soviet corporal had killed 122 Germans with a light machine gun before being killed himself. LeSueur added dryly, "At present, that record stands."

THE RUSSIAN FRONT

Red Army scouts on patrol in Murmansk after the German invasion of June 1941.

LeSueur gathered what information he could from government communiqués, rumors, and other correspondents. There was, he noted later, "no Soviet spokesman to whom an Anglo-American correspondent can direct a question for even semi-official comment." The pickings were slim—one correspondent simply took a translated report from the Soviet newspaper, *Pravda,* and filed it verbatim with the *New York Times.* LeSueur's efforts were little rewarded. In February, he learned that not one of his broadcasts in the preceding three weeks had been picked up by CBS. The Soviet radio signal being used, it turned out, was aimed at England, not New York.

LeSueur wrote: "I have been wasting almost a month walking through the blacked-out, snowbound streets to talk to myself and the censors." LeSueur took the problem to a Soviet official, who in three days juggled the national schedule to open a window for LeSueur's broadcasts. That would have solved things, except that in the meanwhile the United States had gone on "war savings time." The Soviets then arranged for LeSueur's broadcasts to go east through Siberia to San Francisco, rather than west to New York. LeSueur was delighted when, following his next broadcast, he received a CBS cable "informing me that my words were being heard clearly on the West Coast."

LeSueur was well aware of the drama surrounding him. In February, he noted the "gutsiness" of Moscow's population: "They work in stone-cold factories and go home to their unlit apartments at night as though these hardships were a part of the law of nature itself. I hear no complaints." He knew the Herculean effort the Soviet people were making—after invasion, 1,523 factories had been disassembled and relocated east, out of the reach of the advancing Germans. In March, after the invaders had been repelled from the capital, he attended a Moscow exhibit of German armaments captured during the fight for the city. What caught his eye were the German Iron Crosses, thousands of them, intended to be awarded after victory.

The war, at times, was too close for comfort. On March 20, 1942, the Germans bombed Moscow. LeSueur had a sudden longing for "the old tin hat" Edward Murrow had given him, but which LeSueur had left behind as unessential. Shrapnel was falling so heavily that it strummed the trolley wires that ran overhead. Two sentries demanded LeSueur's pass.

> Reassured by my air-raid pass and night pass, we all worked down the streets while shrapnel tinkled on the icy pavement. I had a feeling we ought to take cover fast, but, bound by chains of pride, the two sentries and I sauntered along through the blitz....Suddenly we were all walking faster, almost a trot. Then we three broke into a run simultaneously, gained the shelter of a hallway in a breathless hurry, looked at each other, and began to laugh.

Larry LeSueur
1909–2003
b. New York, New York

Lawrence Edward LeSueur was born on June 10, 1909, in New York, and spent his childhood there and in Chicago, with summers in Indiana on his father's family farm. Both his father (a foreign correspondent for the *New York Tribune*) and grandfather were journalists, and LeSueur began writing at an early age, wanting to follow in their footsteps. He worked his way through college at New York University from 1929 to 1932, graduating with a degree in English.

It was difficult finding work as a reporter during the Depression, and LeSueur took jobs as assistant to a private investigator and a Saturday clerk at Macy's before securing a position as a writer for *Women's Wear Daily*. Less than a year later, however, he was offered a job as a reporter for the United Press wire service. To supplement his meager earnings there, LeSueur wrote and performed scripts for the CBS radio program *We, the People,* and acted as interpreter of the day's news to CBS's controversial commentator, Boake Carter.

In 1939, LeSueur took a leave of absence from UP and sailed to England—even as flocks of people were leaving Europe—convinced that the war would make a real reporter of him. When he first approached Edward R. Murrow about a job, Murrow was impressed with his experience and his voice, but there were no positions available. When LeSueur returned to London a few weeks later, however, Murrow hired him immediately. He was stationed in France and Belgium until the French surrendered in 1940, when he began reporting from London with Murrow and Eric Sevareid. Assigned to cover the war in Russia, he spent a harrowing twelve months struggling to report what he saw to those at home.

In 1943, LeSueur published a memoir of his experiences in the Soviet Union, *Twelve Months That Changed the World,* which became a bestseller in the United States. That summer, on an extended trip home, he broadcast a weekly radio series, *An American in Russia*, from New York for CBS. During that time, he also met and married Joan Phelps, but their marriage didn't last long. They divorced in February 1944,

continued

TRACKS: 22, 26, 39

not having seen each other since their honeymoon. LeSueur was the first radio correspondent to land in Normandy on D-Day, and the first to report the liberation of Paris from that city. He was awarded the Medal of Freedom and the French Legion of Honor.

After the war, LeSueur served as chief CBS correspondent in Washington, then took over Charles Collingwood's post reporting on the United Nations in New York, earning a Peabody in 1949 for his series *United Nations in Action*. In 1946, he married Priscilla Bruce, a Scottish citizen he had met during the war, but they divorced in 1951.

In 1952, LeSueur reported from Korea for *See It Now*, interviewing troops and describing American involvement in the conflict, and for the remainder of the decade, he hosted *CBS Sunday Morning*, which examined the work of the United Nations. In 1957, he married Dorothy Hawkins, and in 1960 prepared with his wife and daughter to return to the Soviet Union as a correspondent for CBS, only to be refused entrance by the Soviet government.

LeSueur left CBS in 1963 and joined the Voice of America, where he would work for twenty years as a news analyst and White House correspondent. In 1984, he retired to northwest Washington with his wife, Dorothy. He died February 5, 2003, of Parkinson's disease.

In May 1942, the grounds dried and the battle resumed. On May 14, CBS announcer Robert Trout reported from London that what "the civilized world is mostly interested in tonight is what is happening in Russia on the decisive eastern front." Fighting, Trout added, focused on Kharkov, an industrial center that the Russians were attempting to recover. Describing that fighting, LeSueur reported, "According to latest communiqués, 150 German tanks have been knocked out in two days. After smashing a German front line whose fortifications were improved for months, coordinated groups of Soviet tanks, artillery, and infantry are exploiting their success, breaking the German defense system in depth."

On May 16, LeSueur reported on the central front, west of Moscow. There, he said, "[Soviet general] Timoshenko's actions nipped in the bud the offensive plans of German general von Bock." The Soviets, LeSueur said, were employing new assault tactics. To keep artillery and infantry from being separated in battle, he said, the infantrymen were riding right atop the tanks. Armed with tommy guns and trench mortars, the infantry would pile off the tank when it reached German lines. "Naturally," he added, "there are casualties among the men riding the tanks into the face of enemy guns—it's the suicide job of the 1942 war." **CD**

TRACK 26

LeSueur wanted to contribute to the struggle. In July, he donated blood, which was sent off with the message: "To the Red Army man who receives this blood: This is a donation from an American in the fight against Hitler. I hope it will bring you back to good health. Sincerely, Larry LeSueur."

Broadcast conditions eased somewhat. With the increase of Lend-Lease aid from America, LeSueur discovered, censorship became less burdensome. Despite that aid, the Russians were keenly aware that they were doing the bulk of the war's fighting. This attitude was summed up in a Moscow joke LeSueur heard. In it, God is awakened by the noise of the war and sends St. Peter to find out who is to blame. Stalin blames Hitler. Hitler blames Churchill. Churchill denies responsibility, saying, "It can't be my fault. You won't find a British soldier fighting anywhere!" LeSueur sought permission to include the joke in his broadcast. To his surprise, the censor had no objection.

LeSueur had no certain way of knowing the merit of the optimistic accounts he had broadcast in May. With summer, the Germans seized the upper hand. They advanced rapidly toward the key city of Stalingrad and oil fields in the Caucasus. In early September, CBS New York announced, "Many experts feel that, saving a miracle, Stalingrad will fall." LeSueur had no firsthand information—no western correspondent was allowed within sixty miles of the battle. He acknowledged the danger. On September 9, he reported, "The greatest threat to [Stalingrad] now comes from the west. The Germans have a featureless prairie for their tanks to charge across."

LeSueur did not stay to learn the battle's outcome. On October 22, 1942, he left the Soviet Union, initially for Cairo. He had been away from America for over three years; his twelve months in Soviet Russia had been a harrowing ordeal. He had a serious stomach ailment, and, according to CBS colleagues, returned looking older and without his usual energy. From Cairo, LeSueur made a final broadcast about the Soviet Union. Living conditions were poor, he said: "I left Moscow in a driving snow squall, but the heat hadn't yet been turned on in a single Moscow apartment." Many items, such as footwear, were hard to obtain: "More and more often I heard the clacking of wooden shoes on the streets of Moscow." Still, he saw a fierce pride behind the Russian resistance. Winter was coming, he noted, and "winter belongs to Russia." He was right. Soviet resistance and the Russian winter would defeat the German army at Stalingrad. In February 1943, the remaining 110,000 German soldiers near the city surrendered.

The Home Front

FOR CBS CORRESPONDENTS other than Larry LeSueur, 1942 was a season of discontent. Ed Murrow returned to London in April of that year, following an extended speaking tour in America. In June, Eric Sevareid was made chief CBS correspondent in Washington, D.C. Each was unhappy with how the war was progressing and with their place in it. One piece of the unhappiness was that America had yet to engage Hitler militarily. The war was still largely defensive. On July 12, Murrow reported from London, "The urgent business for the [Allies] is not victory but survival. Russia and China must be kept in the war, the Middle East defended, and somehow the Battle of the Atlantic must be won."

Murrow and Sevareid took a similar tack—the war effort was in danger both from those who wanted to charge off unprepared and those who did not accept how difficult the struggle would be. In July, Sevareid wrote Murrow from Washington, "Our military people are caught on the horns of the old dilemma. Shall they wait until training and equipment are perfected in order to avoid great casualties or shall we use these men in their present condition and now on the chance that if we wait we will no longer have any place to use them at all?"

Murrow's anguish was deeper. He did not see the war so much as a struggle to be won but as an unfolding catastrophe he could do little to contain.

On December 13, 1942, he broadcast a disturbing report on the realities of the German concentration camps. He began, "One is almost stunned into silence by some of the information reaching London." The reports were "eyewitness stuff," he said. "What is happening is this: millions of human beings, most of them Jews, are being gathered up with ruthless efficiency and murdered." He spoke of the Warsaw ghetto where, beginning in July 1942, "the infirm, the old, and the crippled were killed in their homes....And others were put in freight cars; the floors were covered with quick-lime and chlorine." Those who survived the journey were killed in camps where a bulldozer was used to bury the dead. In sum, he said, it was a story of "murder and moral depravity unequaled in the history of the world." Murrow's broadcast was one of the earliest accounts of the Holocaust that was spreading across Nazi-occupied Europe. One wonders if anyone listening would have been able to comprehend the horror of what was happening—if Murrow himself could even grasp the magnitude of what he was reporting.

Sevareid's concerns were smaller. He pondered his own place, and, on July 24, wrote Murrow to seek advice. He wanted to get near the war, he said, but CBS had no plans to send him overseas as a correspondent. The network, he added, "can get much more out of me here in Washington." CBS was running short of people, and Sevareid's name recognition was of value with advertisers. The upshot, he concluded, was that he thought he should enlist. Sevareid closed, "If you have any happy thoughts in the matter they would be welcomed with appreciation." Soon thereafter, Sevareid wrote a family friend in North Dakota, commenting ambivalently that after several more months in Washington, "I think I will probably decide to go into the Army myself."

Murrow did not respond immediately. His boss, CBS chief William Paley, was visiting London, and Murrow was showing him around. Murrow and Paley admired each other. Each had a restless drive. Murrow was impressed by Paley's success in raising CBS to prominence. Paley was pleased that, with Murrow, CBS had the war's "star." Moreover, Paley was drawn to Murrow's manner—what one writer termed "the eloquence of his voice, the glints of wit, his swashbuckling love of adventure and his Savile Row style." For Paley, Murrow was the perfect host. He seemed to know everyone in London, arranging three weeks of meetings and dinners with the powerful and prominent.

BRINGING THE WAR HOME

Edward R. Murrow's parents, Ethel and Roscoe, listen to one of
their son's broadcasts on the radio at their home in Bellingham, Washington.

With Paley out of London, Murrow replied to Sevareid: "I certainly
would not be too hasty in deciding to join the Army since your sense of frustration there might be even greater than it is at present and at any rate soldiers don't see very much of the foreign countries where they are stationed."
Murrow added that he was "convinced" that "so long as broadcasting enjoys
its present measure of freedom we can do a better job than in any official
capacity." Sevareid got that same advice when he spoke to the Army chief of
public relations. The response did not satisfy Sevareid, who regarded it as
"merely a false balm to the conscience."

The name recognition that gave Sevareid value to CBS made him a
draw on the lecture circuit. In September 1942, he took his message to the
public—what America needed to prosecute the war, he argued, was not
optimism but toughening. The response was mixed. One member of a
Long Island audience wrote him, "It is heartening to hear somebody
speak the simple, unvarnished truth on the attitude of the American peo-

ple. We must somehow be aroused from our national apathy before the bombs begin to fall or millions of our men are locked in the battlefield on the continent of Europe." A second audience member suggested the problem was that "the distance from actual danger is still too great." A Chicago listener wrote to suggest that the problem was people like Sevareid. The newsman's talk, he wrote, was "moral sabotage. Keep on spreading the dead virus of defeat—keep on sniping at the president— keep on pouring out the gloomy bilge." Somewhat archly, Sevareid wrote back, "I have had firsthand experience in Europe of what happens when defeatists take charge of a country and I feel I know a real defeatist when I see one. I don't think you do."

Back in Washington, Sevareid vented some of his frustration when he reported the burning at sea of an American ship that had been pressed into war service. The reported source of the fire was a carelessly tossed cigarette butt. Sevareid broadcast, "Through someone's carelessness, we have lost a...great ship. Defeat of the enemy is set back by that much."

Sevareid had some personal interest in the matter. The ship was the *Manhattan,* the same vessel that had carried the Murrows and Mary Marvin Breckinridge to Europe in 1937, and which had brought Sevareid's wife and infant children back from war in 1940.

Victory in North Africa

AFTER LEAVING RUSSIA, Larry LeSueur made his farewell broadcast from Cairo on November 7, 1942. The day had a greater significance: it marked the start of a British and American offensive that would sweep the Germans from North Africa. The Allied campaign was the story of two armies: one, advancing westward from Egypt; the other, landing nearly two thousand miles away and moving east to join it. The story was to be told by two young CBS correspondents, Winston Burdett and Charles Collingwood.

In the east, it was a case of fight and flight. In mid-1942, the German Afrika Korps under Erwin Rommel had chased the British twelve hundred miles to within striking distance of the Suez Canal. There, the British gathered their forces and broke the Germans at El Alamein. That battle, ending November 7, was Britain's first major victory after three years of war. In the west, the conflict was both political and military. American and British landings were planned for Morocco's northwestern coast and Algeria. These were French colonies. They were ruled from Vichy, France, where, after the French surrender, a government that collaborated with Hitler had been set up. Allied planners did not know whether French garrisons in North Africa would welcome or fight the invasion.

The correspondents were picked less for their experience than because they met some intuitive standard of Murrow's. Collingwood, who covered the western end of the story, was only twenty-five. Thus far, he had worked solely in London, had no military background, and was viewed by some as a dandy. Burdett, who reported from Cairo, was twenty-eight. Before the war, he had written for the *Brooklyn Eagle*. Among other things, he was its Hollywood reporter. In 1940, he headed to Scandinavia as a roving correspondent. There, he replaced Betty Wason as a CBS stringer. He came to Murrow's attention, by one description, as a reporter "who wrote in hard, bright phrases that gleamed like light passing through a jewel." Burdett looked like a sweet-faced kid, but stood near one of the war's great intrigues. In 1941, he married the Italian journalist Lea Schiavi. In early 1942, she was murdered in Iran. A Kurdish militiaman was convicted of the crime, but as he had no plausible motive for the act, it was assumed someone had ordered her death. The fuller story behind her death would not emerge for a decade.

From Cairo on November 8, Burdett reported it was "all over but the shouting." Rommel was in headlong retreat. "Today," Burdett said, "the British are tumbling west so fast they have been unable to list their booty. At one base, we bound five Messerschmitt 109s, with gas tanks full and bomb racks loaded. Someone left in an awful hurry and why they didn't fly away I don't know." Curiously, he said, the British had also seized sixty American Lend-Lease trucks—captured at some point by the Germans and now recaptured, "packed with belongings of German troops."

Winston Burdett
1916–1993
b. New York, New York

Winston Mansfield Burdett was born December 12, 1916, in New York. Perhaps the smartest of all the Murrow Boys, he graduated from Harvard in 1937, after only three years. He soon after joined the staff of the *Brooklyn Eagle*, reporting on culture and writing movie reviews.

In 1940, he went to Finland to report on the Soviet invasion as an unpaid foreign correspondent for the *Eagle*. After Finland capitulated, he managed to get into Norway after the German invasion in April. Betty Wason recruited him to replace her as CBS's correspondent there, and he impressed Murrow with his reporting. After the Norwegian defeat, Burdett ventured to Romania, figuring it to be the next front of the war. There, he met and married the Italian journalist Lea Schiavi, made occasional reports for CBS, and was eventually expelled by the Nazis for his unfavorable reporting after their invasion. They moved on to Yugoslavia, where he was again tossed out by the Nazis, and finally settled in neutral Turkey. He made reports from Ankara and Iran, and was in India when he received the news of his wife's murder in Iran. Though it would not become public knowledge until 1955, the motive behind her murder was wrapped up in Burdett's secret life as a Soviet spy.

Having joined the Communist Party cell of the *Brooklyn Eagle* in 1937, Burdett had become a committed member. In 1940, the Kremlin's chief organizer of espionage in America asked Burdett to go to Finland with Russia's backing. Although he made contact in Finland, Romania, and Yugoslavia with Soviet handlers, he had little to report to them, and focused on reporting for CBS. It was in Ankara that he began to regularly report to a Madame Zhigalova at the Soviet embassy. And it was there that he lost his illusions about communism. He informed Zhigalova that he was quitting. Shortly after, CBS ordered Burdett to India. When he arrived, he learned of Lea's murder in Iran. He discovered later from U.S. Army intelligence that her murder was ordered by Moscow, apparently because she had found out about the Red Army's training of Yugoslav partisans, though it may have been in retaliation for his desertion.

continued

TRACKS: 28, 29, 31, 33

Burdett continued to distinguish himself as a brilliant reporter during the war in North Africa and Italy, and after the war as a correspondent in Washington and then Rome. He remarried in 1945, this time to Giorgina Nathan, the granddaughter of a former mayor of Rome, and had a son, Richard. On June 28, 1955, five years after he had disclosed his past to CBS and the Department of Justice, he told his story and named the names of his fellow Party members to the Senate Internal Security Sub-committee. Whether he was coerced into it or did it of his own free will is still debated, but Burdett was by then a fervent anticommunist. Although Murrow, Collingwood, and Sevareid stood behind him, many of his colleagues had trouble forgiving him, as many careers were ruined by his testimony.

Burdett was CBS's man in Rome until his retirement in 1978. He covered the Arab–Israeli war in 1967, and published the book *Encounter with the Middle East* in 1969. He died on May 19, 1993, of heart failure, and was buried in Rome.

The same day, the American and British landings began—at Casablanca on Africa's northwest coast and at Oran and Algiers in Algeria. From Washington, CBS reported, "A great point to be determined immediately is whether the French will resist at all." Resistance was small, due largely to a last-minute political arrangement. Admiral Jean François Darlan, the Vichy commander in chief, was by chance in Algiers. The U.S. quickly negotiated with him—on November 8, Darlan declared an armistice to ease entry of American forces; in exchange, the U.S. agreed to respect Darlan's authority.

From the west and east, Allied forces advanced. On November 15, Ed Murrow stood on a London rooftop listening to the sound of the city's church bells ringing. They had not been rung for twenty-nine months. In 1940, the bells had been silenced, only to sound in the event of invasion. Now, they were ringing to mark the victory at El Alamein. "The sound was pleasant," Murrow said, "although some of the bell ringers were sadly out of practice."

TRACK 28

From Cairo, Burdett reported continued German retreat. ⓒⅅ On November 16, he said, "Rommel is setting desert records for speed." The advancing British encountered burning gasoline dumps and abandoned trucks. One British pilot sighted "sixteen German officers clinging to a single staff car and driving hell for leather west." Burdett speculated that Rommel would turn and make a stand, but added, "It's true they have passed up every opportunity to stop since they have fled Egypt." From the west, Collingwood reported the scene in Algiers: "Algiers...is a vast showplace," Collingwood said and described two American soldiers' reactions. One had only ever seen anything like it in the movies; the other, Collingwood said, told him he had "never seen anything like this, period." The local population, he said, though nominally loyal to Vichy, "are not treating us like the Germans; they're treating us like Allies." Collingwood went on to describe a successful landing by British paratroops in Tunisia and the bombing of the German-held port of Bizerte.

TRACK 27

There was, however, a cloud on the horizon. The deal with Darlan was creating a firestorm. Murrow led the charge. Darlan, Murrow believed, was no fit associate. Darlan had, Murrow told his audience, turned thirty Frenchmen over to the Germans to be shot in reprisal for the killing of a German officer. He had sent thousands of political refugees interned in France to work in slave-labor conditions in North Africa, and had intensified Vichy's anti-Semitic policies. Murrow stated, "There is nothing in the strategic position of the Allies to indicate that we are either so strong or so weak that we can afford to ignore the principles for which this war is being fought." Sevareid supported Murrow's position in broadcasts from Washington. The controversy spread. The Free French were furious. The British were startled but silent. Others at CBS agreed with Murrow.

Many Americans were, however, prepared to see the match with Darlan as a marriage that was convenient to immediate military needs. One CBS listener in California wrote to William Paley, "Every commentator whom I heard yesterday spoke with satisfaction of this bloodless triumph secured with Darlan's cooperation...save only your Mr. Sevareid." Sevareid, the writer added, "will continue to utter these sneaked-in slurs...unless you or someone curbs him." For emphasis, the writer closed, "A copy of this letter goes to Mr. [J.] Edgar Hoover."

As 1942 drew to a close, fighting slowed. On December 23, Burdett reported, "There's a pause in the desert chase just now, as New Zealanders and others of the British pursuit force refit and refuel for the next dash west." Rommel, Burdett added, faced "a forlorn set of alternatives." Collingwood's story was more seasonal. American soldiers, he reported, had just realized that Christmas was upon them. He added that they were more concerned with giving gifts than with getting them. "When you are away from home," Collingwood said, "buying gifts are a kind of link to everything you are away from. There's isn't much in North Africa to buy, but ferreting around in little shops the men are finding things they think will do—a curious little oriental box; a piece of heavy native jewelry."

Collingwood was proving an excellent reporter. His fluency in French gave him excellent access to local sources. His political instincts were keen—later, *Newsweek* wrote, "sometimes [his reports] caught the turns of events days in advance of official release." His radio manner was polished. One critic wrote, "Each day in the 8 A.M. and 6:45 P.M. newscasts…listeners would hear two and a half minutes of vivid reporting by Collingwood in a firm precise voice."

AMERICAN TROOPS IN NORTH AFRICA

*GIs leave the bombed ruins of a building after they occupied the
area and planted an American flag within the building's walls.*

And Collingwood knew how to compete. This he showed in his handling of the story that closed out the Darlan episode: the Christmas Eve assassination of the admiral by a young Free French adherent. Radio was immediate. In theory, a correspondent's words could be transmitted to listeners in seconds. In practice, this happened only if the studio engineers were monitoring the correspondent's wavelength. This made the broadcasting of a "scoop" difficult—it might come at a time when no one in New York was listening. When the French cleared the Darlan story for broadcast, Collingwood allowed two competing correspondents to speak first. When he gained the microphone, he did not give his report. Rather, he repeatedly urged any ham radio operator who might be listening to contact CBS New York and tell them that Charles Collingwood had a story. The other two correspondents got their stories through only in part; alerted, CBS was able to get all of Collingwood's, and it was his version that was the day's lead story. Collingwood got a second scoop soon after, with a report that Vichy had quickly convicted and executed the assassin.

On December 27, Murrow in London placed the closing year in perspective. In 1942, he said, "The Germans drove for Suez with the Afrika Korps, threw one army across the Don at Stalingrad and another into the Caucasus, and today all three are gravely threatened. They might have achieved victory in one or even two theaters. But they divided their forces, overreached themselves, and are now everywhere on the defensive." This was so—1943 was to be a year of Allied advance in every theater of the war. Murrow spoke of the impact the tens of thousands of American soldiers arriving in England were having on that country. American slang was entering the vocabulary. as were American habits: "A year ago you seldom saw an English girl chewing gum; now, if you visit a town where American troops are stationed, the girls seem to be chewing as though they are making up for lost time." In closing, he acknowledged that while Americans had not yet done the bulk of the war's fighting, "we have brought hope and confidence to a world that was waiting."

There was fighting still to do in North Africa. Rommel retreated two thousand miles to Tunisia, then joined up with forces that had been heavily reinforced there. Standing between the British Eighth Army to the east and the American First Army to the west, he could attack in either direction. In

January, he made a series of attacks west. In February, the Germans inflicted a defeat on American armored forces at Kasserine Pass. Making the best of it, Collingwood said of that fighting, "Veteran soldiers say that troops learn more from a shellacking than they do from a victory." George Patton was given command of the American armor, and the initiative was regained. In April, the British and American forces met, sealing the German army's fate. The two CBS correspondents met as well. Collingwood invited Burdett to a party he was giving at the hilltop villa he was occupying, as described by authors Stanley Cloud and Lynne Olson in *The Murrow Boys*:

> Outside it stood Collingwood, silhouetted against a golden evening sky, dressed in an immaculate dinner jacket, greeting his guests. During dinner, served by white-gloved servants, a dispatch rider rode up to the villa on a motorcycle. He rushed inside and dramatically handed Collingwood a cable from CBS New York, advising him he had been added to the broadcast schedule for that evening.

Collingwood excused himself, wrote the story, and—without removing his dinner jacket—hopped in the dispatch rider's sidecar for the ride to Algiers to make the broadcast.

Ed Murrow might have been amused by Collingwood's style. He was impressed by his work, calling it one of the best jobs of radio reporting since the fall of France. Others agreed. In April, Collingwood received the Peabody Award for his work in North Africa. The citation credited Collingwood's work with having "conveyed to us through the screen of censorship an understanding of the troublesome situation in North Africa." Collingwood was the youngest person ever to receive the award, which was voted to him unanimously.

In early April, Murrow flew to North Africa, in part to congratulate his reporter, but more, to make his first visit to a combat zone. As ever, he set the scene. Hearing the low rumble of supply trucks downshifting their way up to a mountain pass, he said, prompted thoughts of "young boys pushing heavy transports over that road where Roman legions marched more than fifteen hundred years ago." He described fighting near Medjez El Bab, in Tunisia:

The infantry moved off at four A.M. to face mines, mortar fire, and heavy machine guns firing on fixed lines. A quarter of an hour later, the first green Very light plopped in the night sky; that meant someone had reached somewhere. The Germans filled the sky with flares—the red, blue, and green signal lights kept driving in the slight breeze about the valley. It was cold. You shiver, but it isn't that cold.

And he reported the battle's aftermath. A knocked-out tank sat near a stream, where two men were burying a pair of corpses. "A little further along," he said, "a German soldier sits smiling against the bank. He is covered with dust and he is dead." For the Germans in North Africa, the end was approaching. On May 13, 1943, 275,000 enemy soldiers laid down their arms, the largest Axis surrender in the war.

THE DARLAN EPISODE had a larger context. As reporters, the CBS correspondents were privy to a great deal of information not generally known. Most—though they might have denied it—were idealistic; they saw America as fighting not just for victory but for a cause. At the same time, no reporter had power of decision over any aspect of the war effort. The combination bred a frustration—a frustration that at times expressed itself in calls for a tougher war, a war fought for better-articulated ideals.

Sevareid certainly took that line. At times, so did Murrow. In mid-1943, Cecil Brown crossed the line. After his return from Singapore, Brown became a CBS commentator. He was of all the correspondents the one most likely to decry America's war effort as lagging. On August 24, Brown's sponsor—upset with his views—decided to cancel their contract. Brown had not yet received word of this when the following day he delivered a commentary that upset a great many. His topic was the Quebec Conference at which, in Brown's view, President Roosevelt had failed to enunciate clear war aims. "People are in need of words which present a vision of the future in understandable terms," he said. "They are tired of the vague words which came out of Quebec yesterday and today." Brown added, "Any reasonably accurate observer of the American scene at this moment knows that a good deal of the enthusiasm for this war is evaporating into thin air."

CBS News Director Paul White hit the roof. He sent Brown a memo declaring that Brown's words "would be of immense pleasure to Dr. Goebbels and his boys." Under pressure, Brown resigned. CBS, covering its bases, ran full-page newspaper ads in New York affirming its commitment to editorial objectivity.

The War in the Air

ED MURROW HAD advised Eric Sevareid against enlisting. What Murrow did not mention was that he himself had tried to enlist. Following Pearl Harbor, Murrow told his wife that he "ought to be doing something besides sitting behind a microphone." Twice, he discussed obtaining a commission; both times, he was told his reporting was more important.

It rankled him. His brothers were in the service. His own existence, it seemed, was unfairly risk free. Yet Murrow invited risk. During the Blitz, he had, at nobody's insistence but his own, stood exposed on London rooftops, describing the bombing. What Murrow wanted was to ride on a bombing mission over Germany. He lobbied intensively, with the British air ministry, the American Eighth Air Force, and with his superiors at CBS. Urging his case to Paul White, Murrow wrote, "Let me ride in a bomber and I can know a little better how the pilot feels when the tail is shot off."

Murrow's urgings left CBS aghast. Strategic bombing was a key Allied weapon. In January 1943, the British and Americans drew up plans for a concerted bomber assault on German submarine-construction yards, factories, refineries, and other targets. Such bombing could be devastating. On May 24, 1943, Howard K. Smith—broadcasting from Switzerland—described a British raid on Germany's industrial Ruhr. The attack left thirty-seven thousand homeless, Smith reported, and an unknown number dead. The number

OVER NORTH AFRICA

*Two U.S. Navy Curtiss Helldivers (dive bombers) cruise the sky over
North Africa in 1942, the beginning of the end for Rommel's Afrika Korps.*

of dead had been increased, he said, by the order given night-shift factory
workers to remain at their jobs rather than take to the city's shelters. The
official German communiqué acknowledged that "considerable material
damage was caused." That admission, Smith observed, "the first of its kind
in four years of war—is plenty!"

Flying such bombing missions was one of the war's most hazardous
tasks. Losses on a given mission averaged 5 percent—if three hundred
bombers went out, fifteen did not return. CBS executives had no desire to
let Ed Murrow crawl out on that particular limb. In one sense, Murrow had

options. He had been offered the post of president of his alma mater, Washington State College. He was offered the editorship of a Washington, D.C., newspaper. The best—and least likely—offer came in the spring of 1943. Brendan Bracken, the British minister of information, proposed to make Murrow the head of the BBC. The offer came with the knowledge and approval of Winston Churchill. Tempted, Murrow turned it down. To be the American head of a British information agency seemed fraught with conflicts of interest. Possibly, being in London for CBS was the only job Ed Murrow really wanted. What he wanted *more* was for CBS to let him do it as he pleased.

While Murrow agitated for permission, adventure in the air grabbed Eric Sevareid. What put Sevareid in harm's way was a request from President Franklin D. Roosevelt. Roosevelt asked the correspondent to go to China and report as he wished on the three-way struggle there between the Japanese, the nationalist government of Chiang Kai-shek, and the communists led by Mao Tse-tung.

Sevareid flew in stages to India. On August 2, he boarded a C-46 transport plane in India, destined for the temporary Chinese capital of Chungking. Twenty-one men were aboard, including an American diplomat, John Paton Davies. As the aircraft reached the jungle-covered mountains of Burma, its left engine failed. Soon the right engine overheated, and the craft began to sink. All aboard bailed out, except the copilot, who died in the crash. Those jumping included an extremely reluctant Sevareid, who had never previously worn a parachute, much less used one.

On the ground, a dozen of those who had jumped, including Sevareid, gathered to consider their next move. A plane flew overhead, dropping rifles, a radio, and a note instructing them to await a rescue party. Others got there first—fifteen or so local tribesmen, short, naked, and carrying spears. Some, Sevareid noted, "also held wide-bladed knives a couple of feet long, heavy and slightly curved, almost like a butcher's cleaver." Sevareid took charge. He stepped toward the tribesmen and said, simply, "How!" Not long thereafter, a second message was dropped. It instructed them to avoid the local villagers, "as they probably are not friendly." Actually, they were headhunters. This pertinent information arrived too late, as the party was by this time the guests of the Naga.

Three men, including a physician, were dropped to render assistance. Others who had parachuted from the C-46 dribbled in. John Davies led four others into camp in the middle of the night, woke the CBS correspondent, and said, "Dr. Sevareid, I presume?" All were determined not to rile the Nagas. At one point, when the villagers invited their guests to slaughter a goat, one man "closed his eyes and hacked off the goat's head."

To China the Hard Way

John Paton Davies (left), a State Department liaison; William T. Stanton (center)
of the Board of Economic Warfare; and Eric Sevareid (right)
were among the twenty survivors who jumped from a crippled C-46
into the jungle of Burma, on their way to China in August 1943.

After ten days with the Naga, Sevareid was startled by the arrival of an Englishman who "spoke in an Oxford accent and looked like Leslie Howard." The man was Philip Adams, the twenty-nine-year-old British agent in the region. He arrived wearing a blue polo shirt, shorts, and low walking shoes, with a cigarette holder dangling from his mouth. He was the supposed "king" of the region, who brought with him sixty Nagas armed with shotguns and a hundred coolies to act as bearers. Adams had received instructions to find the party and lead them out. He and his troop had hurriedly covered eighty-five miles of jungle in five days, Adams said, because of a rumored attack from a nearby village that had claimed 106 heads in the previous year.

Sevareid considered Adams one of the most remarkable men he'd ever met. Still, the Briton's authority was uncertain. At one point, two Nagas took some canned goods from one of Sevareid's party. Adams decided this was a challenge to his authority. He gathered the Nagas and demanded the cans' return. None were forthcoming. Then, Sevareid wrote, "Adams took a great risk. He collected every man's [knife], carted them away into a pile, and informed the men that none would get his indispensable weapon back until the culprits were produced." This was both an insult and a risk. The Nagas could have killed the entire party or simply abandoned them to death in the jungle. After an hour of wrangling, the canned goods were returned.

On August 18, 1943, Sevareid and the rest of the party set off on an arduous ten-day trek through 140 miles of jungle and mountain to safety. On August 22, Sevareid managed to make a brief broadcast, using a hand-cranked generator for power. His dispatch began, "Burmese jungle headhunters, every one a primitive killer, saved our lives." The story—and the adventure—made minor celebrities of all concerned.

Sevareid made a second attempt. He arrived on September 10 in Chungking, a city he was to describe as "old when Christ was born." On the morning of September 11 (still September 10 in the U.S.), he made his first broadcast, describing the scene: "It is staggering to realize what has happened to China. The immense country has wheeled around and no longer faces to the east. It is as though the United States were rolled in on the east and south, with New York and Charleston, New Orleans and Galveston blocked up, with all travelers from the other side of the world obliged to filter in through the hinterlands and to arrive at St. Paul, Minnesota, and find that little city had taken the place of Washington, D.C." CD

Sevareid's visit proved a disappointment. He was able to meet with U.S. General Joseph Stilwell and others, but Chinese leaders were uninterested. Sevareid was coolly informed that "President Chiang will not be able to receive foreign correspondents in the near future." Broadcast conditions were poor, and little that Sevareid sent out reached America. Complicating everything, Sevareid had dysentery. From the day he landed in the jungle in August to his early November departure from China, he shed thirty pounds. Nine days of plane travel brought Sevareid back to Washington, where frustration continued. Sevareid's "mission for FDR" had been sidetracked. He had expected to write as he pleased. Chiang's armies, he thought, were not really fighting the Japanese, just waiting for them to leave. Chiang's government had little interest in democracy. Sevareid developed these views in a long article intended for publication. When, however, he sought the required clearance from the War Department, Army censors killed it.

IN DECEMBER 1943, permission finally came for Murrow to ride on a bombing raid. The plane was a British Lancaster, *D for Dog*. Its pilot was Jock Abercrombie, and its target was Berlin. Murrow's broadcast account of the flight, known as "Orchestrated Hell," won him a Peabody Award. That account began with the pre-mission briefing and a short wait beside *D-Dog* as the crew was given coffee, chewing gum, oranges, and chocolate. The aircraft took off, climbing to an altitude, Murrow said, "where men must burn oxygen to live." He described encountering flak that looked like "a cigarette lighter in a dark room—one that won't light. Sparks but no flame." He recounted the terse exchanges over the intercom between members of the crew. He told of the sense of vulnerability: "The clouds below us were white, and we were black. *D-Dog* seemed like a black bug on a white sheet."

The last thirty miles to Berlin were, Murrow said, "the longest flight I ever made…*D-Dog* seemed to be standing still, the four propellers thrashing the air. But we didn't seem to be closing in." The pilot put the plane into a climbing turn that dropped Murrow to his knees. "The knees should have been strong enough to support me," he said, "but they weren't, and the stomach seemed in some danger of letting me down, too." Nearing the target, the bomb doors opened, Murrow reported, "And then there was a gentle, confident, upward thrust under my feet." He described the incendiary bombs they'd dropped on Berlin as "going down like a fistful of white rice thrown on a piece of black velvet." With the payload released, the aircraft became lighter and easier to handle. Heading back, Murrow observed a city on fire and painted a vivid picture of it in the minds of his listeners. "I looked down and the white fires had turned red," he said, "they were beginning to merge and spread just like butter does on a hot plate." Minutes later, he reported, "A great orange blob of flak smacked up straight in front of us. And Jock said, 'I think they're shooting at us.'" He added, "I'd thought so for some time."

The navigator announced when *D-Dog* reached the coast. The announcement reminded Murrow of his 1938 flight from Vienna. An older couple, refugees, had been aboard. Murrow recalled that when the copilot announced they were outside German territory, "the old man reached out and grasped his wife's hand." *D-Dog's* mission, Murrow said, "was a massive blow of retribution for all those who have fled from the sound of shots and blows on the stricken continent." 🆔

TRACK 32

It proved to be an exceedingly costly raid—fifty aircraft were shot down. Among those who did not return, and to whom Murrow paid tribute at the end of his broadcast, were Australian reporter Norman Stockton and International News Service correspondent Lowell Bennett. Bennett had bailed out and been taken prisoner in Germany. Stockton was dead. Murrow called his wife from the airport. Janet Murrow later commented, "He sounded shaken."

Mission complete, broadcast made. Murrow received a message from Paul White that ended, "I hope you are cured. Please, please, please don't do it again." Murrow ignored White. He also ignored William Paley. Paley told Murrow he understood the desire to experience a mission, but, he added, "What do you have to gain to do it the second, third, fourth, or fifth time?" Murrow accepted that point, but flew more missions anyway. Murrow, Eric Sevareid commented, was not fearless: "He could be scared plenty, but he wouldn't show it. What he was afraid of was being afraid." Possibly, flying missions was an escape from the strain and constriction of responsibility in London. Those at CBS London could tell when Murrow had just been on a

Flying Combat

Murrow and Lt. M.P. Royston of the RAF prepare for another mission into Germany.

mission—he was calmer. By war's end, Murrow made two dozen bombing runs. Given the odds, he should have been killed—as was Jock Abercrombie, the pilot of *D-Dog,* who was shot down a month after he let Ed Murrow catch a ride.

Italy

BY THE TIME Jock Abercrombie was killed, British and American soldiers were dying in considerable numbers. The theater of war was Italy, where the Allies were painfully working their way up the Italian "boot." Here, again, politics complicated the action. On July 25, 1943, Italy's Fascist Grand Council had ousted Mussolini, then entered into negotiations with the British to take their country out of the war. The Germans intervened. On July 27, Howard K. Smith reported from Switzerland that German divisions had passed through the Brenner Pass "and took over complete control of Trieste, Fiume, and Pola. They are rapidly occupying the rest of the Italian peninsula today. The object, it is said, is to get a firm grip on Italy's flank, in the event that [Italy] should surrender."

Surrender was imminent. In Switzerland, Smith added, editors "told their typesetters and reporters to be on call for extra editions announcing Italy's surrender." Surrender followed, peace did not. German agents rescued Mussolini from captivity. Mussolini then proclaimed the Italian Social Republic, and, with armed forces loyal to him, continued the war. Meanwhile, German forces had occupied the whole of the country.

The German occupation made the Allies' task difficult. The country's mountains, ridges, and deeply cut valleys made it excellent defensive terrain. Having conquered Sicily, the Allies landed on the Italian mainland in early September 1943. They advanced one-third of the way up the peninsula, then were halted south of the major German defensive position, the Gustav Line—a line of fortifications that ran across Italy south of Rome. Rome, barely seventy-five miles away, would not fall for eight months. Trying to break the stalemate, the Americans landed on January 22, 1944, at Anzio, behind the Gustav Line. German counterattacks contained the beachhead, and the stalemate continued.

Winston Burdett covered much of the early fighting for CBS. **CD** Eric Sevareid arrived in March, and soon thought he had a major scoop. Mt. Vesuvius—the volcano that buried Pompeii in A.D. 79—was erupting. On March 20, Sevareid took a jeep and recording equipment, and headed off to record the event. Approaching, he wrote, "You could not see Vesuvius mountain itself; what you saw was a perpendicular river of fire, curving down in the form of an inverted question mark....To the northeast, one could see flashes of fire [from battle], which could not hold a candle to this transaction of the elements." Sevareid came back with the first sound recording ever made of an erupting volcano. It never made the airwaves. CBS New York declared it was not of "network quality."

TRACK 31

Sevareid differed from Murrow. Murrow was a man of high, though rarely articulated, personal standards and continuing doubts as to whether he was meeting them. Sevareid, too, suffered self-doubt, but also had a good many doubts about others. Reaching Naples, not far behind the stagnant front, he wrote, "Weeks go by, and our armies do not advance; and so, inevitably, many soldiers here lose the feeling of fight....Desk officers keep regular hours, and some come to resent any intrusion of the war which might mean overtime work." Some American generals, he thought, were too aware of the limelight, and sought to cajole or coerce reporters into boosting their careers in print. And he wondered whether American soldiers were politically prepared for the war they were fighting. He preferred the attitude he encountered at Free French headquarters: "Those men had a cold implacable hatred of the enemy that was almost frightening." These, of course, were his private ruminations, which never reached the air.

On April 21, Sevareid moved to Anzio and began broadcasting from the beachhead. The long stalemate was about to break. On May 11, the Allies began their fourth and finally successful assault on Cassino, the mountaintop monastery that was a linchpin of the Gustav Line. On May 23, the advance began from Anzio that would link those on the beachhead with the main Allied army.

SEVAREID IN ITALY

Eric Sevareid (left) traveled with a U.S. division in Italy.
He talks with Joseph Duncan of Dallas, Texas.

After almost five years as a war correspondent, Sevareid now got his first close-up look at combat. His reaction—like that of Shirer in France—was of its unreality. "One never saw masses of men assaulting the enemy. What one observed, in apparent unrelated patches, was small, loose bodies of men moving down narrow defiles or over steep inclines, going methodically from position to position between long halts, and the only continuous factor was the roar and the crackling of the big guns." To Sevareid, war was an event in which "unseen groups of men were fighting other men that they rarely saw." On May 23, Sevareid reported from Anzio:

The breakout from the beachhead has begun....Before dawn, this chill cloudy morning, we stood upon a rise in flat prairie among the daisies and the flowing thistles. We listened to the meadowlarks and looked at our watches. A veil of fog covers the German hills. At 5:45, the gun flares spurted from the left, then part of the right, then all around us. There was a faint trembling in the earth. One's jacket flapped from concussions. A few minutes after six we heard the planes and through the one break in the clouds saw the formations coming from several directions. Then fighter-bombers wheeled and darted well under the cloud layer and disappeared in the space dividing the two armies....Sleepy men crawled from their holes. One lay on a sandbag. Another studied and re-studied a page in a book on photography. One man said: "They can hear this in Rome maybe."

He talked of the fighting and talked as well of fighting's consequence, the wounded. He described a young American soldier, "staring at the roof of the tent, blood showing through the bandage on his head. His helmet was on the grass beside his litter, the steel bent back from the hole as though plied with a can opener."

Two days later, the Allied armies linked up, and Sevareid had the "scoop." It was largely a matter of luck. Official announcement of the link-up came May 25 at two P.M. As Sevareid had the next available assigned broadcast time, he got the story out first.

Winston Burdett had a more adventurous day. With two newsmen as companions, he rode in a jeep from the eastern end of the Allied line on the Adriatic all the way to Anzio. They had driven, he broadcast, "up the swerving coast road and around and past the mountains, down again to the plain and the Pontine marshes, and then past rich fields of wheat and barley." Without, he added, "seeing a German." Burdett reported, "the scent of victory [is] in the air today...but victory is not ours yet. Though the Germans have pulled out of the coastal strip, they are still up in the hills." Actually, the German Tenth Army was fleeing. The original Allied plan was to round up the retreating Germans and let Rome fall when it may. Now, a controversial change of direction made Rome the first priority, and Allied armies advanced on that city.

Sevareid, in his writing and broadcasting, returned often to the cost of war—in destruction and in lives. On Memorial Day, he attended a service at a military cemetery. Afterward, he came upon six unburied bodies. A burial assistant told Sevareid that one got used to death. The burial sergeant corrected him: "It isn't true—I never get used to it. With a thousand," he added, "it would be just a matter of sanitation. With six, it seems like a tragedy."

On June 3, Sevareid made his last broadcast from Anzio, and headed toward Rome. The city fell the following day. Exhausted, Sevareid broadcast just a brief announcement from outside the city. At six A.M., Winston Burdett pushed him awake. Burdett had of his own volition driven into and around Rome. Now, he awakened Sevareid to read him the broadcast he had made. Sevareid called it "one of the most dramatic and beautiful broadcasts I've ever heard." Sevareid was the only one to hear it. Operators at the Naples relay station had not been monitoring Burdett's frequency.

The formal entry into Rome occurred on June 5. Sevareid rode in a jeep at a snail's pace through the throng. Later, reporters typed out their stories to be cleared and carried back to Naples for broadcast. Sevareid recalled a conversation with an Army radio sergeant, who said the transmitter mounted on his half-truck could reach Naples. Sevareid tracked down the sergeant. His broadcast—transmitted rather than carried to Naples—was the first to reach New York. Sevareid was greatly pleased. He was generally considered a "commentator," and liked to show he could on occasion outrun the pack.

Hours later, Burdett gave a further report on Rome. "The people of this ancient and still splendid capital," he said, "have seldom celebrated such a riotous holiday as they did today." TRACK 33 The city was in the streets. Burdett and two other correspondents made slow progress through the crowds in a jeep. "Our jeep could not stop," he said, "without at least twenty persons gathering around it—men who wanted to see our equipment; boys who wanted a ride; women who wished to kiss our feet. All of them asking questions, all of them telling us how much they hated the fascists." That afternoon closed in the piazza near St. Peter's Cathedral, where Pope Pius XII blessed the throng. Rome, the pope said, "had escaped the unimaginable destruction of war and had entered a new era." Burdett closed, "Here in Rome, today, no one asked how far the Germans had retreated from Rome; everyone acted as though the war was over." It wasn't. Allied forces in Italy would require another eleven months to reach the French and Austrian borders in the country's north.

In late 1944, Sevareid published in *The Nation* a surprisingly blunt assessment of the Italian campaign. His writing was hedged, but his points were clear. Sevareid, a military amateur, questioned the wisdom of fighting up the length of the heavily defended Italian peninsula and of entering

Rome rather than moving to capture the fleeing Germans. The piece was notable on two counts. First, the points Sevareid made were supported by some later military historians. And second, Sevareid—who complained continually of censorship—in the end got his version of the story told.

The taking of Cassino, the breakout at Anzio, the fall of Rome—coming in quick succession, each of these stories claimed the headlines. In the Pacific, Allied forces had been steadily recapturing islands from the Japanese in 1944. In February, the Marshall Islands fell to U.S. forces; in April, American GIs helped the Australians liberate New Guinea. Saipan, in the Mariana Islands, would be the next target for Allied invasion in June—a key battle of the war in the Pacific. The bigger story, however, was elsewhere.

"STERNER STUFF LIES AHEAD."

Murrow, always a two-finger typist, prepares a report for broadcast wearing his U.S. War Correspondent uniform.

The bigger story was the pending Allied invasion of France. On June 5, Ed Murrow broadcast from London that Rome's capture had produced little excitement there. It was simply "the first flash of lightning preceding a storm" and Murrow spoke of Londoners' "realization that sterner stuff lies ahead." **CD** The storm would come with D-Day. Its date was a matter of intense speculation, "and while the speculation continues, Allied fliers are memorizing the landmarks on the fringes of Europe" for bombing runs to come. Murrow reported on a squadron of New Zealanders who flew reconnaissance over the French coast: "They have a favorite farmer on the other side of the channel. For weeks now he has been plowing a field. They call him Lazy Louie. Each day they report how many furrows he has plowed. Progress is slow. He spends too much time watching the Allied planes overhead." By June 5, the farmer had little longer to wait.

In Rome on June 6, Sevareid was at an Army press facility where correspondents were typing out their stories. A BBC man ran in and shouted, "Eisenhower has announced the invasion of France." Sevareid recorded the reaction: "Every typewriter stopped."

TRACK 34

5

INVASION AND LIBERATION

You will bring about the destruction of the German war machine, the elimination of Nazi tyranny over the oppressed peoples of Europe, and security for ourselves in a free world.

Your task will not be an easy one. Your enemy is well trained, well equipped, and battle-hardened. He will fight, fight savagely. But this is the year 1944. Much has happened since the Nazi triumphs of 1940–1941....

The tide has turned.

—General Dwight D. Eisenhower
June 6, 1944

TRACKS: 35–46

Previous page: Soldiers disembark from a landing craft and wade in toward Omaha Beach on D-Day, June 6, 1944.

D-Day

THE ANNOUNCEMENT THAT history's greatest seaborne invasion was underway came, appropriately, from Ed Murrow, the war's preeminent reporter, who was selected to read Eisenhower's Order of the Day over radio. He spoke on June 6, 1944, at 3:33 A.M. Eastern Time, delivering a message that ended: "We will accept nothing less than full victory. Good luck. And let us beseech the blessing of almighty God upon this great and noble undertaking." 🔘

TRACK 35

D-Day was the largest military operation of all time. In April, Murrow had rightly broadcast that its planning was "complex beyond description." CBS, to the extent security permitted, broadcast reports on the planning. In one, a variation of the CBS Roundup, Charles Collingwood, Larry LeSueur, and others reported from ports, airfields, and a matériel center. The Allied command did its preparation; Murrow did his own. He hired Richard C. Hottelet—the reporter arrested and expelled from Germany in 1941—and brought Bill Downs, first hired to provide coverage from Russia, back to London for D-Day. Murrow used his standing to get his people ringside for the coming invasion. Of five hundred reporters in London, twenty-eight were permitted to take on-scene part in D-Day. Five of them were from CBS. And, largely for the occasion, standards changed. CBS would now permit some use of tape recorders on the battlefront. Both wire and celluloid tape recorders were by then available; both were bulky and sensitive. D-Day was to be "pool" coverage. That is, given the large number of news agencies pushing to cover the story, and the small number of reporters actually allowed on the scene, reports coming in would be shared. Radio coverage from London would move through CBS and Murrow.

Across the Channel, Erwin Rommel was also preparing. The German general, given command in December 1943, took the view that if the invasion was not stopped on the beaches, Germany would lose the war. At his direction, crews were soon laying one million mines per month along the coast.

Some while after four A.M., on June 6, 1944, Murrow and other select reporters were telephoned, awakened, and summoned to briefings held on the campus of London University. By that time, Larry LeSueur and Charles Collingwood were riding on landing craft headed for Utah Beach, Bill Downs was on a British craft, Richard Hottelet was with a Marauder aircraft, and Willard Shadel was with the Navy in the British Channel. They were specks in a vast undertaking. Historian John Keegan wrote of D-Day: "The spectacle that confronted those embarked—and those ashore—was perhaps more dramatic than any soldiers, sailors, or airmen had ever seen at the beginning of any battle." The Normandy coast was filled with ships as far as the eye could see, "the sky thundered with the passage of aircraft; and the coastline had begun to disappear in gouts of smoke and dust as the bombardment bit into it."

Collingwood noted and passed back to Murrow a story that Murrow used several days after the landing. Pre-invasion, some Americans were stationed near a dormitory that housed a group of British Wrens, women who were trained to use signal flags. The Americans learned just enough about signal code to try to ask the women out. According to Collingwood, Murrow reported, the night before the invasion, a lone Wren came out of the dormitory and broadcast a single word in code. The one word was "courage."

All was ready. Still, as Eisenhower said in another context, war is chaos. And the chaos of D-Day overmatched CBS's efforts to cover the story. Of CBS reporters who witnessed the invasion, only Richard Hottelet managed a broadcast that day. ⓒ Hottelet had ridden on a Marauder aircraft, low under the cloud cover over Utah Beach. Deeply airsick, he dashed back to London by car to report his experience, broadcasting with a slop bucket at the ready.

At Utah Beach itself, Collingwood was finding that his fifty-five-pound tape recorder was not well suited to the conditions of a beach invasion. Larry LeSueur reached Utah Beach with the second wave, coming ashore from a landing craft that had spent over twenty-four hours at sea, leaving the soldiers so seasick that he did not see how they could fight. The resistance at

TRACK 36

Richard C. Hottelet
1917–
b. Brooklyn, New York

Richard C. Hottelet was born on September 22, 1917, in Brooklyn, New York, the son of recent German immigrants. In 1937, he graduated from Brooklyn College with a degree in philosophy, and that same year left for Berlin, where he lived with his uncle and attended classes at Friedrich-Wilhelms Universität. He left college in 1938 when he realized the university had become a vehicle for Nazi propaganda, and though he had not thought of becoming a journalist, he went to work as a correspondent for the United Press wire service because they were hiring.

Following troops through Germany, Hottelet's naturally assertive nature made him a fearless reporter. He was arrested and interrogated by Nazi officials several times for asking what they deemed inappropriate questions. At seven A.M. on March 15, 1941, he was arrested by the Gestapo at his apartment in Berlin. "I was taken by car to the old police presidium at the Alexanderplatz," he reported. "A member of the secret police there informed me I would have to be their 'guest' probably over the weekend." Three days later, Hottelet was finally informed at his first formal hearing what he had been arrested for: "suspicion of espionage," a charge he flatly denied. After four months of questioning, he was released along with another journalist—the two of them traded for two Germans charged with espionage in the United States.

After a hero's welcome at home, Hottelet went to work as a UP Washington correspondent. In 1942, he married his girlfriend, Englishwoman Ann Delafield, and shortly thereafter left the UP for the Office of War Information (OWI), which soon sent him to London to broadcast the war to German-speaking countries. Upon leaving the OWI in 1944, Hottelet was hired by Murrow. He was the youngest of the Murrow Boys.

When the war ended, Hottelet served as CBS correspondent in Moscow, the United States, and, beginning in 1950, Bonn. He returned to the United States in

continued

1956, continuing to report for CBS and taking part in Murrow's celebrated annual roundup *Years of Crisis,* during which he could be counted upon to argue with David Schoenbrun about the superiority of Germany over France, and conservative politics over liberal.

In the late 1950s, Hottelet hosted an early-morning program, *Richard C. Hottelet with the News,* and in 1960, he took over United Nations news coverage for CBS but, despite his vast knowledge of world politics, was underused by the network until his forced retirement amid cutbacks in 1985.

Hottelet then worked as spokesman for the U.S. ambassador to the United Nations. In 1993, he created a weekly National Public Radio program, *America and the World*, which was funded by the Council on Foreign Relations and for which he served as moderator until 1995.

Hottelet, who lives in Connecticut, continues to lecture, produce documentaries, and write, and is a frequent contributor to the *Christian Science Monitor* and other American newspapers.

Utah was comparatively light—the Allies suffered 197 first-day casualties among the twenty-three thousand soldiers put ashore. Germans began surrendering. One was an immaculately dressed captain who disdained taking cover when Germans elsewhere opened fire on the beach. LeSueur watched as the German officer was shot dead by fire from one of his own men.

CBS and other pool reporters were raking in news from landing zones, but little was getting back to London. Murrow read a report from Collingwood describing the waves of landing craft: "The first craft onto the beaches was a little LCT [Landing Craft Tank]....[T]hey came in doggedly looking very small and gallant with their heads up. Offshore several miles loomed the silhouettes of the big ships." The landing craft arrived, then backed off to make room for others. Collingwood described the assortment of amphibious "ocean-going vessels," like the LST [Landing Ship Tank]: "She's a floating garage....When she reaches shore, her mouth opens and trucks and vehicles of every description roll out of her and are lifted by dabbits from her hold."

The invasion, in fact, went considerably more smoothly than CBS's efforts to cover it. At four of the five beaches, the German defenders were second-rate troops, and lodgments were soon secured. At Omaha Beach, the German 352nd Division put up a determined defense—here, the Americans suffered the bulk of the 4,649 casualties they sustained that day. By nightfall, all five beaches were in Allied hands.

With little filtering back from the beaches, CBS from London and New York filled the air by repeating earlier announcements and talking to each other. From New York, Robert Trout reported Winston Churchill's invasion announcement to the House of Commons as Churchill's words arrived, sentence by sentence, by wire service to Trout's desk.

"Airborne landings successfully effected behind German lines....

"Landings in beaches are proceeding at various points....

"The fire of shore batteries has been largely quelled....

"Obstacles constructed in the sea have not proved so difficult as we apprehended."

Trout then cut to Murrow, who announced a report from the English coast from reporter Stanley Richardson. No Richardson; no report. Murrow covered, "Hello, New York, we are having technical difficulty, we will try again."

There was a huge hunger for news, but, as yet, little to feed it. At another point, Murrow spoke live by transatlantic phone call with CBS News Director Paul White, who was making a rare on-air appearance. Murrow told White that CBS London would pass along pool reports as they arrived. There were, however, no pool reports available at the moment. With much of the nation listening, Murrow found he had nothing to say. Awkwardly, he filled time: "Things have been a little bit confused. An elderly charwoman in the hallway, scrubbing the floor, is the most unconcerned person in this building."

Even more awkwardly, White responded, "I had a young woman come in with a vacuum cleaner."

Collecting himself, Murrow said there would be news soon. He ticked off its sources: Charles Collingwood was with a landing craft, he said, and Larry LeSueur was with the American ground forces. Bill Downs was with the British; Bill Shadel was with the Navy. "We'll be here," Murrow closed, adding, "...most of us look on this as something more than just a way to make a living."

If there was little hard news, there was still much that was momentous. In New York, Robert Trout interrupted other coverage to play a just-received recording of General Eisenhower's announcement to the people of Nazi-occupied western Europe. Eisenhower began: "People of western Europe, a landing was made this morning on the coast of France by troops of the Allied expeditionary force. This landing is part of a concerted United Nations effort for the liberation of Europe, in conjunction with our great Russian allies." He urged those near the invasion to follow the lead of local resistance groups. To others, he said, "Continue your passive resistance, but do not needlessly endanger your lives. Wait until I give you the signal to rise and fight the enemy. The day will come when I will need your united strength."

Away from the eye of the storm of battle, an odd calm reigned. Reporter Kent Stevenson arrived mid-morning at an airfield on the English coast to be greeted with the words "Of course, you've heard the news." That was how he learned of the invasion. There was, Stevenson added, no shouting or cheering, "not even when loud speakers relayed the words of Winston Churchill." Everyone was busy. Murrow reported that bombers operating in support of the ground troops had encountered little opposition from German aircraft: "As a matter of fact, the refusal of the Germans to commit their air force is one of the principal subjects of conversation here tonight." **CD**

TRACK 35

By evening, Murrow had a coherent commentary to present. He spoke, first, of the morning of the invasion:

> Early this morning we heard the bombers going out. It was the sound of a giant factory in the sky. It seemed to shake the old gray stone buildings in this bruised and battered city beside the Thames. The sound was heavier, more triumphant than ever before. Those who knew what was coming could imagine that they heard great guns and strains of the "Battle Hymn of the Republic" well above the roar of the motors.

Murrow, too, was struck by the calmness around him. Most Londoners seemed to be going about their everyday business. "You almost wanted to shout at them and say, 'Don't you know that history is being made today?'" Once again, he announced that reports from beachheads should be coming

NORMANDY LANDING

*American soldiers disembark from an LCVP (Landing Craft–Vehicle,
Personnel) in Normandy after the beach had been secured.*

in soon. He assessed the situation as a race against time: "We are attempting
to consolidate our positions to withstand the inevitable German counterat-
tack, while the Germans are attempting to regroup their forces and prepare
to strike before we are well established." Murrow was greatly in the dark
about his own operation. Rumors reached him that LeSueur and Collingwood were both dead at Utah Beach. As the reports expected from them
failed to arrive, those rumors gained credibility.

On June 7, the invasion's second day, things were only marginally clearer.
Murrow reported, vaguely but reassuringly, "The latest word about Allied

operations in France…is that things are going according to plan and running to time." It would be unwise, he added, "to expect speedy or spectacular results." Enemy counterattacks were expected. He commented on the military's continuing policy of suppressing news coverage "to keep the enemy in the dark." Murrow added, "Those who are impatient of hard news might reflect that no story is worth the life of a single soldier."

Collingwood's first recorded report from D-Day on Utah Beach was broadcast on June 8. Though resistance at Utah was "light," Collingwood captured some of the reality of the fighting. "This beach…is still under considerable enemy gunfire," he reported. "These boys are apparently having a pretty tough time in here on the beaches. It's not very pleasant, it's exposed, and it must have been a rugged fight to get it." **CD** On June 9, a second account taped by Collingwood on the beachfront June 7 arrived, to be played and replayed frequently. "Yesterday," Collingwood began, "I was in France; not very far in France, just on the beaches." There was, he added, "Quite enough going on the beaches to occupy one's mind with." The invasion, he said, was going well: the German defenses were not as strong as expected, American troops were fighting magnificently, and supplies were arriving smoothly. He described a single American soldier, a "sergeant in his foxhole in the beach [with] the picture of his wife at one end and a glamour-girl calendar turned to June tacked up at the other." His foxhole's only other decoration was "a little pattern of concentric circles made with cigarette butts, while the Germans were shelling the beach with eighty-eights."

Collingwood described the confusion. Wherever he went, he said, soldiers would ask him for the latest news. He mentioned one peculiarity: "A persistent rumor on the beaches [is] that we had invaded Norway." He described the hazards. At one point, Collingwood was standing near a half ton of explosives when his site came under enemy fire. And he described the stretcher-borne casualties:

> Men, with infinite tenderness, lift the stretchers down to the ship. One man, with a slight head wound, proudly carrying his helmet on his middle with a bullet hole right through the steel, from back to front. Another man who was hurt bad, not saying anything, just looking at the sky as they brought him indoors.

TRACK 37

Bill Downs
1913–1978
b. Kansas City, Kansas

William Downs was born in 1913 and grew up in Kansas City, Kansas, the son of a railroad engineer and a housewife. Downs dreamed of being a reporter from the time he was a boy, and he served as sports editor for his high school newspaper and manager for the paper at Wyandotte College, which he attended for two years. When he transferred to the University of Kansas, he was integral in reviving the bankrupt University of Kansas paper, the *Daily Kansan*, which, under his care, even turned a profit.

After graduating in 1935, Downs worked for the United Press wire service in Kansas City, Denver, and New York City, transferring in 1941 overseas to the UP's London bureau, where Charles Collingwood spotted him and recommended him to Murrow as a replacement for the dissatisfied Larry LeSueur in Moscow. Murrow hired Downs in September 1942. His faith in Downs's ability to get a good story outweighed any reservations about the young reporter's delivery and loud, gravelly voice. Downs covered with distinction the war in Russia, the D-Day landings, the liberation of Nazi death camps, and the Japanese surrender. Once, during the German counteroffensive near the Dutch town of Arnhem in September 1944, Downs and his old UP colleague Walter Cronkite scrambled for cover in a ditch. "Just think," Downs said to Cronkite, "if we survive them, these will be the good old days."

Downs was more at home with the common soldier than he was with generals or politicians; he wasn't the most elegant wordsmith, and he never sought glamour. Murrow nicknamed Downs "Wilbur," and Downs always called Murrow "Doctor." Known for his integrity and outspoken opinions, Downs was dubbed "Murrow's conscience" at CBS.

Not a favorite at CBS despite his ties to Murrow, Downs spent a year after the German surrender travelling the Pacific, assigned to cover the Japanese surrender and other stories throughout Southeast Asia. On his return home in 1946, Downs

continued

was assigned the difficult, unglamorous task of reporting on labor issues for CBS on *Cross Section—USA*. In 1947, he was asked to open a Detroit bureau for the network, and he reluctantly agreed.

Downs was assigned to Korea in the early 1950s to cover the war for *See It Now*, which became televised in November 1951. During the McCarthy era, Downs reported for CBS-TV, and his everyday exposure to fear-mongering, blacklisting, loyalty oaths, and book burnings led him to harass Murrow to confront the infamous senator—which Murrow eventually did twice, on the radio in 1953 and in an electrifying television documentary in March 1954. By that time, Downs was CBS bureau chief in Rome, and he showed tapes of the documentary every evening in his home to crowds of Americans.

In 1956, Downs was reassigned to Washington against his will, replaced by Winston Burdett, who was being sent "into exile" in Rome. Downs resigned from CBS in 1962 to write novels. When his novels didn't sell and his money ran out in late 1963, he became a reporter for ABC in Washington, where he remained for the rest of his life.

When Downs died in 1978, his family and friends buried his ashes behind his house and drank a toast to his memory.

One invasion aim was to advance northwest down the Cotentin peninsula to capture the port of Cherbourg. On June 9, Richard Hottelet reported that the Allies were one-third of the way to their goal. "Weather today has been rotten," he added, and "air activity has been cut to a minimum." Their opponents were a somewhat motley array of soldiers drawn or impressed from various countries. Thus far, nineteen hundred prisoners had been taken and processed; these, Bill Downs had told Hottelet, included "Germans, Russians, Poles, Belgians, Czechs, and even one Japanese."

Cherbourg fell on June 26. From that city, Larry LeSueur reported, "Men are shaving again. They are polishing their boots. Makeshift clotheslines of underwear, shirts, and socks dangle in the breeze." The soldiers, he said, had a newly found confidence. They had not doubted the American army, "the only thing they weren't sure of was themselves." With the capture of Cherbourg, LeSueur added, "they know that they themselves have been tested under fire and made the grade."

While the western end of the advance had reached Cherbourg, the eastern end had been bottled up by the region's centuries-old hedgerows, largely impenetrable by tanks and easy to defend with infantry. On July 25, the Allies began to achieve a breakthrough at St. Lô. On August 1, George Patton's Third Army broke through the westernmost end of the line and started a sprint across the body of France that carried 175 miles in seventeen days, helping break the main German defenses in France.

With the invasion, CBS coverage focused almost entirely on the fighting in France. News from the Pacific Theater was scant, limited in the week after D-Day to a few reports from Douglas Edwards in New York on American bombings of Japanese-held islands.

Invading the South of France

ONE MORE CBS correspondent had a beach landing to make. Eric Sevareid was picked by lot for a spot aboard a landing craft in Operation Anvil, the August 15 assault on the Mediterranean coast of France. Three American and five French divisions were gathered for the invasion, with Sevareid set to land with the American Forty-Fifth Division near the village of Saint-Maxime.

Infantrymen and correspondent boarded their craft the night before the dawn assault. Sevareid later wrote: "Nobody on board this LST had the remotest notion of how it would all go off." During the night of waiting, Sevareid found his fear melting away. He could not account for this. Perhaps it was "the spectacle of power that one saw all around or the immediate sense of strength derived from comradeship with the men." Perhaps the reason was simpler. Stuck on a tiny craft in a night sea, he had no alternative but to proceed.

The landing was a letdown; few Germans were anywhere in sight. Sevareid felt "almost disappointed." The infantrymen, he noticed, were not. They tossed their lifejackets and talked with relieved boisterousness. Sevareid spotted a French girl trying "between bursts of self-conscious laughter" to pin a handful of flowers to the uniform shirt of an American infantryman. Later that day, Sevareid broadcast from "a pine-covered hill several miles inland." He reported, "We landed almost without opposition." For the moment, Sevareid added, the scene was quiet: "Where the Germans are now, the bulk of them I cannot tell you, though we may find out very suddenly."

Sevareid did find Germans very suddenly, though not because they were looking for him. Hearing an unofficial report that Cannes had been liberated, he and five others bounded into a jeep to investigate. The road ran along a cliff. Rounding a curve near the city, they encountered two American paratroopers running back toward them and shouting of German artillery fire. All eight took very crowded refuge in a cut into the cliff abutting the highway. Theirs was the only vehicle in sight, and the German battery had it targeted. Sevareid described this as "a relatively new experience for me." To be near shellfire intended for others was distressing, he wrote, "but to know that you are the target is quite another sensation."

One shot clipped the jeep. There were two options, Sevareid thought. They could scamper back down the road pursued by shellfire, or they could stick to their cramped hideaway until sunset, then make their exit under cover of darkness. Sevareid favored the latter option. The paratroopers were not so patient. They headed into the open, crawled over and under the damaged jeep, and decided that the only real problem was a severed ignition wire. They located and spliced in some replacement wire, and got the vehicle running. All jumped in the vehicle and cleared out to safer terrain. Sevareid discovered that a shell fragment had punctured his typewriter case and nicked the space bar.

The invading French-American forces moved rapidly north through the Rhone Valley. Their advance was aided, Winston Burdett reported from Rome, by members of the French resistance, who, Burdett added, "are guiding our forces through the hills and fighting with them." Opposition was half-hearted: in the first week, the Allied army advanced 125 miles, taking twenty thousand prisoners and reaching Grenoble on August 22.

Sevareid found himself a minor hero. When French farmers or innkeepers learned that he was with American radio, he wrote, "they would burst into loud cries, summon the neighbors, and throw their arms about us." The French men and women had been listening to broadcasts on the sly, in backrooms and basements, to avoid detection.

Sevareid saw the dirty underside of war. With the advance, he moved against a wake of atrocities committed by the retreating Germans. At La Chapelle, twenty-two civilians had been executed; 147 more at Vaissux. And he witnessed the pattern of French revenge—German soldiers summarily executed and women collaborators shaved, stripped, and ridiculed by mobs. Sevareid viewed this as just revenge. In an October 7 broadcast, he stated, "I would like to make one thing clear—this is not civil war in France. At the worst, a few murderers have been murdered, without trial—except as four-years' trial by their neighbors."

The moral landscape was clearer than the battlefield. Once again, Sevareid exhibited his strange facility for wandering into the wrong place. Thus far in this war, he had escaped France under fire, been in London for the Blitz, parachuted into the Burmese jungle where he had been rescued by headhunters, and been targeted by German artillery. One further episode now occurred. German forces, in retreat, inadvertently surrounded parts of the infantry division to which Sevareid was attached. Five correspondents, including Sevareid, were given the option to clear out. They considered the matter for what Sevareid later called "the most distressing" twenty minutes of his life. Sevareid was for staying and joining the fight: "I felt at first that we could not leave—that it would involve an insupportable loss of face." The opposing view was that the reporters were incompetent as soldiers and more likely to look like idiots than heroes.

The latter view won out. The reporters took a jeep and headed in the direction of safety. Down the road, they were approaching a tunnel when a tank emerged heading straight for them. Scooting to the side of the road, the jeep avoided a collision in which it would have been pancaked. As the vehicles passed, Sevareid looked through an aperture in the tank and saw its commander. The commander looked back. Sevareid couldn't tell if he was German or American.

Another surprise waited several days later in Culoz. An Army colonel tipped off Sevareid that the American writer Gertrude Stein was living in the village with her partner, Alice B. Toklas, where they had spent most of the war unharmed under Nazi control (remarkable in that they were lesbian, Jewish, and American). Before the war, Sevareid had interviewed Stein, found her a remarkable talker, though less of a prophet: she had argued that

Hitler was too much of a romantic ever to go to war. Now, she told Sevareid that the Germans never understood the French: a German officer had roomed with the French railway stationmaster without ever figuring out that he was the head of the local resistance. A few days later, Sevareid arranged for Stein to broadcast to America. "What a day is today that is what a day it was day before yesterday, what a day!" was how Stein began, in her singular poetic idiom. She closed her talk: "I can tell you that liberty is the most important thing in the world more important than food and clothes more important than anything on this mortal earth."

Liberation of Paris

PARIS WAS THE great prize not simply to the Allied armies, but to Charles Collingwood and Larry LeSueur. Each had vowed to make the first report from the city following its liberation. For LeSueur, who, along with Sevareid, claimed to be the last American correspondent to broadcast from a free Paris, that goal was especially dear. That day was nearing. On August 19, Collingwood reported that American troops had "reached the River Seine, twenty-six miles from Paris." That same day, LeSueur reported, without explanatory comment, that French radio in Paris had gone silent: "The last signal heard on the Paris wavelength were eleven bars of music played on a reed instrument—a song favored by the French underground." Both Collingwood and LeSueur missed that report's significance: Paris was rising in rebellion against the German garrison.

Later that day, LeSueur chipped a tooth on a stale K-ration. When he tried to speak, he whistled, making it impossible for him to broadcast. Neither gum, his finger, his tongue, nor floury paste could cover it up. Assured by General Courtney Hodges of the U.S. First Army that Paris would not be freed for another two weeks, LeSueur reluctantly returned to London to see a dentist. On August 21, Collingwood was outside Paris with

American forces. When word of the rebellion arrived, the Second French Armored division was ordered to move immediately on the city. Collingwood saw an opportunity. He wrote and recorded a hold-for-release story announcing that Paris had been liberated, and filed the tape and transcript on the assumption that liberation would occur before his story worked its way through censorship. But the story was cleared just two days later, August 23.

In London, Richard Hottelet, who couldn't have known that fighting was still going on in Paris, read Collingwood's story announcing the city's liberation on the air:

> Columbia's Charles Collingwood reports tonight that the Second French Armored Division has entered the capital....It was the people of Paris who really won back their city....The people of Paris had risen and so hounded the Germans that the German commander requested an armistice. 🆑

TRACK 38

FIGHTING IN THE PLACE DE LA CONCORDE

Hundreds of Parisians look on as the Second French Armored and Fourth U.S. Infantry Divisions flush the Germans from their strongholds during the struggle to liberate Paris.

The dispatch was a bombshell, setting off celebrations in America and England. CBS played Collingwood's recorded version over and over again that night. At New York's Rockefeller Center, Lily Pons sang "The Marseillaise" to a throng of twenty thousand. Meanwhile, however, the fighting in Paris continued.

The truth soon became obvious. CBS beat a hasty and embarrassed retreat. Larry LeSueur, whom Collingwood had "beaten" for the first report from Paris and who was back in France on August 24, had the consolation of reading the CBS correction: "Paris has not yet been entered by Allied troops. Their French Second Armored Division is still outside the city. It's believed here that the French resistance groups are in possession of the center of Paris, but it's also certain that it's thick with Germans on the outskirts." **CD** LeSueur also had the consolation of being the first American reporter to broadcast from a liberated Paris on August 25.

After the war, an American censor explained what had occurred. When Collingwood's account reached London, the CBS office there phoned it to censors for clearance. The officer taking the call later said that Collingwood's story "was the first inkling that the Allies were in Paris. We immediately assumed that because Collingwood was filing the story from Paris…that Americans were in Paris." When the BBC aired a separate rumor that Paris had been entered by the Allies, CBS felt it had confirmation of Collingwood's story. The censor requested a written text of the story, approved it, and Hottelet told the world.

Collingwood's was the most infamous journalistic error committed by a Murrow reporter during the war. It was one he more or less got away with. Perhaps his youth, his charm, his recent Peabody Award—and the fact that Paris did indeed fall the following day—were enough to get him off the hook.

Paris was the main story, but from New York, announcer Douglas Edwards told listeners of events elsewhere—a Russian advance in Bessarabia and initial bombings of an island U.S. Marines would make memorable, Iwo Jima.

But Paris was the lure for Howard K. Smith and Bennie, his pregnant, Danish-born wife. The couple had been holed up in Switzerland since Smith's last-minute exit from Germany on the eve of Pearl Harbor. Now, with Paris liberated, they decided it was their time to join the main Allied advance. Their first attempt failed. The Smiths simply walked across the

TRACK 39

ALLIES LIBERATE PARIS

American troops march down the Champs-Elysées on
August 26, 1944, the day after the German occupation ended.

French border, reaching a small restaurant in provincial Annecy. Soon thereafter, well-armed French partisans burst in and placed them under arrest.
The French were looking for a German collaborator, thought to be holding
a false passport and accompanied by a red-haired mistress. Smith's American
passport seemed suspect; Bennie's hair was red. Captive, they were marched
through town as a rapidly swelling crowd jeered. Smith expected summary
execution. At a fortuitous moment, the regional resistance leader arrived,
and the Smiths were released. Once bitten well shy of Paris, the Smiths
returned to Berne.

There, a Norwegian businessman offered to drive them to Lyon, from
which Smith hoped they could hitch an airplane ride to Paris. Smith stood
on the runway for seven hours before finding a willing pilot. The ride was

bumpy, as the pilot flew low to escape detection from German positions. Descending into Paris, Bennie Smith was violently ill, and, Smith wrote, her vomit ran in a rivulet the length of the plane. On the ground, the pilot gave Smith "a short, burning essay on what he thought of a man who would take his wife in that condition into a theater of war."

In Paris, the Smiths headed for the Scribe Hotel, where many journalists stayed. Charles Collingwood invited them up. The Smiths were much the worse for travel—their clothing was a mess, and, Smith wrote, his wife's hair was "rather like dead seaweed cast up on an untidy beach." Collingwood answered the door in the red silk robe he had been carrying in his knapsack since D-Day, puffing on a cigarette in a six-inch ivory holder. Half-a-dozen crates stood in his suite. These, he told Smith, contained Picassos that Collingwood had purchased on the wartime cheap. Collingwood, however, knew how to come to the aid of a colleague. He found the couple lodging, and, the following day, cut through red tape to get Smith press credentials and dog tags.

Collingwood thoroughly enjoyed the reporter's life in Paris. Smith noted that you could attend a morning briefing, write and transmit your broadcast, and then be free for afternoon strolls and evening parties where correspondents swapped drinks and stories with John dos Passos and Ernest Hemingway. Smith quoted one editor as saying, "I gave my man an unlimited expense account, and he exhausted it in three days."

Smith wanted back to the war. In September, the man who made those decisions, Ed Murrow, arrived. He and Smith had never met. When Murrow walked in, Smith said, "I did not think it was possible, but he was more suave than Charles [Collingwood], very tall, very slim, very dark and handsome, and wearing an at least as handsomely tailored British officer's uniform." At Smith's request, Murrow assigned him to the American Ninth Army.

Murrow had not seen Paris since 1940. Unlike Shirer or Sevareid, he'd had no love affair with the city. Broadcasting his impressions of the liberated city, his ambivalence showed. What he noticed in Paris, he said, were the shortage of transport, the high prices of luxury goods, and the fact that the city had suffered far less damage than London. But he pointedly added, "There was the memory of those familiar, well-fed but still empty-looking faces around the fashionable bars and restaurants—the last four years seemed to have changed them very little."

Howard K. Smith
1914–2002
b. Ferriday, Louisiana

Howard Kingsbury Smith Jr. was born in the Mississippi River town of Ferriday, Louisiana on May 12, 1914. His family relocated to New Orleans when he was still a child, which is where he spent most of his life until graduating from Tulane University in 1936. While at Tulane, Smith was a standout scholar, track star, and student-body president. He worked for the *New Orleans Item,* his first real foray into the world of journalism, until winning a Rhodes Scholarship to study at Oxford. From there he pursued post-graduate study at Heidelberg University in Germany, then signed on as a United Press correspondent in London and Copenhagen. He joined the CBS news team a year later as their Berlin correspondent. Smith remained in Berlin until December 6, 1941, before fleeing just in time to the safety of Berne, Switzerland. Smith continued reporting from Switzerland, and became known as the last American correspondent to leave Berlin. He published a memoir of his experiences there a year later in the bestselling *Last Train from Berlin.*

Smith remained in Europe throughout the war—Switzerland, then France and Germany after the post D-Day liberation—often accompanying Allied troops and reporting on events for Murrow and CBS. In 1945, he wrote a firsthand account of the German surrender to Russia, then went on to cover the Nuremberg war-crime trials. Although Murrow had not personally hired Smith, he always thought of him as one of his "Boys." Smith even succeeded Murrow as chief London correspondent after the war, a post he held for eleven years.

Smith was perhaps the best known of any of "Murrow's boys" following the war. Upon returning to the states, he was named chief of the CBS Washington Bureau in 1960, and hosted the popular news shows *Face the Nation* and *The Great Challenge.* Smith moderated the pivotal 1960 Nixon–Kennedy presidential debate, the first to be televised. But Smith's tenure at CBS ended in 1961 following the broadcast of a special report on the civil rights movement called *Who Speaks from Birmingham?*

continued

Smith had wanted to close the report with a line from an Edmund Burke poem that reads, "All that is necessary for the triumph of evil is for good men to do nothing." The line was cut by network censors, which resulted in a confrontation with CBS Chairman William S. Paley and Smith's subsequent resignation. From there, Smith signed on with ABC, where he hosted a myriad of news shows and covered the most pressing stories of the day, including the Cuban Missile Crisis and the war in Vietnam. Smith believed that it was not just a journalist's job to report the news, but to offer judgment and analysis as well. Smith's outspoken style, along with his often-controversial political views, made his role as a television broadcaster increasingly uncomfortable. After numerous attempts to start new shows, followed by numerous cancellations, Smith resigned from ABC News in 1979.

Smith retired to his home in Bethesda, Maryland. In 1996, he published a memoir of his life in broadcasting, *Events Leading up to My Death*. He died on February 18, 2002, and is survived by his wife, Benedicte; a daughter; a son; and three grandchildren.

"War Is Still War"

MURROW WAS SKEPTICAL of Parisians. The uprising aside, he wasn't certain they had risked or suffered enough. He had come to Paris after being with others who were risking greatly. In mid-September, the Allies made a bold gamble for a quick end to the war in the west. By paratroop drop, they would seize the bridges on a road that led across the Rhine, Germany's last major bastion. An armored column would then dash up the road to secure what the airdrops had taken. If successful, the plan—Market Garden—would open a corridor of attack into Germany.

Murrow rode on one of the troop transports, an unarmed, unshielded C-47 that skimmed in at five hundred feet to release its cache of paratroops. In a recorded broadcast on Murrow's return, he described the soldiers, "looking out the window rather curiously" like passengers in peacetime. Tension was barely submerged: "You occasionally see a man rub the palm of his hand across his trouser leg," Murrow added. "There seems to be a sort of film over some of the faces, as though they were just on the verge of perspiring, but they aren't."

He described the drop: "In just about thirty seconds now our ship will drop and these nineteen men will walk out onto Dutch soil. You can probably hear the snap as they check the lashing on the static line....There goes, you hear them shout—" Murrow counted as the paratroops exited "—three...four...five...six...seven," up to nineteen. Then he added, "Every man out—I can see their chutes going down now, every man clear. They're dropping just beside a little windmill near a church, hanging there. Very gracefully. They seem to be completely relaxed...like nothing so much as khaki dolls hanging beneath a green lampshade." **CD**

Market Garden came to grief. American paratroopers seized the first two bridges and linked up with the armored column. By ill chance, when the British landed near the more distant Rhine bridges at Arnhem, they dropped almost on top of recently arrived German Panzer units. The armored column could not reach them. After a weeklong battle, three-quarters of the British were killed or captured.

In the end, Market Garden was a failure. However, far from the stumbling advance of the Allies in Europe, General Douglas MacArthur and the American army made ready to recapture the Philippines.

TRACK 40

MURROW WAS PERIODICALLY near the fighting. But the bulk of the frontline coverage in fall 1944 came from Richard Hottelet, Bill Downs, Howard K. Smith, Ned Calmer, and Bill Shadel. Reports were dispatched from the field, a process Smith likened to "carefully writing a script and dropping it in the nearest manhole." In early November, Smith broadcast on the attack on Aachen. Here, as elsewhere, the main firepower was delivered by the artillery. Artillery, Smith reported, was terrifying even when it was yours: "For fifteen, twenty, twenty-five yards in front of their yawning muzzles and phantom cloak of camouflage they wear, the grass is burnt away by the heat of their blasts."

Interviewing German civilians in the area, Smith found that while he flinched with each distant crash of the artillery, the civilians "didn't flutter an eyelid. They were the personification of utter indifference, weariness, sick-to-death tiredness." They had, he learned, no interest in the war beyond the fact that they were out of it.

On November 17, the attack on Aachen was renewed. Smith, Hottelet, and Calmer did a lengthy joint broadcast on the resumption of the offensive. Smith was struck by the weakness of German resistance: "The infantry boys say the village strong points literally fell in their hands after the usual soft-ening-up process." Calmer begged to differ. While he was making a tape-recording earlier that day, soldiers near him came under artillery fire, with some of the shells dropping near the highway upon which American units were advancing.

The broadcast had a tone of morale building for the people back home. Hottelet cited "the precision" of the advance: "The way one part of the operation fitted so smoothly into the other—[was] what impressed me most." Smith reported that the attack, though slow in preparation, took the enemy by apparent surprise: "Today's results seem to indicate that Jerry's information service was not as good as we feared." Hottelet added that the enemy was yielding. As his jeep reached a town, nine German prisoners were being escorted out of a building. "All of them had fought in Russia," he said. "They had decorations, and all of them had been wounded at least once. They had surrendered without a fight." Calmer quoted a comment made by an American soldier during the artillery barrage: "I sure wish my ma and pa could hear that—they'd find out where their war bonds are going." Calmer spoke of the flood of supplies efficiently reaching the front lines. In contrast, Hottelet stated, Germany was "scraping the barrel." He closed, "The Germans still have a fight left in them. But we're matching our strength against theirs, and I think we've got too much for them."

The battle for Aachen turned into house-to-house fighting. Hottelet took a tape recorder to capture it. "Right down below us," he reported, "the houses still are in German territory, and if anybody is leaning out a bay window and draws a bead on this recorder, you will probably never hear it." **CD** Hottelet's account was something new: play-by-play coverage from a battle zone, including the distorted, but jarring, noise of machine-

HOUSE-TO-HOUSE FIGHTING IN AACHEN

Richard C. Hottelet captured on tape some of the sounds of battle in the streets of Aachen,
Germany, in October 1944, as CBS began to open up to the possibilities of recording.

gun fire. CBS, which had resisted tape recorders, was beginning to appreciate their value.

It is uncertain how close to the realities of combat reporting ever comes. Hottelet in Aachen, and Murrow, in his 1943 account of the bombing raid, likely came as close as any. Eric Sevareid sensed this. In October 1944, *Time* magazine urged that planning begin for "Victory Day." Addressing his remarks to those on the home front, Sevareid broadcast:

> Your map tells you that the going has been rapid, but you seem to have forgotten that war is still war, that feet still swell in wet boots, that one can still shiver and ache on the ground all night, that the stomach still contracts when a shell bursts nearby, and that a dead boy with punctured lungs, with the little rivulet of blood dried on his chin, remains a sight that does not bring thoughts of gaiety, organized or otherwise.

There was, he said, an unbridgeable difference between soldiers and civilians. "We shall see the difference, no doubt, on that Victory Day. The civilians will want to make noise for once, and the soldiers will want to be quiet for once. They are so very, very tired of noise."

The noise of war continued around the world. From the Pacific, William J. Dunn on October 25 reported the major American naval victory at Leyte Gulf, which helped ensure the success of the invasion of the Philippines, then in its early stages.

London

PARIS WAS FREED, but London remained home base for the CBS correspondents and Murrow remained the hub through which the others spoke. His leadership and stature were unquestioned. Winston Burdett wrote of watching Murrow enter a room: "There was a shock of recognition, and what they instantly recognized was a man of stature. There was something sovereign about him." Reporters returned to London to rest or be briefed on a new assignment. Murrow had not shared Sevareid's affinity for Paris; likewise, Sevareid did not entirely feel Murrow's love for the British capital. Back in

London briefly in October 1944, Sevareid drew a portrait of a tired, careworn place. The city, he wrote, "was like a famous hotel gone seamy and thread-bare after an interminable business convention that gave no chance for redecoration." The city was tired, he added, and its universal heroism had become a bore: "For Londoners, life had the consistency and taste of the powdered eggs on which they fed."

London was once again a city under attack. Beginning in June, Hitler had targeted the British capital for his "vengeance" weapon—the V-1 flying bomb. Each carried a ton of explosives and reached the city from launch sites in the Netherlands at four hundred miles an hour. In September, the V-2 was introduced, which, because it traveled supersonically, arrived without audible warning.

Murrow, in a November 12, 1944, broadcast, described the weapon, but spoke to its larger meaning: "This demonstration of German skill and inge-nuity," he said, "makes complete nonsense out of strategic frontiers, moun-tains, and river barriers." No country, he said, could be adequately defended against such weapons, which he said serve "to make more appalling the prospect or the possibility of another war." The V-2s, he suggested, should "inject an added note of urgency into the rather casual conversations" the Allied nations were then having about the creation of a postwar world organ-ization to maintain peace.

America, Murrow increasingly urged, had a special responsibility to shape that peace. In his November 26 broadcast, he argued that America had "fought this war in the light," without bomb shelters, and would emerge with its industrial plant unscathed. "We are—we must be—less tired than the peoples of Europe. And as our strength is greater, so must our responsi-bility be." He welcomed the 1944 reelection of Franklin Roosevelt as a con-tribution to this end. In late November, Murrow—claiming his prolonged stay in England had put him out of touch with America—left with his wife, Janet, for the United States. There, he all but dropped out of sight for sev-eral months, planning to return to Europe for the war's close.

Battle of the Bulge

EVENTS DID NOT wait upon Murrow's return. And for the American soldiers who Sevareid said wanted quiet, things were about to get noisier. In early December 1944, frontline forces were suffering something of an emotional lull, or so Howard K. Smith thought. In six months, they had secured landing, swept across France, liberated Paris, and driven the Germans back toward their own borders. With this achieved, Smith reported, "The war was anticlimax...and frankly, GIs appeared to be getting sluggish and indifferent."

Hitler had one more card to play. In mid-December, he threw his last reserves against a weakly defended sector of the American line in the Ardennes. His target was Antwerp, the key port that lay sixty miles into Allied territory. Its capture would disrupt the flow of Allied supplies, buy time, and protect the sites from which the German V-1s and V-2s were launched. On December 16, the Germans hurled two Panzer armies against four American divisions. Richard Hottelet got the news as quickly as anyone. That morning, he had driven to the headquarters of the American Fourth Division to see what was happening. The response was definite: "For Christ's sake, don't you know? The Germans have been attacking us since this morning."

Except for Market Garden, the story since D-Day had largely been one of advance. Now, with the American line punctured and troops reeling backward, the story and the rules for telling it were different. On the battlefield, American leaders responded promptly. North of the breakthrough, American armor took the crossroads of Saint Vith, slowing the German advance toward the Meuse. South, lightly armed U.S. paratroopers of the 101st Airborne Division, with elements of the Tenth Armored Division, resolutely held the crossroads town of Bastogne against superior German forces.

None of this was reported in detail, as the army slapped a forty-eight-hour news embargo on reports from the front. Howard K. Smith, traveling with the Ninth Army just north of the breakthrough, made it to First Army headquarters in Liege looking for the news. There, United Press reporter Jack Frankish gave him the latest and warned Smith against believing any of the rumors that were swirling across the battlefield. Somewhat tempered, Smith headed back to write a broadcast. Smith lost confidence in the UP

MARCHING INTO BELGIUM

American troops of the Eighty-Fourth Infantry advance through a field of snow in France toward La Roche, Belgium, during the Battle of the Bulge.

man's opinion, he later wrote, "when I heard that, half an hour after I had left him, German planes attacked...and he was killed."

One rumor—which also proved true—was that Germans dressed in American uniforms had infiltrated English-speaking infantry. For security, American sentries fell back on popular culture. They dropped formal passwords and asked questions only an American would know: Who was married to Blondie? Who won the 1944 World Series? Challenged to name Betty Grable's husband, Smith got a barely passing mark for blurting out Jackie Coogan—actually, Coogan was Grable's *former* husband.

By December 21, the Allies had nineteen divisions facing the Bulge. News remained scant. On December 23, CBS New York reported, "Today, there were no dispatches from the front lines." That same day, Richard Hottelet offered marginally informed grounds for optimism: "Even though it's necessary to guess at how things are going and to hope for the best, we certainly can see some cause for optimism." He was not specific. Hottelet could, however, paint for those in America a fair picture of the battle conditions: "It's icy cold on the front tonight. And the men...have had to chop at the ground with their shovels and axes." And everything, he added—the grass, the roads, the trees, and the corpses in wrecked tanks—was encrusted with frost. Periodically, the sense of cold was interrupted by "artillery fire and the nervous chatter of German guns." The American soldiers, he added, were on the alert: "They're waiting for the German attack, the next big attack which we know will come."

Actually, the German attack was passing its crest. Early in the battle, cloud cover prevented the Allies from employing their air superiority. On December 26, Smith reported, weather cleared. The only clouds over Belgium, he said, were "the tiny strings of frozen vapor that mark the wake of

DEAD GERMAN SOLDIERS

January 1945 in Belgium: Private Vakasin reloads his rifle while
two dead German soldiers wearing camouflage suits lie dead in the snow.
The tide of battle turned in Belgium after skies cleared in December.

the thousand of our fighters and bombers that have gone out in force again today." The Germans were running out of steam—and running out of fuel. Smith broadcast a report of a German spearhead the Allies would not have to break off: "It fell off all by itself when the thirteen vehicles that composed it simply ran out of gas deep in our territory." The report proved true.

On December 28, Bastogne was relieved. News flowed more readily. On December 30, Smith broadcast that it was "now permissible" to say that the first two days of the German offensive brought as great a scare as any American armed forces had known since Pearl Harbor. During those two days, the American line was threatened with being cut in two. Briefly, German general "Gerd von Rundstedt rode again....New German armies tasted the drunken joy, and the freed lands of Europe again knew the paralyzing fear, of 1940."

Battlefield initiative was shifting. On January 3, 1945, the American counteroffensive began; in the next several weeks, all German gains were reversed. The common view of military historians is that the Battle of the Bulge brought Germany only a brief delay in the Allied advance, and at heavy cost. Losses included eight hundred tanks, enough to supply five armored divisions. With ground recovered, the Allies made ready to advance.

As winter came, fighting in France subsided. At the same time in the Pacific, U.S. Marines were spending twenty-six days bloodily capturing the eight square miles of Iwo Jima.

Crossing the Rhine

BY MID-MARCH 1945, British, French, American, and Canadian armies stood ready to force a crossing of the Rhine. It was the largest, most meticulously planned Allied operation since D-Day, and aimed to break open the heart of Nazi Germany. Germany was nearing exhaustion. On March 6, Cologne on the Rhine's west bank had fallen. After touring the city, Howard K. Smith broadcast a description of its residents as modern cave- and dungeon-dwellers: "They were pale, almost blue, in the face, and their eyes were rimmed with red." They had lived, slept, and eaten in dark cellars for months, said Smith, and the first question they asked was, "The bombers won't come anymore, will they?" The city was a netherworld. Smith met a Yugoslav partisan who had been building a weapons cache, a Jew who had hidden in cellars for a year, and a Polish laborer who had scored revenge by killing a German sniper. And he learned that the preceding Thursday, Nazi authorities had hanged ninety-four German citizens for, Smith said, that "elastic crime which the Gestapo designates as treason."

CBS was also gathering its force. Smith returned from a reconnaissance one night to find a total stranger on the cot next to his. The stranger rose until he towered over Smith and said, "I'm Eric Sevareid. I've come from London to work with you on the crossing." The crossing was set for March 23. Anticipating success, Sevareid ruminated the evening before: "Tomorrow, the great German raid on the human race would be all over save for the meaningless odds and ends." That evening brought a titanic artillery assault. Sevareid wrote of it: "Seven o'clock. Eight o'clock. Nine o'clock. The barrage did not cease for so much as ten seconds. It was not night, nor was it day. It was a ghastly mixing and overlapping of…flares, spots, waves, sparks, flames, and streamers." Smith reported that the bombardment was "the single most terrifying spectacle I have ever seen." The morning following, tens of thousands of infantry in assault boats crossed the Rhine; thousands of paratroopers landed behind German lines. Bill Downs witnessed and described two paratroopers entangled in midair. He overheard a British soldier mumble, "Come on, come on, break it up—break away, for God's sake." Downs added, "Their bodies seemed to hit the earth with the gentleness of raindrops. But from a thousand feet, you could tell they were dead."

Richard Hottelet rode in an observation plane that was hit twice by German flak. He watched the flames caused by the flak "eating a larger and larger hole in the left wing like a smoldering cigarette." All parachuted out. Hottelet, unhurt, got himself and the day's best first-person story to an army press camp, where Eric Sevareid was broadcasting. Accounts of what happened next vary. Hottelet was to claim that Sevareid refused to yield his time for Hottelet's remarkable news; Sevareid claimed that Hottelet never asked for it.

TRACK 42

TRACK 43

THE BRIDGE AT REMAGEN

The Allies crossed the Rhine on March 23, 1945, after relentlessly shelling
the east bank the night before. The Remagen bridge was captured intact by
U.S. First Army troops, who used it to pour men and materials into their
east-bank bridgehead. The smoke in the photograph is from enemy shellfire.

Taking a large view, Bill Downs described the vast battlefield: "As far as
the eye could see there was smoke: smoke laid down by our artillery; smoke
from burning German houses; smoke from the enemy ack-ack [antiaircraft
fire]." These reports came as a special news bulletin. Incongruously, at their
close, the CBS announcer in New York stated, "We now resume our scheduled program, *The Carolina Hayride*, with the Tennessee Ramblers singing
the 'Columbus Stockade Blues.'"

By now, Allied strength was overwhelming. The Allies placed on the
Rhine eighty-five well-supplied divisions backed by enormous air power.

The Germans defended it with twenty-six of uneven quality. At the north end of the line, the crossing was readily achieved. The Allies were into the German mainland. On March 25, Winston Burdett reported on "a drive due east toward the heart of Germany [that gained] six and one-half miles by afternoon." Bill Downs added, "The new bridgehead is old news; this may be the real beginning of a road to Berlin."

While Germany was yielding, tough fighting continued in the Pacific. On April 1, the Americans landed on Okinawa, site of the largest and last island battle in the Pacific.

Buchenwald

WITH THE RHINE cracked open, the seamiest underside of Nazi Germany was laid bare. Reports and rumors had circulated for years about Nazi concentration camps. Ed Murrow had, in late 1942, broadcast one of the first major media accounts on the subject. It was a subject of special interest to him, going back to the years when Murrow helped relocate scholars and others, many of them Jewish, out of Germany and to the United States.

For Murrow, April 12, 1945, would be a very bad day, a day that led to a broadcast often ranked with "Orchestrated Hell" as his finest. The day's advent was auspicious enough. The night before, Murrow—generally regarded as a lousy poker player—won hand after hand in a correspondents' game, and left the table with his uniform stuffed with currency.

On April 12, Murrow and Charles Collingwood went to the recently liberated Nazi concentration camp at Buchenwald. There, he was appalled almost beyond his substantial powers to describe. He did not broadcast his account of the camp until three days later, so troubled was he by what he'd seen. As a result, his report was not the first, nor the most graphic, but it was the most eloquent and memorable:

Permit me to tell you what you would have seen, and heard, had you been with me on Thursday. It will not be pleasant listening. If you are at lunch, or if you have no appetite to hear what Germans have done, now is a good time to switch off the radio, for I propose to tell you of Buchenwald. It is on a small hill about four miles outside Weimar, and it was one of the largest concentration camps in Germany, and it was built to last....

There surged around me an evil-smelling horde. Men and boys reached out to touch me; and they were in rags and the remnants of uniform. Death had already marked many of them, but they were smiling with their eyes. I looked out over that mass of men to the green fields beyond where well-fed Germans were ploughing. CD

TRACK 44

BARRACKS AT BUCHENWALD

Survivors of the concentration camp at Buchenwald remain in their barracks after liberation by Allies in April 1945. Ed Murrow toured the camp on April 12, reporting what he saw three days later.

Two hundred men were dying every day—from, a camp doctor told him, "Tuberculosis, starvation, fatigue, and there are many who have no desire to live." He entered a barracks that "had once stabled eighty horses. There were twelve hundred men in it, five to a bunk. The stink was beyond all description." As he entered, he added, "There was applause from those too weak to stand. It sounded like the hand clapping of babies; they were so weak." Celebrating their release, inmates tried in vain to lift Murrow to their shoulders, but were too feeble.

Reaching the center of the barracks, a man came up to Murrow and said, "You remember me, I'm Peter Zenkl, one-time mayor of Prague." "I remembered him," reported Murrow, "but did not recognize him." Zenkl asked about former Czech president Eduard Benes and foreign minister Jan Masaryk. The last time Murrow had seen Zenkl was in 1938, before the Czechs had been sold out at Munich.

Back outside, he watched a man fall dead in the courtyard. "Two others— they must have been over sixty—were crawling toward the latrine. I saw it but will not describe it." The camp was out of coal, and the dead were no longer cremated. Instead, Murrow reported, they were simply stacked like cordwood. Viewing the bodies, he said, "They were thin, and totally white. Some were shot through the neck, but they bled but little...I concluded that all that was mortal of five hundred men and boys was what lay there in two neat piles."

Murrow was furious at the meticulousness of German record keeping— each little red tab on a chart marked off another ten dead. He was furious at the relative comfort of Germans living nearby—they were, he reported, "well clothed, they appear well fed and healthy, in better condition than any other people I have seen in Europe." Tens of thousands had died at Buchenwald, he told his listeners, in conditions as he had described. In another part of the camp, Murrow was shown the children:

> ...hundreds of them. Some were only six. One rolled up his sleeve, showed me his number. It was tattooed on his arm. D-6030, it was. The others showed me their numbers; they will carry them till they die.
>
> An elderly man standing beside me said, "The children, enemies of the state." I could see their ribs through their thin shirts....The children clung to my hands and stared.

Murrow recounted the many men who came up to speak with and touch him, "professors from Poland, doctors from Vienna, men from all over Europe." His days with the Emergency Committee, helping to place European scholars in American universities, was no doubt on his mind. Three hundred thirty-five men he and the committee had been able to save—out of more than six thousand who had been seeking refuge.

Murrow urged his listeners: "I pray you to believe what I have said about Buchenwald. I have reported what I saw and heard, but only part of it. For most, I have no words....If I've offended you by this rather mild account of Buchenwald, I'm not in the least sorry." **CD** The broadcast would be re-aired on the BBC and the text printed on the front page of the *London Express*, as well as in many other papers. A translation of the report was broadcast in Allied-controlled areas of Germany six to eight times a day.

TRACK 44

Yet, in later years, Murrow would confess to feeling that the broadcast had failed. To Ben Gross, a columnist for the *New York Daily News*, he confided that it was a heap of children's shoes that had unnerved him. "I could have described three pairs of those shoes...but hundreds of them. Well, I just couldn't. The tragedy of it simply overwhelmed me."

The visit traumatized Murrow. Collingwood reported a stricken Murrow, passing out to inmates the money he had won at poker the night before and breaking into uncharacteristic tears. Murrow was not the only correspondent to visit a concentration camp—Larry LeSueur went to Dachau. And his was far from being the only account printed in newspapers or broadcast by air. But the integrity of his outrage was clear.

The day, remarkably enough, got worse. That evening, Murrow learned that Franklin Roosevelt had died in Hot Springs, Georgia. In Murrow's mind, Roosevelt stood with Churchill as one of the irreplaceable leaders of the Allied cause, and as perhaps the single world leader most committed to seeking the postwar world Murrow hoped could be achieved. For Murrow and for many Americans, Roosevelt was close to being the only president of their adult lives. A shared interest in FDR had been a common bond between Ed Murrow and Janet Brewster when they were courting. The twin events—Buchenwald and Roosevelt's death—wrenched Murrow's views on life's good and bad possibilities. Murrow's beliefs on many subjects were murky. One matter he was clear on was personal responsibility. He rejected the idea that Germans had been ignorant of what was being done at Buchenwald and elsewhere. At one point, Murrow said, "I do not believe that the facts were wholly unknown to the German people in the mass. Certainly many people in Weimar knew not only where Buchenwald was but what it was."

Surrender

WITH THE ALLIES across the Rhine, Nazi Germany imploded—collapsing into a vacuum that pulled the American, British, French, and Soviet soldiers onward. Murrow returned once more to the front. Often, he observed, German defenders fired off a few rounds for show, then surrendered. At other times, resistance was stubborn. From Leipzig on April 22, Murrow described an assault made on the City Hall by units of the American Sixty-Ninth Division:

> When they began to roll, they were hit with bazookas and machine guns. When they turned a corner, the wounded slipped off. The medium tanks were traveling about thirty miles an hour, and no man turned back. Lieutenant Ken Wilder started with a total of thirty-nine men, and when they reached the City Hall he had eight. They had a company of infantry riding on the tanks, 185 men. Sixty-eight reached the City Hall. The tanks were marked with machine-gun fire, and they were splattered with blood. An hour after reaching the City Hall, those boys were driving German cars and motorcycles about the streets. In the place where we were sitting, a sniper's bullet broke a pane of glass in a window. A doughboy said, "My! My! Somebody done broke a window. Things are getting rough around here. Folks are destroying things." The Germans had given up. A few had shot themselves. One said he couldn't be taken prisoner by the Americans. He must commit suicide. A young lieutenant said, "Here's a gun." The German took it and shot himself just under the right ear.

When Army censors refused to approve the script, Murrow pulled rank. He took the script to General Omar Bradley. When Murrow assured Bradley that he witnessed the assault and aftermath, Bradley initialed his approval.

Five days later, Richard Hottelet broadcast the meeting of the American and Russian armies. There had been, Hottelet reported, some skittishness about this. Fearing incidents if the two armies simply collided on the battlefield, Bradley had ordered a halt to the American advance. The nearest Russian commander had done likewise. Hottelet reported that jeep patrols had been sent out scouting, passing crowds of German refugees and German soldiers who offered no resistance. Near a small town, he added, "a Sixty-Ninth Division patrol spotted some Russians, and that was it." Some hours later, an American lieutenant "crawled out to the middle of a wrecked bridge and brought back some Russian officers to division headquarters and that made it official....Just some men meeting and shaking hands."

American forces halted on the Elbe. Howard K. Smith did some exploring, hopping into a motorboat and heading up river. "From over a ridge on the east bank, German soldiers began running towards us, dozens and scores, their hands up, begging to surrender. Some of our divisions were accumulating more prisoners than could be handled." Hottelet was more adventurous. On May 4, he and several other reporters claimed a jeep and drove unhindered into the German capital. They were the first Americans to reach Berlin. They were beating a retreat the following morning when they were picked up by a Red Army unit, which treated them as prize guests.

On May 5, the remains of two German armies surrendered to a single American division. Near Czechoslovakia, a Panzer division surrendered unconditionally. On May 7, Germany threw in the towel. With Charles Collingwood present, German representatives surrendered to the British and Americans.

Collingwood returned to Paris for V-E Day celebrations. They were, he reported, more tempered than might be expected. Parisians "are physically too tired and emotionally too exhausted to throw themselves in the wild and uproarious celebration one might have expected." London, Murrow reported earlier in the day, was likewise largely quiet. Murrow said he was struck by the number of serious faces—people were reflecting, perhaps, on the memories of friends who had died and buildings that had fallen. He closed, "Six years is a long time. I have observed today that people have very little to say. There are no words."

Murrow broadcast a number of times that day. In one, he looked beyond victory and sought to rally Americans to the task of rebuilding. "Europe," he said, "has no doubt that America is mighty in battle. Our nation, which was created by people who wanted to leave Europe, is the center of the hopes and some of the fears of millions who are in Europe today."

London's initial quiet gave way to celebration. Douglas Edwards reported the scene from the Stag Head pub. The Stag Head, Edwards said, was normally one of the city's more sedate pubs, but today "the walls were bulging, packed to the rafters." In the pub's front right corner, he said, "about fifteen people were holding high their beer glasses and singing what I'm told is 'Take Me Back to Blighty.'" A second bunch was singing of "Mother McCrea" and a third was concentrating on "When Irish Eyes Are Smiling." The Americans present, he added, either hummed along to the words they didn't know or broke into occasional bursts of "Marse Doats" and "Don't Fence Me In."

For V-E Day, CBS rolled out hour after hour of coverage. There were moments of solemnity. Fleet Admiral William D. Leahy paid tribute to President Franklin D. Roosevelt, who had not survived to see victory. In New York, William Shirer noted that he had been in Berlin on September 1, 1939, when the war began. "Some twenty-five million human beings who were alive on that day have perished," he said.

TRACK 45

Most of the day was exuberant. Congratulations flowed in from everywhere, and were read—interviews with leaders of the U.S. Senate and House; talks with aircraft workers in Seattle; reports on celebrations from around the country, including one at Hollywood and Vine in Los Angeles; patriotic music, including many renditions of "You're a Grand Old Flag."

By evening, Murrow was at Piccadilly Circus. "Believe me," he said, "tonight there is no traffic in Piccadilly Circus." He could recall nights, Murrow said, when the spot was empty and "you could read a newspaper by the light of flares dropped from German bombers." Tonight, it was so crowded that you could "walk on the heads of people from one side to the other." Murrow broke off from his line of thought, and with a rare, full laugh said, "They're throwing confetti at me."

TRACK 46

One further surrender remained. Pointedly, the Germans had not surrendered to the Russians. The Russians now informed them that they would. On May 9, representatives of England, America, and France joined the Russians in Berlin for the final German surrender. Howard K. Smith was the sole radio reporter present. The surrender scene was dominated by two men, Soviet military commander G.K. Zhukov and German Field Marshal Wilhelm Keitel. Keitel, Smith reported, made a show of arrogance. Other Germans present wore whatever military decorations they had won; Keitel, alone, also wore the Nazi Party golden badge of service to Hitler. At the

GERMANY SURRENDERS TO SOVIET UNION

*Field Marshal Wilhelm Keitel signs surrender terms at Russian headquarters
in Berlin. Keitel was later executed at Nuremberg for war crimes.*

actual signing, Keitel paused, waiting for someone to give him a pen. No one on the Allied side stirred, so Keitel used his own. The surrender was followed by an Allied banquet at which, by Smith's count, there were twenty-four vodka toasts, and the reticent Marshall Zhukov autographed a hundred-mark note that Smith carried.

Smith, back in Berlin just a few hours, wanted to tour his former city of residence. He told an American officer that as he knew the city well, he could tour it unescorted. The officer replied, "You will find that it is not the city you knew. It is not the city that anyone knew." On May 9, Smith broadcast his description of what remained of Berlin: "The place was not just ruined. The ruins themselves had been pounded, then re-pounded and re-pounded, until there's no more rubble of bricks and parts of bricks." A pale red dust from pulverized brick covered everything. A car fifty yards ahead of Smith's tossed up so much dust that it disappeared from view. Smith and the others tied handkerchiefs around their faces to keep from inhaling the dust of defeat.

The Allied representatives, plus Smith, then flew out of Berlin, bearing last-minute gifts from the Russians of bread, sausage, and vodka. Smith returned to the Scribe in Paris where, as pool reporter, he was obligated to make seventeen separate broadcasts. Generals, political figures, and commentators of all nations were speaking their thoughts on the fall of Germany. Few comments matched those of Bennie Smith, Howard K. Smith's wife, who told her husband: "No matter what terrible things happen in the future, we must remember this: we won. We might not have. They might have won. Think of what the world would have been like if they had won. Nothing can ever be as terrible as that."

6

MURROW'S LEGACY

There is a danger that the individual comes to believe
that, just because his voice is amplified and reaches
halfway around the world, he is therefore more intelligent, more discerning, than he was when his voice only
reached from one end of the bar to the other.

—*Edward R. Murrow*

TRACK: 47

Peace

WAR WAS CHAOS. But the end of the war in Europe did not bring order. The day after V-E Day dawned on an exhausted continent containing millions it could neither feed nor house. Worldwide, more than fifty million soldiers and civilians had been killed in the struggle. In Germany, the cities of Berlin, Hamburg, Cologne, and Dresden had been reduced to rubble. Murrow had little sympathy for the defeated Germans. They had, he wrote Janet, allowed the Nazi government to rise, had supported it to the bitter end, and had denounced it "only after its downfall...and then only to save their own skins."

Writ small, the question that faced Europe faced Murrow as well: What next? Murrow talked of heading to the Pacific for the final phase of the war. He did not go. It smacked, perhaps, of anticlimax—Murrow considered Europe to be the war's center stage; the fight against Japan he regarded as secondary. It smacked, as well, of pushing the odds. Murrow told Howard K. Smith that he worried he had "used up my good luck in Europe," and feared he would be shot down in the Pacific. More likely, he was approaching the reportorial equivalent of combat fatigue. In July 1945, Murrow wrote Janet: "I am sick of tired people and bombed towns and misery and hate. There just doesn't seem to be any emotion left."

Murrow was, notoriously, a pessimist. Once, during the war, CBS News Director Paul White called for Murrow from New York, only to be informed that his star broadcaster was out somewhere, "wearing his customary crown of thorns." A later writer observed that Murrow delivered his broadcasts in a manner that "often conveys the impression that he knows the worst but will try not to mention it." Still, his pessimism was a

V-E DAY IN NEW YORK

A throng of joyous people celebrates victory in Europe on Wall Street, May 8, 1945.

BOMBED-OUT BERLIN

The ruins of Berlin in May 1945: "The place was not just ruined,"
said Howard K. Smith. "The ruins themselves had been pounded,
then re-pounded and re-pounded, until there's no rubble of bricks."

defense against disappointment, not a rejection of hope. From the Battle of
Britain on, he—though somewhat less than Sevareid—had seen the war as
something that would transform Britain into a better place.

Visions of a better Britain faded as the emergency of war passed. Peace
did not end the fighting. The liberation of Greece in late 1944 ushered in a
civil war in which the British were fighting the pro-communist forces that
had led the resistance against the occupying Germans. Visions were further
compromised by the dropping on August 6 of the atomic bomb on
Hiroshima, and a second bomb on Nagasaki three days later. This new and
unmatched power brought Japan's unconditional surrender on September 2,
1945, but it inaugurated an era in which the horror of future war was expo-
nentially increased.

In a broadcast following Hiroshima and Nagasaki, Murrow reflected on the reaction of George Kistiakowsky, one of the leading Manhattan Project scientists, to the detonation of the first atomic bomb in the New Mexico desert. "I am sure that on doomsday," Kistiakowsky said, "in the

MUSHROOM CLOUD OVER NAGASAKI

August 9, 1945, three days after obliterating Hiroshima, the U.S. dropped a second atomic bomb on Nagasaki. Emperor Hirohito announced six days later that Japan would surrender unconditionally to the Allies.

last millisecond, the last man on earth will see what we have just seen." In contrast, Murrow pointed out, William Lawrence of the *New York Times* compared the experience of witnessing that explosion to being present at the Creation, when God said, "Let there be light." The last thirteen years, Murrow said, were but an instant, "Nineteen thirty-three's unemployment, September at Munich, that June 10 at Lidice [a town in Czechoslovakia whose inhabitants were massacred by the Nazis in 1942], December 7 at Pearl Harbor, 9:15 over Hiroshima, were all part of the identical moment. The one question remaining then: Was it 23:59 o'clock or 00:01? Was there to be still another cycle of affliction, appeasement, and annihilation? Or had we walked through midnight towards the dawn without knowing it?" **CD**

TRACK 47

Visions faded elsewhere. In 1945, the surrender of the Japanese in China brought new fighting between Mao Tse-tung's communists and Chiang Kai-shek's nationalists—fighting that State Department expert John Paton Davies, who had bailed out with Sevareid over Burma, rightly thought the nationalists would lose. And in eastern Europe, the Soviet Union used its military presence to establish satellite governments in country after country, until there fell across the continent what Winston Churchill would call an "iron curtain."

Churchill fell, too. In a July 1945 election, Churchill—indispensable in war—was dispensed with by the British electorate. As a Labor Party friend of Howard K. Smith explained, Churchill had been great in war, but England could not keep having wars just to make Churchill great. The two men central to Murrow's worldview had in a few months departed the scene—Roosevelt by death, and Churchill by electoral defeat. Step by step, the postwar world was a letdown. The war's end, Charles Collingwood said, brought "euphoria"—Hitler was defeated; all things seemed possible. "Then, as these [hopes] became progressively disappointed, it seems to me that it was then that Ed became more disillusioned."

What was next for Murrow was framed by two events. On November 6, 1945, Janet Murrow gave birth to a son, Charles Casey, whom his parents were to call by his middle name. The Murrows had wanted children for years. Casey's arrival came when Janet was thirty-five, then a somewhat advanced age for a first child. His son's birth brought out in Murrow domestic qualities not previously notable in his nature. Then, in late December, he accepted the position of vice president and director of public affairs for CBS, the most important post in news broadcasting.

Murrow had lived primarily in England since arriving as CBS's chief European correspondent in 1937. In February 1946, he made a final broadcast that was a salute to his second home. Years earlier, Adolf Hitler argued that the strength of totalitarianism was that it forced those who opposed it to adopt its means. This Murrow now disputed: "I am persuaded that the most important thing that happened in Britain was that this nation chose to win or lose this war under the established rules of parliamentary procedure." It had feared the Nazis, but had not imitated them. The democratic essentials—parliamentary government, trial by jury—had survived. England had retreated in battle, Murrow noted, but the debates in the House of Commons demonstrated that there had been "no retreat from the principles for which your ancestors fought."

Howard K. Smith was in London, and watched Murrow put together his parting broadcast. Murrow, Smith noted, did not write, but paced and smoked and dictated his remarks to a secretary: "As I heard those shaped, immaculate glowing sentences, I knew that this was something you did not learn, you had to be born with it." The following day, a British radio reviewer wrote, "When I hear a broadcast like that I want to give up and throw my typewriter away."

Smith was in London because Murrow had picked him as his successor, in the plum position of chief CBS correspondent in Europe. Murrow could not—occasional impulses to the contrary—fix the continent of Europe. But he could try to protect his own band. Postwar, Murrow wrote Collingwood this typically self-deprecating note: "For a few brief years a few men attempted to do an honest job of reporting under difficult and sometimes hazardous conditions and they did not altogether fail." Murrow doubted he would in the future have "the high privilege of working intimately and harmoniously with a crew such as the one we gathered together in Europe." But he intended to try.

The task took some doing. Smith got London because Shirer and Sevareid had turned it down. Shirer, Murrow's first colleague in Europe, had all but given up on reporting. Late in the war, he broadcast commentaries from London and Paris, but made only brief forays to the front. With the great success of *Berlin Diary*, he no longer saw himself as a reporter chasing after breaking news, but as an author and news analyst, whose comments were regularly broadcast by CBS in New York. Sevareid wanted to pursue the submerged literary ambitions he carried through the war. He settled for a time in California, where he wrote a memoir, *Not So Wild a Dream*. In literary terms, the book was the best produced by any Murrow correspondent, telling with grace and candor the story of his growing up, loss of naïveté, and the war he went to witness.

Even the selection of Smith for the London post took some doing. First, Murrow had to persuade Smith to pass up an offer from Henry Luce of *Time*. Then, when Smith objected that he lacked the wardrobe for the London post, Murrow threw into the bargain three of his own suits (which Smith wore after he had the trouser legs shortened).

In New York as CBS vice president, Murrow had greater success in gathering his crew. His book written, Sevareid came to Washington, D.C., as CBS bureau chief. Collingwood surfaced in Los Angeles, where he married the actress Louise Allbritton and served initially as West Coast correspondent. Richard C. Hottelet took the key post of Moscow; Winston Burdett went to Rome; Larry LeSueur covered the United Nations. Murrow hired others who were knowledgeable observers and sharp writers: Alexander Kendrick went to Vienna; David Schoenbrun went to Paris, and George Polk to the Middle East.

In bringing CBS his reporters, Murrow gave the network its identity. Eric Sevareid stated that before the Murrow Boys reached the scene, CBS was largely "a collection of leased phone lines and cables [and] contracts with a lot of scattered actors and others." Murrow's correspondents ended the war with enormous public recognition and stature. With their arrival, Sevareid added, "the news people became…the personality of the network."

Murrow's reporters tended to cut a wide swath. Larry LeSueur stated, "We not only got special privileges but we were upset if we didn't get them." This was their due, they felt, because they had been present at the creation of CBS News, and, LeSueur added, "everybody else were Johnny-come-latelies." Later, some others in the newsroom, feeling shortchanged, formed a "Murrow Isn't God" club. Learning of its existence, Murrow promptly applied for membership.

Delivering the News

WHATEVER THEY SUBSEQUENTLY achieved, the Murrow Boys would always be most associated with their coverage of World War II. Fairly so, as during that conflict, they were the most significant source of news to the American people—outshining both their radio competition and the printed press. (The two-volume *Reporting World War II*, which anthologized much of the best print coverage of the war, included fifteen articles and broadcasts by Murrow Boys, including accounts from Murrow, Shirer, Sevareid, Smith, Brown, LeSueur, and Hottelet.)

CBS gained primacy within radio despite having entered the field of international reporting as a definite underdog. When Edward R. Murrow went to England as CBS's chief European correspondent in 1937, he was competing with an NBC that was far better established. In England, the chief NBC correspondent, Fred Bate, was a friend of the Prince of Wales, and enjoyed excellent access to government and other high circles. On the continent, NBC had secured exclusive arrangements with several governments. In Germany, it held first-refusal rights on all broadcasts: CBS could cover a story only if NBC wasn't interested. In gaining its position, NBC had made use of its name: it was the *National* Broadcasting Corporation, implying that it was the official government-affiliated network, and therefore the only one worth dealing with. All this had consequences. At the time of the Anschluss in 1938, William Shirer, desperately trying to broadcast from the Vienna transmitter, was marched out of the building at bayonet point. While Shirer flew to London and Murrow scrambled to Vienna to take his place, NBC's Max Jordan was given ready access to Austrian broadcast facilities. It was NBC's scoop that led to Paley (or White) mounting CBS's revolutionary "European News Roundup" on March 13. The roundup was a huge success and became the model for broadcast news coverage for years to come.

Further events led to CBS's advantage in news: when war opened in September 1939, NBC abruptly cancelled its news coverage from Europe. The network feared that by covering the war it would somehow run afoul of the U.S. Neutrality Act and jeopardize its broadcast status. Key, though, was that Ed Murrow and William Shirer immediately moved into the vacuum that departure created, filling it with a new style of reporting—incisive, intelligent, immediate, and engaged.

NBC returned to the field, but never caught up. The network presented some fine reporting. Radio historian Erik Barnouw, for example, calls attention to several broadcasts. One was George Hicks's description of landing craft hitting the beach on Normandy. Another was W.W. Chaplin's report on the advance into France, in which a woman—transporting to the cemetery by wheelbarrow a child killed in the shelling—stops to listen to an impromptu speech being given by Charles de Gaulle.

Murrow and his crew were not only strongest within radio, but more influential than newspapers, as well. The differences between print and radio are readily apparent. One difference is length. A newspaper report might stretch to three thousand words or more; a radio reporter with a two-minute time segment must hold the script to about 250 words. There are exceptions, of course. Murrow's "Orchestrated Hell" broadcast ran to several thousand words, as did his report on Buchenwald.

A more important difference is immediacy. A newspaper can be scanned, put down, and picked up later; a radio report happens *now*—just as the listener hears it. Radio is also more personal—no editors or producers filter the reporter's words. A radio correspondent "writes his own headlines." And he speaks to his audience in his own voice. Murrow advised his broadcasters to be aware of radio's essential intimacy—an announcer's voice heard in the privacy of a listener's imagination. Radio was a storyteller's medium, one that invited listeners to fill in the scene in their minds. Conveying his sense of exposure while flying over Germany, Murrow wrote: "The clouds below us were white, and we were black. *D-Dog* seemed like a black bug on a white sheet."

The power of radio was startling. As early as the Munich crisis of 1938, Robert Landry noted in *Scribner's*, Murrow's reporting had more influence "than a shipful of newspapermen." The public preference was clear: a 1941 survey of nineteen American cities showed that two-thirds of those queried ranked radio news and analysis more important than newspaper. By 1942, a government-sponsored poll reported that, by a margin of 46 to 18 percent, respondents put more faith in radio than in newspaper reporting.

Compare Murrow with the war's leading print journalist, Ernie Pyle. Pyle covered the war on the ground in North Africa, Sicily, and Italy, winning a

ERNIE PYLE

*The premier print journalist of World War II, Ernie Pyle eats what
the soldiers ate—slop from a tin can—in Anzio in the spring of 1944.*

Pulitzer Prize, then landed on Omaha Beach the second day of the invasion
of France. Pyle took the common soldier as his text; likely, he was the reporter
held in highest regard by the average GI. In early 1945, he exercised the
option Murrow had declined; he went to cover the Pacific war. Early in the
battle for Okinawa, he was killed by hostile machine-gun fire. The difference
between Murrow and Pyle is not one of quality. Both were excellent. The difference is that while Pyle mastered the forms of newspaper journalism, Murrow invented the forms for radio.

Through radio, Murrow's reporters had a larger daily audience than did print reporters. Their standing as correspondents gave them better access to the event—five CBS reporters were selected to cover D-Day. Their reputation as a group gave credence to their work as individuals. And Murrow's example and leadership gave them focus.

Murrow Considered

WHAT MOST SEPARATED CBS from its competitors in radio and print was Edward R. Murrow. Murrow stands out even though, as his biographer Joseph Persico suggests, Eric Sevareid and Howard K. Smith were better writers, Robert Trout and Charles Collingwood were smoother at the microphone, William Shirer was a sharper analyst, and Richard C. Hottelet was a more hard-nosed reporter. Murrow's influence traces to his nature, his work, and the talent he recruited and led.

Murrow was a hero to those who worked for him. Winston Burdett noted "something sovereign" to Murrow. Howard K. Smith described Murrow as "the most impressive male person I was ever to know." Meeting Murrow in London before the war, Eric Sevareid, who "loved" and "adored" Murrow, said Murrow possessed "that rare thing, an instinctive, intuitive recognition of the truth." Murrow had strong loyalties, but he was not a joiner. He stood always somewhat apart. "His camaraderie was superficial," Richard Hottelet said. "He was always his own person. You never had a road map of the mind of Murrow."

Murrow has been called an American original. More likely, he was that American archetype: the self-made man. That making began with a renaming: born Egbert Roscoe, he became known as Edward R. That remaking was thorough. On first encountering Murrow, Howard K. Smith made a comment made by others: "It was hard to believe that this natural aristocrat was born in the impoverished hollows of the North Carolina Appalachians and worked in his youth in the logging camps of the northwest."

Sevareid regarded Murrow as a natural broadcaster who was "simply born to the new art," a blessing that was Murrow's alone. More accurately, Murrow's was a case of unintended preparation. Indeed, had he at age eighteen decided that his life's ambition was to be a foreign radio correspondent, he could hardly have planned better. In high school, he was drawn to debate; in college, his best grades came in speech and military training. Biographer and postwar Murrow Boy Alexander Kendrick writes, "All through school he had never been interested in the written word, except as a reader, but in the spoken." He wrote only as required, but declaimed, debated, and orated from interest. Murrow was not a great student, but he was a student leader, a class president. His presidency of the NSFA, during and after college, brought responsibility; his work with the Institute of International Education gave him an awareness of European politics uncommon to Americans in the early 1930s.

With CBS in England, Murrow adopted from BBC broadcasters the practice of dictating his scripts, an approach that freed him to use his rhetorical training. Winston Burdett said of Murrow's style: "Accurate diction, economy, filed sentences, firm phrasing—these gave to his scripts a kind of magnificent clarity that bordered on the epigrammatic." Murrow was a nervous wreck while broadcasting, but his on-air voice conveyed an engaging informality. This, Kendrick wrote, had the result that "people who heard him felt they knew him."

Leadership is a much-debated quality. One view is that it is a willingness to focus on what is central. Murrow and those he trained did not simply cover the story; they *identified* the story. When Murrow reached England, its rulers, in the words of scholar A.L. Rowse, were deliberately ignorant of the menace of Nazism, an ignorance sustained by "a certain superciliousness, a lofty smugness, as well as superficiality of mind." The English public and, more so, the American dismissed Hitler as some wayward fanatic with a Charlie Chaplin moustache. Murrow saw Nazism from the first as a gathering threat not simply to peace but to civilization. Others who worked with him agreed. Shirer wrote in his diary in 1937 that "the shadow of Nazi fanaticism, sadism, persecution...has hung over all our lives, like a dark brooding cloud that never clears." Howard K. Smith, on visiting prewar Germany, was appalled by the unthinking militarism.

It began as a hard view to sell. Smith was also appalled when in Britain people he knew to be intelligent dismissed out of hand the notion that Germany posed any hazard. In New York, five months prior to the invasion of Poland, Shirer wrote in his diary that Tess, his wife, "says I'm making myself most unpopular by taking such a pessimistic view.... They *know* there will be no war."

Officially, Murrow was neutral, just as CBS demanded. After the war, he stated, "News programs are broadcast solely for the purpose of enabling listeners to know facts—so far as they are ascertainable—and so to elucidate, illuminate, and explain facts and situations as fairly as possible to enable the listener to weigh and judge for himself." He had said as much in 1938 during the Munich crisis and on a dozen occasions thereafter. Yet Murrow simultaneously held a second view. He was not simply looking for the facts of a story, but looking for its core.

This, if conscientiously applied, sets a higher standard. Working within the strictures of journalism, a reporter who with reasonable skill tracks down the pertinent facts and enlivens the report with quotes and anecdotes has met the minimum requirements of the job, but has not provided context and meaning. True, standards differ in wartime. Candid reporting was limited by government censorship in each country from which correspondents broadcast, as well as by CBS's insistence on editorial objectivity. Virtually everything Murrow and his correspondents wrote had to pass through the screen of the censor—Shirer was particularly troubled by his inability to report honestly within the constraints of the Third Reich. With American entry into the war, their task changed: they went from being independent voices whose sympathies, as it happened, lay with Britain and France, to being citizens of a nation at war, and therefore required to support the war effort (though, of course, they all did, and had been anyway). Among other things, this meant that while they saw, they rarely reported war's casual brutality, its incompetence, its vainglorious seeking after honors. Cecil Brown criticized the British and American war effort to the point of losing his job; Eric Sevareid never went that far in his criticism, although clearly, it went too far for some.

But censorship and the tugs of patriotism were not the only limits. Murrow saw reporting as a sort of seeking after truth. And the limits on that search lie as much within as without. They lie in the limits of the reporter's perceptiveness and honesty; the distance between the observer and the event. Sevareid understood something of this. In a late 1944 commentary, he spoke about the gap between those who fought the war and those who covered that fight. The soldier, he wrote, lives the war; the reporter does not. The reporter "may share the soldier's outward life and dangers," but not his inner life. The reporter is free to leave; the soldier is not. The "mere knowing" of this makes a crucial difference. Reaching across that divide, Sevareid added: "War happens inside a man. It happens to one man alone. It can never be communicated. That is the tragedy—and perhaps the blessing....And, I am sorry to say, that is also why in a certain sense you and your sons from the war will be forever strangers."

Murrow sought to bridge that strangeness. This explains in part his seeming recklessness in boarding two dozen bombing missions to Germany. What pleased him about his famed "Orchestrated Hell" broadcast, he said, was when members of its crew commented that Murrow got the feel and tone of the in-air chatter over the intercom about right.

As a reporter, Murrow was doubly pressed. He was pressed, first, by his urge to get at any story's truth. But he was also pressed by his awareness of the depth of the tragedy that was befalling Europe. He could put names, faces, and voices to that tragedy. The names included those of scholars with whom he had dealt during his days with the Emergency Committee. The faces and voices included that of his friend Jan Masaryk, the Czech foreign minister who spent the evening with Murrow the day his country was betrayed at Munich.

William Paley biographer Sally Bedell Smith wrote of Murrow's "inner turbulence." She quoted one Murrow colleague as saying that even at the peak of his fame and fortune, "Ed couldn't sleep....He was exhausted, but the will was driving him on. There was a lot of anguish in him that he couldn't get out."

Murrow's influence can be judged in stages. When he joined CBS in 1935, radio news was a marginal undertaking; serious foreign reporting was unknown. In 1937, when Murrow first arrived in London as CBS's European director of "talks" and tried to join the American Foreign Correspondents' Association, his application was rejected because, as he later put it, he "was involved in that ridiculous thing called 'radio'." (During the war, Murrow would become the president of the association.) The Austrian crisis of March 1938 abruptly changed his, and radio's, status. Suddenly, Murrow and

Murrow on "Person-to-Person"

*In the era of television in the 1950s, Murrow became a TV star—
for his continuing work as a serious journalist and as host of various
programs, including the celebrity-interview show,* Person-to-Person.

William Shirer were recast as reporters and on-air performers. CBS New York devised the "roundup" format; Murrow and Shirer brought that format to life and gave it legitimacy. Shirer spoke of the Anschluss as the "birth of the 'radio foreign correspondent,' so to speak." He spoke correctly.

Murrow's greatest fame came during the Blitz of 1940–1941. The strongest image of Murrow is probably of him on a London rooftop, describing live the crashing bombs and the toppling buildings. As the Germans gathered for invasion, radio historian Eric Barnouw wrote, "Americans began to hear, night after night, a voice from London. Murrow—calm, never arguing, never urging an opinion—began to refer to himself as 'this reporter.' He narrated—and in so doing, had historic impact."

That influence was rooted in Murrow's ability not just to tell the story, but bring it to his listeners. This was the point Archibald MacLeish stressed at the December 1941 dinner that honored Murrow for his work. Murrow, MacLeish said, was speaking in the kitchens and living rooms and all the casual settings in America. Murrow made London's story America's, MacLeish said, laying the city's dead at America's doorsteps, and "we knew [they] were all men's dead were mankind's dead and ours."

During the war, Murrow's chief duty was to replicate himself. CBS President William Paley claimed that in hiring correspondents, he preferred good newsmen to those with a "pleasant speaking voice." Not so. Murrow hired Shirer and Sevareid over considerable objections from CBS New York, which complained that Shirer spoke in a monotone and Sevareid mumbled. Murrow knew what he was looking for. He once told the head of a British journalism school that the best news analysis in England came "from men who spent most of their university career studying the classics." Murrow wanted reporters who could "think and write." He chose a very bright group—Smith and Collingwood were Rhodes Scholars; Burdett, Shirer, and Sevareid were at least as sharp. And, having chosen them, Murrow was their model. Sevareid acknowledged that he imitated Murrow, but then so did everybody else.

The Future of Broadcast News

IN JULY 1948, Ed Murrow reported from the Republican National Convention in Philadelphia. The convention would nominate Thomas E. Dewey for president, for what at that moment was considered an all but certain victory over incumbent Harry S. Truman. The hall, lacking air-conditioning, was sweltering. Murrow was sweltering, too. In place of his usual microphone, he was lugging around a thirty-pound backpack that carried the transmitting equipment then necessary to broadcast his voice by television. Television, indeed, was the main reason Philadelphia had been chosen as the convention's site. An early coaxial cable linked that city with New York and Washington, creating the then impressive television audience of more than one million viewers. Murrow was not greatly impressed. Doing a wrap-up his first evening, he told viewers, "We've been [talking] here ten minutes and all we've said is that nothing much happened today, or if it did, we don't know about it."

During the era in which Americans heard most of their news by radio, the introductory words, "This is Edward R. Murrow…" was the best-known phrase. That era was brief. When Murrow joined CBS in 1935, radio news existed in not much more than name. By 1941, radio was foremost. By 1952, however, the Nielsen rating service determined that more Americans watched late-evening television than listened to radio. Early television leaned heavily to entertainment over news, but the trend was clear.

Television was the transforming "new thing" of the postwar years. In 1947, the country had 190,000 television sets. By 1949, it had ten million. By the early 1950s, standard home blueprints included a place for a television, which in many middle-class homes replaced the piano as the thing around which the family gathered. Talent that had gone from vaudeville to radio now moved to television: George Burns and Gracie Allen, *Our Miss Brooks*, and *Dragnet*. Television presented its own star attractions—Milton Berle in 1948; Sid Caesar and Imogene Coca in 1950.

Murrow and his correspondents were not anxious to be transformed. Initially, they were disdainful of television. They were writers and journalists. Television showed pictures and entertainers. The pull of the new medium, however, was simply too strong. On November 18, 1951, Murrow's radio documentary *Hear It Now* moved to TV as *See It Now*. The move from radio to television carried with it many of radio's forms, such as the format of news "anchor" coordinating reports from correspondents in the field. It carried many of the faces: at CBS, Sevareid, Smith, and Collingwood among them. And it carried to CBS television news much of the reputation the network had on radio.

Radio and television are commonly lumped together as broadcasting. Both, indeed, then used the airwaves. The differences, however, are as great as the commonalities. Radio is individual. A reporter, working alone, can develop a story and send it by shortwave transmission for broadcast. As one correspondent said, you just flip the switch and talk. Television news is collective, involving the efforts of writer, film crew, soundman, director, editor, and producer. It involves, as well, considerable equipment. Radio is unobtrusive: its correspondents can be inconspicuous at the scene of an event. When television arrives with its baggage of cameras and lights, it is in danger of becoming a competing event in itself. Television is greatly more expensive to present—one can equip a decent radio studio for less than the cost of a single television camera. Commenting on the relative costs, Howard K. Smith noted that when the radio game show *The $64 Question* moved to television, it emerged as *The $64,000 Question*. When, during the war, Murrow tried to hire reporter Walter Cronkite away from United Press, he offered a salary of $125 a week—substantially more than Cronkite was making at UP, but, as it turned out, not enough to lure him away. Radio was still in the same league as print—television was a whole new ball game.

The differences between radio and television are not simply those of scope, but in kind. Radio is active; the listener completes the story by filling in the scene in his or her own imagination. Television is passive—even television's essential helpmate, the remote control, exists to raise that passivity. This was recognized early on. A 1950s survey of television-owning families showed that families enjoyed television, watched it in increasing amounts, and generally watched it together. They were not, however, paying each other much attention: "They just sat in silence and watched."

Murrow had been outstanding in radio; he remained outstanding in television. His show, *See It Now*, was the finest documentary series on the air. While it is remembered for such landmark episodes as its investigation of migrant labor and its challenge to the methods of Senator Joseph McCarthy, it was consistently excellent. He continued to hire those who could think and write. A 1953 *New Yorker* profile stated that it was largely through Murrow's influence "that CBS hires correspondents who are inclined to approach the news with an open mind and by and large leaves them free to report it as they see it."

Television changed CBS, as well, making it a major corporation. Murrow's relationship with William S. Paley rested on the mutual regard they had for each other and their wartime camaraderie, but also in the instrumental role each had played in creating the network. Growth changed each man's circumstance in different ways. When Murrow was first hired by Ed Klauber,

Paley, who controlled about 42 percent of CBS, along with his father and uncle, who owned another 9 percent, owned a majority share in the company; Paley was in most matters answerable only to himself. By 1945, Paley—having sold off shares as the network's worth had sykrocketed—had reduced his ownership stake in CBS to 19 percent; it would continue to decline as the corporation grew. Personal relationships remained, but they became secondary to stockholder concerns and the imperative for profit.

ED MURROW AND BILL DOWNS IN KOREA

Murrow and many of his "boys" would continue as war
correspondents for radio and TV in Korea and Vietnam.

It would be a mistake to think that Paley ever ran CBS as anything less than a business. He was one of the century's great visionaries, but he had always been first and foremost an astute businessman. Murrow, in a very different way from Paley, had also been integral in making the network what it was. But as the company flourished and continued to build on the foundation they had each helped establish, any individual became less important. It's not that there was no place in the corporate world for Ed Murrow: at one point, CBS took the very unusual place of putting Murrow, an employee, on its board of directors. It was that the place itself was getting so large that no employee, Murrow included, could shape it. No one person was any longer indispensable.

Television, with its emphasis on images over words, was less suited to what Murrow viewed as the essentials of news presentation: reporters who could think and write. The Murrow Boys, on balance, were extremely well educated and broad of view. At the same time, they could take their perspectives and render them into a language and an idiom that was accessible to the full range of their audience. What joined thought and writing was intent: the desire to get at the heart of a story simply to learn that heart's nature.

While radio demands the listener's participation and imagination, television requires less involvement—its images stir emotions with equal effectiveness, but much more quickly and with much more ease. In the 1984 presidential campaign, CBS reporter Leslie Stahl did what was, by television standards, a sharply critical piece on Ronald Reagan. In the voiceover, she pointed out his opposition to government funding of public health and his funding cuts for children with disabilities, while showing images of Reagan speaking at the Special Olympics and at a nursing home. Stahl was surprised when a White House official called to praise her for the story. She naturally wondered why the White House wasn't upset about the piece. "You television people still don't get it," the official replied. "No one heard what you said. Don't you people realize that the picture is all that counts?" In an age dominated by moving images, journalists would need to learn to write with pictures, not just words—just as Murrow had had to invent a new language for the radio reporter.

By the time of that election, Ed Murrow had been gone almost two decades. He had spent his last few years serving not altogether happily as director of the United States Information Agency, having been appointed by President John F. Kennedy. Long a heavy smoker, he died of lung cancer in 1965 at the age of fifty-seven.

TELEVISION CHANGED MUCH, but did not greatly change Ed Murrow. With CBS television in New York, as with CBS radio in Europe, he continued to work himself to the point of exhaustion. Given a one-month vacation in 1951, for example, he spent it in Korea, covering the war. In 1963, one colleague said that Murrow was "all wound up and can't slow down." He offered this explanation: "I think that...he hit his high spot emotionally...during the Battle of Britain, when he was living in the midst of disaster, and that sepulchral 'This is London' of his was the voice of England telling America about it. I wouldn't be surprised if he's been trying to recapture some of that—the danger, the exhaustion."

Beginning in 1938, Edward R. Murrow created and legitimized serious foreign news reporting on the radio. More significantly, he created the forms and fashions of broadcast-news delivery—and became its greatest practitioner. He was able to combine the finest attributes of print reporting—knowledge of the subject matter, exceptional writing, the ability to get at a story's essence and to discern the important from the unimportant—with the most compelling features the new medium offered: to humanize the story with one's voice, and to tell that story as it is happening. Murrow transformed news by changing the way we received it. His vivid word pictures, his choice of detail, the homey, yet earnest, tenor of his voice—these all formed a new idiom for communicating the day's news. In a way, he was simply doing what Ida Lou Anderson had taught him. But he was doing it for an audience of millions, and he was speaking about the most important events of the twentieth century as they occurred. He was trying to uncover the truth that mattered, to shed light on the darkest corners of the world, at the darkest hour in our history.

Murrow's creation has become a mixed blessing: all that often remains in modern broadcast journalism of his model is the part that stirs our emotions, but circumvents our critical faculties. Images of a mother roughly spanking her young daughter may move us to outrage, but a spanking—even one judged to be abuse—is hardly news. The things that can so quickly grab our attention can also easily distract us from the things to which we really ought to be paying attention. The model Murrow set for today's broadcasters is not an easy one to follow.

Murrow's greatest achievement may have been his role in making real for his fellow Americans the Battle of Britain, and dramatizing what was at stake. In that moment of world crisis, Ed Murrow reached into the as yet unrealized capacities of radio and into his own, in some ways, unrealized character, and told the story that most needed telling. He not only invented a new form, he was on hand to put it to its best use.

HOWARD K. SMITH WITH MURROW
Smith (left) replaced Murrow as chief
CBS correspondent in Europe after the war.

He also inspired others to do the same. After a war-weary Eric Sevareid returned to New York in 1940, he by chance overheard the voice of Larry LeSueur, broadcasting from an underground studio in London, come forth from the radios of passing cars. The experience, Sevareid wrote, was "thrilling beyond compare. I wanted to write to them that the whole thing was real after all, and not a pantomime in an empty room."

The "whole thing" was, arguably, the most real thing to happen in news broadcasting. It continued. During the war, Murrow directed the team he had largely hired and trained and set it to the task of making real and clear for millions in America the enormous undertaking in which their country was engaged. During World War II, the Murrow Boys set the standard for wartime news coverage. They continued to set the standard in broadcast journalism for decades to come.

Murrow and his "boys" not only entered a journalistic tradition, but the specialized tradition of war reporting, which included the likes of Ernest Hemingway, who took part in and wrote about World War I and the Spanish civil war; Winston Churchill, who as a reporter during the Boer War in South Africa, escaped enemy capture and crossed twelve hundred miles of Africa incognito; William Howard Russell, whose coverage of the charge of the Light Brigade in the Crimean War inspired Tennyson; and even the legendary Pheidippides, the Greek messenger who in 490 B.C. ran twenty-six miles to report the triumph at Marathon (and summarily dropped dead). It also included a fair list of rogues and adventurers, many of whom had no qualms about distorting the truth to lure readers—the yellow journalists of the late 1890s, who promoted war with Spain at the behest of William Randolph Hearst and others, are perhaps the most memorable example.

Radio journalism was an oxymoron when Murrow arrived in England in 1937. Thanks in large part to Murrow and Paul White, CBS's crop of broadcast war correspondents began a tradition of integrity, artistry, and courage that would serve as an exemplar for the journalists who followed. The televised reports from Vietnam that horrified a nation in the 1960s were a descendent of those rooftop broadcasts of Murrow's in the fall of 1940. When CNN's Bernard Shaw and Peter Arnett broadcast live from the enemy's capital of Baghdad in 1991 (in what was essentially a televised radio report), it had its roots in Shirer's reports from Berlin and Cecil Brown's reports from Rome.

The reporting of war has taken on greater significance as reports have become instantaneous, live broadcasts. Governments and military leaders have always exerted a great deal of pressure on news networks, producers, and individual reporters about what they report, how they report it, and when. At the same time, journalists must examine the fundamental questions on the purpose of their reporting, because since the days of Murrow, Shirer, Sevareid, Grandin, Breckinridge, LeSueur, Brown, Collingwood, Smith, Burdett, Downs, and Hottelet, our expectations are higher from those reporting on armed conflicts, wherever in the world they may be.

"WE WERE LIKE a young band of brothers in those early radio days with Murrow," said Eric Sevareid in his final broadcast in 1977. Edward R. Murrow and the group of reporters he assembled leading up to and during the Second World War were remarkable in many ways. Their contribution to the war effort, however, was far greater than simply as messengers, or morale boosters. "They might have won," said Bennie Smith. "Think of what the world would have been like if they had won. Nothing can ever be as terrible as that." Hitler had believed that, to fight totalitarianism, a nation would have to employ totalitarian methods. And it might have happened that way—"They might have won." But the Murrow Boys, the leading broadcast journalists of the war, never used the public's airwaves for propaganda. Nor did they simply pass along a series of dry facts. Murrow set, and followed, a higher standard than that. And in creating the new form, he also created a new weapon in defense of free societies: a forum for spreading the truth, or at least to search for the truth; "to elucidate, illuminate, and explain;" to allow the people to weigh and judge for themselves and so determine their own fate.

Notes

Prologue: August 1940

1   **Epigraph:** letter from Murrow to Charles Collingwood, dated January 2, 1946, Tufts University special collection.

London After Dark

3   **Murrow at St. Martin's:** Sperber, *Murrow: His Life and Times* (New York: Bantam Books, 1986), p. 163.

3   **Murrow, "Here comes one of those big buses":** CBS broadcast, August 24, 1940.

3   **"walking along the street"..."sirens holler":** CBS broadcast, August 24, 1940.

4   **Latry: "my friends in America" and Savoy menu:** *Time* magazine, September 2, 1940, p. 40.

4   **"brought around in"..."airplanes":** CBS broadcast, August 24, 1940.

5   **LeSueur report:** CBS broadcast, August 24, 1940.

5   **Transmission from London:** "Covering a War for Radio," Paul W. White, p. 4. Unpublished 1941 manuscript located in Eric Sevareid papers, U.S. Copyright Office (manuscripts division), Madison Building, Washington, D.C.

5   **115 CBS affiliates:** H.V. Kaltenborn, *Fifty Fabulous Years* (New York: G.P. Putnam's Sons, 1950), p. 208.

6   **Sevareid, "Few spots are":** CBS broadcast, August 24, 1940.

6   **Vincent Sheean at Piccadilly:** *Time* magazine, September 2, 1940, p. 40.

6   **Whitehall history:** Sidney Dark, *London* (New York: Macmillan Company, 1936), p. 19.

6   **J.B. Priestley:** *Time* magazine, September 2, 1940, p. 40.

6   **Murrow and Sheean view fire:** Edward R. Murrow, *This Is London* (New York: Simon & Schuster, 1941), p. 148.

7   **Air war:** John Keegan, *The Second World War* (New York: Penguin Books, 1989), p. 96.

7   **Bombing mistake:** Philip Knightley, *The First Casualty* (New York: Harcourt Brace Jovanovich, 1975), p. 237.

Our Man in Berlin

7   **Shirer, "like hail falling":** Shirer, *Berlin Diary*, p. 487.

7   **Potatoes, tennis in German:** William S. Shirer, *"This Is Berlin"* (Woodstock, New York: The Overlook Press, 1999), p. 385.

7   **Shirer broadcast during bombing:** William L. Shirer, *Berlin Diary* (New York: Alfred K. Knopf, 1941), p. 487–488.

8   **Elmer Davis in New York:** Shirer, *Berlin Diary*, p. 488.

8   **German claim of sixty-four:** Shirer, *"This Is Berlin,"* p. 385; confirmed count of 22: Keegan, *The Second World War*, p. 96.

9   **Murrow and others avoid shell casing:** Eric Sevareid, *Not So Wild a Dream* (New York: Atheneum, 1978), p. 170.

Chapter 1: The Gathering Storm

11   **Epigraph:** Shirer, *"This Is Berlin,"* p. 13.

Radio Days

13   **Founding of KDKA:** Sally Bedell Smith, *In All his Glory* (New York: Simon and Schuster, 1990),p. 53.

13   **$650 million in radio sales:** Erik Barnouw, *A Tower in Babel* (New York: Oxford University Press, 1966), p. 210.

13   **Innumerable small stations:** Barnouw, *A Tower in Babel*, p. 179.

13   **Sarnoff organizes NBC:** Barnouw, *A Tower in Babel*, p. 184.

13   **CBS organized:** Barnouw, *A Tower in Babel*, p. 222.

14   **Paleys purchase CBS:** Barnouw, *A Tower in Babel*, p. 223.

14   **Paley on son:** Erik Barnouw, *The Golden Web* (Oxford University Press, New York, 1966), p. 56.

14   **Paley discovers Bing Crosby and Kate Smith:** Raymond A. Schroth, *The American Journey of Eric Sevareid* (Steerforth Press, 1995), p. 132.

14   **Paley signs up NBC stars:** Joseph E. Persico, *Edward R. Murrow: An American Original* (McGraw-Hill, New York, 1988), p. 95.

14   **Popular shows:** Barnouw, *A Tower in Babel*, p. 273–274.

15   **WILLIAM S. PALEY, 1901–1990:** biographical material for Paley was drawn from Smith, *In All His Glory*; "William Paley: 1901–1990," *Macleans*, Nov. 5, 1990 (obit.); and Persico, *Edward R. Murrow*.

17   **Sun Oil prepares the news:** Sally Bedell Smith, *In All His Glory* (Simon & Schuster, New York, 1990), p. 161.

17   **Kaltenborn joins CBS:** Barnouw, *A Tower in Babel*, p. 245.

17 **Boake Carter bio and mannerisms:** Stanley Cloud & Lynne Olson, *The Murrow Boys* (Houghton Mifflin, New York, 1996), p. 13–14.

17 **Trout, "Nobody ever had":** Cloud & Olson, *The Murrow Boys*, p. 14.

17 **Saerchinger broadcasts:** Persico, *Edward R. Murrow*, p. 110–111.

18 **Radio impact on newspaper advertising:** Smith, *In All His Glory*, p. 164.

18 **AP, "Not allow any news":** Smith, *In All His Glory*, p. 125.

18 **CBS hires Klauber & White:** William S. Paley, *As It Happened* (Doubleday, New York, 1978), p. 119.

18 **CBS news operation:** Paley, *As It Happened*, p. 126.

18 **Radio–press agreement:** Paley, *As It Happened*, p. 128.

18 **Murrow interview and job offer:** Persico, *Edward R. Murrow*, p. 99.

A Man in the World's New Fashion

19 **Epigraph:** this quote from Shakespeare's *Love's Labour's Lost* was printed under Murrow's senior photo in the *Mazda*, the Edison High School yearbook.

19 **"Egbert," a name he loathed...saved him from having to fight every lumberjack:** Sperber, *Murrow: His Life & Times*, p. 24.

19 **"She was cruelly dwarfed":** Robert Sandberg, speech of April 22, 1983, Washington State University Symposium: "Commemoration of the seventy-fifth birthday of Edward R. Murrow"; recollections of Ida Lou Anderson by one of her students. As quoted in Sperber, *Murrow*, p. 25.

21 **Murrow did audition...with NBC:** Persico, *Edward R. Murrow*, p. 64.

22 **Murrow managed to...integrate black students:** Persico, *Edward R. Murrow*, p. 67–69.

22 **Murrow's service with IIE:** Sperber, *Murrow: His Life & Times*, p. 51–54.

22 **Duggan was a reform-minded pioneer:** Sperber, *Murrow: His Life & Times*, p. 45.

23 **He would...bring 335 scholars:** Sperber, *Murrow: His Life & Times*, p. 64.

24 **Frustration with the committee:** Sperber, *Murrow: His Life & Times*, p. 72–74.

24 **Fred Willis...arranged a meeting for Murrow:** Sperber, *Murrow: His Life & Times*, p. 77.

24 **"It is Murrow whose work":** Persico, *Edward R. Murrow*, p. 102.

25 **White rivalry with Murrow:** Cloud & Olson, *The Murrow Boys*, p. 30, and Sperber, *Murrow: His Life and Times*, p. 83.

25 **Sioussant on Murrow's looks:** Persico, *Edward R. Murrow*, p. 101.

25 **Murrow–White drinking contest:** Persico, *Edward R. Murrow*, p. 108.

25 **Murrow offered London post:** Smith, *In All His Glory*, p. 169.

Foreign Correspondent

25 **Murrows sail for London:** Persico, *Edward R. Murrow*, p. 113.

25 **Janet Murrow background:** Sperber, *Murrow: His Life & Times*, p. 50.

25 **Murrow bio note:** "The World on His Back," by Charles Wertenbaker, *The New Yorker*, December 26, 1953, p. 33.

26 **Meets Mary Marvin Breckinridge:** Persico, *Edward R. Murrow*, p. 158.

26 **Breckinridge/Murrow NSFA tie:** from "Notes for a Book" by Mary Marvin Breckinridge, on file with the Edward R. Murrow papers [on microfilm], Ohio University, Athens, Ohio.

27 **Chamberlain, "Human nature":** William R. Rock, *British Appeasement in the 1930s* (New York: W.W. Norton & Co., 1977), p. 28.

27 **Murrow watching coronation:** Alexander Kendrick, *Prime Time: The Life of Edward R. Murrow*, (Boston: Little, Brown & Company, 1969), p. 144.

27 **Murrows at Hallam Street:** Sperber, *Murrow: His Life and Times*, p. 101.

27 **Murrow's secretary, Katharine Campbell:** Kendrick, *Prime Time*, p. 146.

27 **Murrow's "democratic" broadcasts:** Kendrick, *Prime Time*, p. 144.

28 **Dawson, "I do my utmost":** A.L. Rowse, *Appeasement* (New York: W.W. Norton & Co., 1961), p. 10.

28 **Chamberlain, "I got the impression":** Rowse, *Appeasement*, p. 83.

28 **Smith, "comical looking man":** Howard K. Smith, *Last Train from Berlin* (New York: Alfred A. Knopf, 1942), p. 31.

28 **"a harmless and annoying zealot":** Smith, *Last Train from Berlin*, p. 32.

28 **Smith picketing Downing Street:** Smith, *Last Train from Berlin*, p. 35.

28 **Churchill, "decided only to be":** Roy Jenkins, *Churchill: A Biography* (New York: Farrar, Straus and Giroux, 2001), p. 406.

29 **Shirer, "Wish I could":** William L. Shirer, *Berlin Diary* (New York: Alfred A. Knopf, 1941), p. 11.

29 **Shirer, "A man could":** Schroth, *The American Journey of Eric Sevareid*, p. 136.

29 **Universal Service hires Shirer:** Shirer, *Berlin Diary*, p. 13.

29 **Shirer's coverage of Garmisch Olympics:** Shirer, *Berlin Diary*, p. 45.

29 **Shirer laid off:** Shirer, *Berlin Diary*, p. 78.

29 **Murrow telegrams Shirer:** Shirer, *Twentieth Century Journey: Vol. II, The Nightmare Years, 1930–1940* (Boston: Little, Brown & Company, 1984), p. 273.

29 **Account of Murrow/Shirer dinner:** Shirer, *Berlin Diary*, p. 80.

29 **Shirer's Hindenberg broadcast:** Shirer, *Berlin Dairy*, p. 72–73.

30 **White, "little thought is given":** "Covering a War for Radio," Paul W. White, p. 4. Unpublished 1941 manuscript located in Eric Sevareid papers, U.S. Copyright Office (manuscripts division), Madison Building, Washington, D.C.

30 **CBS hires Shirer:** Shirer, *Berlin Diary*, p. 82.

30 **"Murrow had fired me with a feeling":** Shirer, *The Nightmare Years*, p. 281.

30 **Shirer's early assignments:** Shirer, *Berlin Diary*, p. 88–89.

31 **WILLIAM L. SHIRER, 1904–1993:** biographical material was drawn from Library of America, *Reporting World War II: Part One: American Journalism 1938–1944* (New York: Literary Classics of the United States, 1995); Shirer, *Twentieth Century Journey: The Start, 1904–1930* (Boston: Little, Brown & Company, 1976); Shirer, *Berlin Diary*; and Shirer, *The Nightmare Years*.

Anschluss

33 **Murrow in Poland, Shirer in Yugoslavia:** Kendrick, *Prime Time*, p. 154.

33 **Austrian political situation:** Kaltenborn, *Fifty Fabulous Years*, p. 205.

33 **Shirer, "A bit comical":** Shirer, *Berlin Diary*, p. 97.

34 **Schuschnigg capitulation:** Shirer, *Berlin Diary*, p. 98–99.

34 **Shirer, "argued, pleaded, fought":** Shirer, *Berlin Diary*, p. 95–96.

34 **Shirer, "opposing team"…"paid to be sure":** Sperber, *Murrow: His Life and Times*, p. 115.

35 **Murrow hires plane:** Barnouw, *The Golden Web*, p. 77.

35 **Idea for news Roundup:** Sally Bedell Smith, *All His Glory*, p. 171.

35 **Difficulties in organizing Roundup:** Kendrick, *Prime Time*, p. 157.

35 **White phones Shirer:** Shirer, *Berlin Diary*, p. 104.

35 **Organizing Roundup:** Sperber, *Murrow: his Life and Times*, p. 117.

35 **Trout, "A program of St. Louis blues"… "The world trembles":** CBS broadcast, March 13, 1938.

35 **Shirer, "after the delirious mobs":** CBS broadcast, March 13, 1938.

36 **Wilkinson, "People are asking"…"the situation here":** CBS broadcast, 1938.

36 **Reports from Paris/Berlin/Italy:** Kendrick, *Prime Time*, p. 157.

36 **Murrow, "riding about in trucks":** Paley, *As It Happened*, p. 135.

36 **Murrow, "No one seems to know":** CBS broadcast, March 13, 1938.

36 **Trout, "moving as full speed":** CBS broadcast, September 13, 1938.

36 **New French government:** William R. Rock, *Appeasement on Trial*, (Archon Books, London, 1966) p. 51.

36 **Chamberlain, "severest condemnation":** Rock, *Appeasement on Trial*, p. 64.

36 **Schwellenbach, "is today Europe's leader"…"We will be":** CBS broadcast, March 13, 1938.

37 **Murrow, "It was called a bloodless"…"I'd like to forget":** Sperber, *Murrow: His Life and Times*, p. 122.

37 **Shirer, "birth of the 'radio foreign correspondent'":** Shirer, *Berlin Diary*, p. 112.

37 **Murrow from Maginot Line:** Sperber, *Murrow: His Life and Times*, p. 124.

37 **Shirer interviews Benes, CBS engineers work with Czechs:** Kendrick, *Prime Time*, p. 162.

37 **Tess Shirer strip-searched:** Shirer, *Berlin Diary*, p. 118.

Munich

37 **Munich crisis background:** Keegan, *The Second World War*, p. 40.

38 *Times* **[of London] editorial:** Rowse, *Appeasement*, p. 77.

38 **Approval to broadcast from Prague:** Shirer, *Berlin Diary*, p. 126.

38 **German headlines:** Shirer, *"This is Berlin,"* p. 17.

38 **Shirer broadcast interference:** Kendrick, *Prime Time*, p. 166.

38 **Masaryk, "I tell you our powder is dry":** Kendrick, *Prime Time*, p. 164.

38 **"Under the most urgent":** Robert J. Landry, "Edward R. Murrow," *Scribner's*, December 1938, p. 8.

38 **Murrow, "Well, the only way":** Edward Bliss Jr., editor, *In Search of Light: The Broadcasts of Edward R. Murrow, 1938–1961* (Da Capo Press, New York, 1962), p. 6.

39 **Shirer, "It was simply a terrific":** Shirer, *"This is Berlin,"* p. 16.

39 **Shirer in Godesberg:** Shirer, *"This is Berlin,"* p. 20.

39 **Shirer, "Every few steps":** Shirer, *Berlin Diary*, p. 137.

39 **Murrow, "that Herr Hitler will":** Bliss, *In Search of Light*, p. 8.

39 **Hitler position at Godesberg:** Jenkins, *Churchill*, p. 524.

39 **Shirer, "We have six days":** Shirer, *"This is Berlin,"* p. 24.

39 **Shirer, "Not a soul outside":** Shirer, *"This is Berlin,"* p. 29.

39 **Shirer, "No one in that vast":** Shirer, *"This is Berlin,"* p. 29.

39 **Five hundred CBS broadcasts:** Smith, *In All His Glory*, p. 135.

39 **102 Kaltenborn commentaries:** H.V. Kaltenborn, *Fifty Fabulous Years* (New York: G.P. Putnam's Sons, 1950) p. 107.

39 **Interruption of horse race:** Kaltenborn, *Fifty Fabulous Years*, p. 210.

39 **Crowds at taxicabs:** Kaltenborn, *Fifty Fabulous Years*, p. 208.

40 **Murrow, "Throughout most of the night":** Bliss, *In Search of Light*, p. 8.

40 **British mobilization urged:** Rock, *British Appeasement in the 1930s*, p. 12.

40 **"Rose to its feet":** Jenkins, *Churchill*, p. 525.

40 **Murrow, "Last night it appeared":** Bliss, *In Search of Light*, p. 9.

40 **Murrow and Masaryk:** Persico, *Edward R. Murrow*, p. 142.

40 **Murrow first to report Munich settlement:** Persico, *Edward R. Murrow*, p. 143.

40 **Shirer, "Fears to return":** Shirer, *Berlin Diary*, p. 145.

40 **Sevareid, "I watched him":** Eric Sevareid, *Not So Wild a Dream* (New York: Atheneum, 1976),p. 98.

41 **Murrow, "International experts":** Bliss, *In Search of Light*, p. 10.

41 **Shirer, "A bushel of flowers":** Shirer, *"This is Berlin"*, p. 35.

42 **Near-explosion and "they never would have":** Shirer, *"This is Berlin,"* p. 37.

42 **Shirer, "We try to get it":** Shirer, *Berlin Diary*, p. 150.

42 **Shirer takes up golf:** Shirer, *Berlin Diary*, p. 151.

42 **$190,000 spent on coverage:** Landry, *Scribner's*, p. 8.

42 **CBS "stole the radio spotlight":** Barnouw, *The Golden Web*, p. 80.

42 **Murrow as "tall without being lanky":** Landry, "Edward R. Murrow," p. 9.

42 **Murrow drive car up Capitol:** Persico, *Edward R. Murrow*, p. 108.

42 **"he must deal":** Landry, "Edward R. Murrow," p. 50.

42 **"the scattering bits of wireless":** *Newsweek*, September 11, 1939, p. 43.

42 **Murrow's influence and advantages:** Landry, *Scribner's*, p. 8.

43 **England's military position:** Rowse, *Appeasement*, p. 83–84.

43 **Churchill, "sordid, squalid":** Jenkins, *Churchill*, p. 526.

44   **Relief followed by shame:** William R. Rock, *British Appeasement in the 1930s*, p. 82, 88, 91.

44   **Listeners panic:** Brian Holmsten & Alex Lubertozzi, *The Complete War of the Worlds* (Naperville, Illinois: Sourcebooks, 2001), p. 6, 8–10.

44   **Were actually Germans:** Cantril, Hadley, *The Invasion from Mars* (Princeton, New Jersey: Princeton University Press, 1940).

44   **Underground BBC facility:** Kendrick, *Prime Time*, p. 171.

44   **Murrow, "Whether we like it":** Kendrick, *Prime Time*, p. 172.

Chapter 2: War in Europe

45   **Epigraph:** A.J. Liebling, *Reporting World War II, Part One*, p. 174.

Poland

47   **Paul W. White, "Covering a War For Radio":** p. 4.

47   **"center-parted, lacquered-down look of an oversize Dink Stover":** Sperber, *Murrow: His Life and Times,* p. 82.

47   **Sevareid childhood:** Sevareid, *Not So Wild A Dream*, p. 4.

47   **Sevareid opposes ROTC:** Sevareid, *Not So Wild A Dream*, p. 60.

47   **Sevareid to London:** Sevareid, *Not So Wild A Dream*, p. 74.

47   **Sevareid, "a tall thin man":** Sevareid, *Not So Wild A Dream*, p. 82.

48   **Murrow, "I don't know":** Sevareid, *Not So Wild A Dream*, p. 107.

48   **Audition & Murrow, "Quit your other jobs":** Sevareid, *Not So Wild A Dream*, p. 107.

48   **Appointment letter; "Incidentally":** Letter dated August 16, 1939, with Eric Sevareid papers, Library of Congress, Washington, D.C.

48   **CBS press announcement:** Letter dated August 22, 1939, with Eric Sevareid Papers, Library of Congress.

48   **German–Polish boundaries:** Keegan, *The Second World War*, p. 41.

48   **German–Soviet Pact:** Keegan, *The Second World War*, p. 41.

48   **Kaltenborn refused entry:** Kaltenborn, *Fifty Fabulous Years*, p. 217.

49   ERIC SEVAREID, **1912–1992:** biographical material was drawn from Schroth, *The American Journey of Eric Sevareid*; and Library of America, *Reporting World War II: Part Two: American Journalism 1944–1946* (New York: Literary Classics of the United States, 1995).

51   **"Europe Dances":** Persico, *Edward R. Murrow*, p. 154.

51   **Shirer, "The entire press":** CBS broadcast, August 28, 1939.

51   **Kaltenborn, "The odds [are] still":** Kaltenborn, *Fifty Fabulous Years*, p. 219.

51   **Murrow, "The man on the street":** Murrow, *This Is London*, p. 4.

51   **Sevareid, "carted out in wheelbarrows":** CBS broadcast, August 30, 1939.

51   **London air raid:** Murrow, *This Is London*, p. 17–18.

52   **Smith applies for job:** Smith, *Last Train from Berlin*, p. 40.

52   **Sevareid broadcast of French declaration:** Sevareid, *Not So Wild A Dream*, p. 110–111.

53   **Sevareid, "Apparently all America":** Sevareid, *Not So Wild A Dream*, p. 111.

53   **Grandin, "abandoned and destroyed":** CBS broadcast, September 16, 1939.

53   **False reporting:** Philip Knightley, *The First Casualty*, p. 219.

53   **Early censorship:** Philip Knightley, *The First Casualty*, p. 219.

53   **Polish retreat:** Keegan, *The Second World War*, p. 44.

53   **Shirer reports Germans at Warsaw:** Shirer, *This Is Berlin*, p. 85.

53   **Competitors stop broadcasting:** Persico, *Edward R. Murrow*, p. 157.

53   **Polish army, "in a very strong position":** CBS broadcast, September 16, 1939.

54   **Shirer, "The Polish war is over":** Shirer, *This Is Berlin*, p. 85.

54   **Shirer, "I'll be frank":** Shirer, *This Is Berlin*, p. 91.

54   **Shirer, "watching the killing":** Shirer, *This Is Berlin*, p. 92.

The Phony War

54   **British claim on *Royal Sceptre*:** Shirer, *Berlin Diary*, p. 225–226.

54   **Captain, "I sank the *Royal Sceptre*":** Shirer, *This Is Berlin*, p. 99.

54   **Captain's message to Churchill:** Shirer, *This Is Berlin*, p.100.

55   **Shirer, "One good break":** to Browning reaches port: Shirer, *Berlin Diary*, p. 227.

56   **Murrow on Little Barfield:** CBS broadcast, November 12, 1939.

56   **Sevareid village report:** CBS broadcast, November 12, 1939.

57   **Klauber, "elucidate and illuminate":** Schroth, *The American Journey of Eric Sevareid*, p. 140.

57   **Murrow, "I thought your streets":** Bliss [ed.], *In Search of Light*, p. 3.

57   **Murrow predicts Britain will fight:** Persico, Edward R. Murrow, p. 155.

57   **Sevareid's views on broadcast content:** Schroth, *The American Journey of Eric Sevareid*, p. 141.

57   **Shirer, "they bomb the hell":** Shirer, *Berlin Diary*, p.198–199.

58   **Shirer, "are certainly the least":** Shirer, *Berlin Diary*, p. 173.

58   **Berliners feeding ducks:** Shirer, *Berlin Diary*, p. 324.

58   **"heavy laborers":** Shirer, *This Is Berlin*, p. 189.

58   **"worked like a magic wand":** Smith, *Last Train From Berlin*, p. 50.

58   **German woman denounces friends:** Shirer, *Berlin Diary*, p. 288.

58   **Shirer, "I note that you":** Shirer, *Berlin Diary*, 200.

58   **New correspondents:** White, "Covering a War for Radio," p. 4.

58   **Breckinridge speech:** Breckinridge, "Broadcasting from Europe to America," p. 1.

59   **"equipped with a dressing-case":** Breckinridge, "Notes for a Book," 1952, p. 1.

59   **Breckinridge in France, Savoy:** Breckinridge, "Notes for a Book," p. 2.

59   **Breckinridge dinner with Murrows, "partly because"** Breckinridge, **"Broadcasting from Europe to America":** p. 4.

59 **Breckinridge broadcast career:** Breckinridge, "Broadcasting from Europe to America," p. 5.

59 **Shirer, "I am speaking to you":** Shirer, *This Is Berlin*, p. 170–171.

59 **Sevareid, "The men sang"…"so perhaps it was":** Sevareid, *Not So Wild a Dream*, p. 107.

60 **Murrow's report on King's Christmas message:** CBS broadcast, December 26, 1939.

60 **"familiar, very American":** Sevareid, *Not So Wild a Dream*, p. 178.

60 **Murrow, "street lights, automobiles" and "The British think":** CBS broadcast, January 18, 1940.

61 MARY MARVIN BRECKINRIDGE, 1905–2002: biographical material was drawn from Persico, *Edward R. Murrow*; Cloud and Olson, *The Murrow Boys*, "Jefferson Patterson Park & Museum History" (website: *www.jefpat.org*); and "Women Come to the Front: Journalists, Photographers and Broadcasters During World War II" (Library of Congress Exhibition).

62 **Shirer, "only two alternatives":** CBS broadcast, January 18, 1940.

62 **Snowball fight:** Breckinridge, "Broadcasting from Europe to America," p. 11.

62 **Shirer, "I've invited Marvin":** Shirer, *Berlin Diary*, p. 278.

63 **Breckinridge studies German:** Breckinridge, "Broadcasting from Europe to America," p. 11.

63 **Murrow illness:** Schroth, *The American Journey of Eric Sevareid*, p. 146.

64 **Breckinridge, "I sat at one desk":** Breckinridge, "Broadcasting from Europe to America," p. 10.

64 **Breckinridge reports on night club; brides' school; and coal shortage:** from her broadcast scripts for February 4, 1940; February 15, 1940; February 4, 1940, on file with Edward Murrow papers, Aldon Library, Ohio University, Athens, Ohio.

64 **Sevareid, "While France is at war":** CBS broadcast, February 5, 1940.

64 **Breckinridge report on German press censorship:** Breckinridge broadcast script of February 8, 1940.

Scandinavia

65 **British interception of *Altmark*:** Keegan, *The Second World War*, p. 50.

65 **Breckinridge reports on funeral:** Breckinridge broadcast script for February 19, 1940.

65 **Breckinridge, "Under the gangway":** Breckinridge broadcast script for February 21, 1940.

65 **Breckinridge, "was cold feet":** Breckinridge cable to CBS New York, February 22, 1940, on file with Edward r. Murrow Papers, Athens University.

65 **Shirer, "from thirty-five cents to three dollars":** Shirer, *This Is Berlin*, p. 231.

65 **Breckinridge on defenses in the Netherlands:** Breckinridge, broadcast script of March 26, 1940.

65 **Murrow, carpenters' strike:** CBS broadcast, April 1, 1940.

66 **German invasion of Norway and Denmark:** Keegan, *The Second World War*, p. 50.

66   **Shirer reports attack on Denmark & Norway:** Shirer, *This Is Berlin*, p. 236.

67   **Shirer, "Danes…were amazed":** Shirer, *Berlin Diary*, p. 318.

67   **Sevareid, "The atmosphere in government":** CBS broadcast, April 9, 1940.

67   **Shirer, "Neutral naval attachés":** Shirer, *This Is Berlin*, p. 242.

67   **Shirer, "It has even been reported":** Shirer, *This Is Berlin*, p. 247.

The French Invasion

67   **Shirer, "Not two hundred yards":** Shirer, *Berlin Diary*, p. 324.

67   **Shirer, Gasoline rationing:** Shirer, *Berlin Diary*, p. 327.

67   **German travel restrictions:** CBS broadcast, May 9, 1940.

68   **Shirer, "The decisive battle of the war":** CBS broadcast, May 10, 1940.

68   **Murrow, "History has been made"…"plump, bald with massive round shoulders":** CBS broadcast, May 10, 1940.

68   **British general, "men unshaven":** Keegan, *The Second World War*, p. 62.

68   **Junker 52 transports:** capture of Eben Emael: Keegan, *The Second World War*, p. 65.

68   **Rommel crosses the Meuse:** Keegan, *The Second World War*, p. 71.

68   **Sevareid tour cancelled:** Sevareid, *Not So Wild a Dream*, p. 139.

68   **Companion times shellfire:** Sevareid, *Not So Wild a Dream*, p. 141.

68   **Davis, "usually well-informed":** Sevareid, *Not So Wild a Dream*, p. 142.

68   **Shirer, "Last night, for instance":** Shirer, *This Is Berlin*, p. 278.

69   **Grandin, "not far from Paris":** CBS broadcast, May 16, 1940.

69   **Sevareid, "landed in a row":** CBS broadcast, May 16, 1940.

70   **Murrow, "the whole history":** Murrow, *This Is London*, p. 120.

70   **Murrow, "The British Parliament":** Murrow, *This Is London*, p. 105.

70   **Murrow reports on *Peace News*:** CBS broadcast, May 16, 1940.

70   **"Shoot the murdering swine!":** Murrow, *This Is London*, p. 107.

70   **"could hold out" and "Increased help":** Murrow, *This Is London*, p. 107–108.

70   **White writes correspondents, "you have absolute confidence":** Paul White to CBS correspondents, May 25, 1940, in Eric Sevareid papers, Library of Congress.

70   **Breckinridge casualty report:** Breckinridge, broadcast script of May 21, 1940.

70   **Shirer, "first round":** Murrow, *Berlin Diary*, p. 389.

70   **Sevareid decides French have lost:** Sevareid, *Not So Wild a Dream*, p. 143.

71   PAUL WHITE, 1902–1955: biographical material was drawn from Cloud & Olson, *The Murrow Boys*; Persico, *Edward R. Murrow*; and RTNDA website (*rtnda.org*).

72   **Shirer, "Before we start":** Shirer, *Berlin Diary*, p. 375.

72   **Shirer, "I, at least"…"seemed to be going on":** Shirer, *This Is Berlin*, 291.

72   **Shirer, "The Germans now believe":** Shirer, *This Is Berlin*, p. 295.

73   **Breckinridge reports Reynaud's resignation:** Breckinridge broadcast script of May 28, 1940.

73   **Brown, "in the Mussolini tradition":** CBS broadcast, May 20, 1940.

73   **Davis, "is ready to go":** CBS broadcast, May 20, 1940.

73 **Dunkirk evacuation:** Keegan, *The Second World War*, p. 81.

73 **Murrow report on the Blackburn Rovers:** CBS broadcast, June 3, 1940.

73 **Murrow, "I saw more grave, solemn faces":** Murrow, *This Is London*, p. 113.

The Fall of France

74 **Shirer, "Church bells":** Shirer, *Berlin Diary*, p. 313.

74 **"Perhaps the English":** Shirer, *Berlin Diary*, p. 393.

74 **Churchill, "We shall go on to the end":** Martin Gilbert, *Churchill: A Life* (New York: Henry Holt & Co., 1991), p. 656.

74 **Murrow, "I have heard Mr. Churchill":** CBS broadcast, June 4, 1940.

74 **Citroën factory bombed:** Schroth, *The American Journey of Eric Sevareid*, p. 153.

74 **"Everyone in the room":** CBS broadcast, June 3, 1940.

76 **Breckinridge, "stuffed with treasures"…"We must lie down":** Breckinridge broadcast script of May 14, 1940.

77 **Lois Sevareid gives birth:** Schroth, *The American Journey of Eric Sevareid*, p. 149.

77 **Sevareid finds ambulance, nurse:** Schroth, *The American Journey of Eric Sevareid*, p. 150.

77 **Lois Sevareid, "seemed to move":** Schroth, *The American Journey of Eric Sevareid*, p. 151.

77 **Passage on *Manhattan*:** Schroth, *The American Journey of Eric Sevareid*, p. 152.

77 **Breckinridge takes final train from Brussels:** Breckinridge, "Broadcasting from Europe to America," p. 13.

77 **Breckinridge, "going to follow"…"marrying a Nazi":** Breckinridge, "Broadcasting for Europe to America," p. 13.

77 **Breckinridge purchases bicycle:** Schroth, *The American Journey of Eric Sevareid*, p. 152.

77 **Breckinridge marries:** Schroth, *The American Journey of Eric Sevareid*, p. 154.

77 **Breckinridge marriage ends career:** Breckinridge, "Broadcasting from Europe to America," p. 13–14.

77 **Burdett replaces Wason:** Cloud & Olson, *The Murrow Boys*, p. 73.

78 **Sevareid, "We talked to everyone":** Sevareid, *Not So Wild a Dream*, p. 142.

78 **Sevareid, "Paris was dying":** Schroth, *The American Journey of Eric Sevareid*, p. 155.

79 **Sevareid, "would be under jurisdiction":** Sevareid, *Not So Wild a Dream*, p. 146.

79 **Sevareid, "had no heart":** Sevareid, *Not So Wild A Dream*, p. 146.

79 **Mussolini declares war:** Keegan, *The Second World War*, p. 85.

79 **Sevareid on the lam:** Sevareid, *Not So Wild a Dream*, p. 145.

79 **Broadcasting from perfume factory:** Sevareid, *Not So Wild a Dream*, p. 149.

80 **Sevareid, "the transmitter crew":** Sevareid, *Not So Wild a Dream*, p. 151.

80 **Sevareid, "Regardless of what":** Sevareid, *Not So Wild a Dream*, p. 153.

80 **Sevareid broadcasting without clearance:** Sevareid, *Not So Wild a Dream*, p. 153.

80   **Broadcast, "now" v. "not":** Sevareid, *Not So Wild a Dream*, p. 153.

80   **Grandin's departure:** Cloud & Olson, Murrow's Boys, p. 80.

80   **Murrow, "entirely justifiable":** Cloud & Olson, Murrow's Boys, p. 80.

80   **Germans enter Paris:** Keegan, *The Second World War*, p. 84.

80   **Shirer, "I had an ache":** Shirer, *Berlin Diary*, p. 409.

80   **Shirer, "are still dazed":** Shirer, *This Is Berlin*, p. 327.

80   **Shirer, "I stood in a throng":** Shirer, *This Is Berlin*, p. 327.

81   **THOMAS GRANDIN, 1907–1977:** biographical material was drawn from Cloud & Olson, *The Murrow Boys*; Persico, *Edward R. Murrow*; and Sperber, *Murrow: His Life and Times.*

82   **Surrender set for Compiegne:** Shirer, *Berlin Diary*, p. 414.

82   **Shirer, "By a super-human":** Shirer, *Berlin Diary*, p. 444.

83   **Shirer, "clear as a bell":** Shirer, *Berlin Diary*, p. 444.

83   **Shirer, "German army engineers":** Shirer, *Berlin Diary*, p. 414.

84   **Shirer, "Everything ... everything":** Shirer, *This Is Berlin*, p. 329.

84   **Inscription, "Here on the eleventh":** Shirer, *Berlin Diary*, p. 422.

84   **Shirer, "I have seen that face":** Shirer, *Berlin Diary*, p. 422.

84   **Shirer arranges for broadcast:** Shirer, *This Is Berlin*, p. 333.

84   **Shirer, "The armistice has":** Shirer, *This Is Berlin*, p. 333.

85   **Captain, "I don't care whether":** Sevareid, *Not So Wild a Dream*, p. 159.

85   **Sevareid, "The grizzled old Frenchmen":** Sevareid, *Not So Wild a Dream*, p. 159.

85   **Sevareid hears Shirer broadcast:** Sevareid, *Not So Wild a Dream*, p. 159.

85   **Murrow, "an Englishman who":** Murrow, *This Is London*, p. 129.

85   **Announcement, "Think of your":** Murrow, *This Is London*, p. 132.

85   **George VI, "Personally, I feel happier":** Keegan, *The Second World War*, p. 87.

Chapter 3: This Is London

87   **Epigraph:** Murrow, "A Reporter Remembers," farewell broadcast from London, 1946.

London Is Burning

89   **Sevareid, desertion:** Sevareid, *Not So Wild a Dream*, p. 159.

89   **Porter, "Air raids, ye know":** Sevareid, *Not So Wild a Dream*, p. 169.

89   **Shirer, "the suspense":** Shirer, *This Is Berlin*, p. 343.

89   **Sea Lion planning ordered:** Taylor, *Breaking Wave*, p. 214.

89   **Shirer, "Three hundred Germans":** Shirer, *This Is Berlin*, p. 353.

89   **Hitler peace offer:** *This Is Berlin*, p. 355.

89   **Shirer, "depressed":** *This Is Berlin*, p. 459.

90   **"The Few":** Taylor, *Breaking Wave*, p. 99.

91   **"First, that the Swastika":** Shirer, *Berlin Diary*, p. 462.

91   **Aircraft comparison:** Keegan, *The Second World War*, p. 94.

91   **British advantages:** Keegan, *The Second World War*, p. 94.

91   **Shirer, "Once in Belgium":** Shirer, *This Is Berlin*, p. 380.

91   **Shirer, "Nearby, a French":** Shirer, *This Is Berlin*, p. 380.

91   **Murrow, "Much of it":** Murrow, *This Is London*, p. 147.

91   **Shirer, "a gigantic, illuminated map"…"that map":** Shirer, *This Is Berlin*, p. 391.

92   **Hitler, quoted:** "The English ask": Shirer, *This Is Berlin*, p. 394.

92   **Shirer, Invasion rumor:** Shirer, *Berlin Diary*, p. 504.

92   **Attacks of August 24, 1940:** Keegan, *The Second World War*, p. 96.

92   **Aircraft losses:** Keegan, *The Second World War*, p. 96.

92   **Switch to London as target:** Keegan, *The Second World War*, p. 96.

92   **LeSueur, "a typical day":** LeSueur broadcast script for September 6, 1940, located in Eric Sevareid papers, U.S. Library of Congress.

92   **Murrow, "On the airdrome"; "The hollow grunt"; "told us these raids"; and "Vincent Sheean":** CBS broadcast, September 8, 1940.

94   **London casualties:** Shirer, *This Is Berlin*, p. 399.

94   **Shirer, "All this combined":** CBS broadcast, September 8, 1940.

94   **Attack of September 15, 1940:** Knightley, *The First Casualty*, p. 236.

From the Streets to the Rooftops

94   **LeSueur, "It was a sad sight":** CBS broadcast, September 29, 1940.

95   **Shirer, "I was talking":** Shirer, *This Is Berlin*, p. 413.

95   **Churchill approves broadcasts:** Persico, *Edward R. Murrow*, p. 173; CBS News Archives, *Edward R. Murrow: Reporting Live*, "Farewell to Studio 9," interview with Robert Trout, 1963.

95   **Sevareid, "will probably never know":** Sevareid, *Not So Wild a Dream*, p. 177.

95   **News media survey:** White, "Covering a War for Radio," p. 2.

96   **Sevareid:** "not trying to sell: Sevareid, *Not So Wild a Dream*, p. 177.

97   **Saerchinger opening:** Persico, *Edward R. Murrow*, p. 145.

97   **Ida Lou Anderson suggestion:** Persico, *Edward R. Murrow*, p. 145.

97   **Murrow, "I spent the day":** CBS broadcast, September 9, 1940.

97   **Murrow, "I saw a man":** Murrow, *This Is London*, p. 201.

97   **Murrow, "Walking down the street":** Murrow, *This Is London*, p. 16.

98   **Murrow, "This afternoon, I followed":** Murrow, *This Is London*, p. 220.

98   **Murrow, "a row of automobiles":** Murrow, *This Is London*, p. 178.

98   **Murrow, "Two cans of peaches":** Murrow, *This Is London*, p. 173.

98   **Murrow, "Watching that system":** Murrow, *This Is London*, p. 200.

98   **Hotel keeper, "That's right":** Murrow, *This Is London*, p. 190.

98   **Murrow, "old dowagers and":** Bliss (ed.), *In Search of Light*, p. 34.

98   **Murrow, "Just as I reached":** Murrow, *This Is London*, p. 143.

98   **Murrow, "The girls in light":** Murrow, *This Is London*, p. 173.

99   **Sevareid, "simply born to":** Sevareid, *Not So Wild a Dream*, p. 177.

99   **Murrow, "will engage":** Persico, *Edward R. Murrow*, p. 103.

99   **Murrow, "I have an old-fashioned":** Murrow, *This Is London*, p. 71.

99   **Murrow, "What I think":** Murrow, *This Is London*, p. 135.

99   **Murrow, "We are told today":** Murrow, *This Is London*, p. 163.

101   **Pyle, "As a nervous censor":** Schroth, *The American Journey of Eric Sevareid*, p. 166.

101   **Murrow coffee and cigarettes:** Sperber, *Murrow: His Life and Times*, p. 182.

101   **Janet Murrow broadcasting:** Kendrick, *Prime Time*, p. 188.

101   **Janet Murrow & Bundles for Britain:** Kendrick, *Prime Time*, p. 230.

101   **LeSueur's dressing in closet:** Sevareid, *Not So Wild a Dream*, p. 171.

101   **LeSueur, "would walk along":** Persico, *Edward R. Murrow*, p.175.

102   **Murrow on bomb shelter:** Persico, *Edward R. Murrow*, p. 172.

102   **Golf:** Perscio, *Edward R. Murrow*, p. 179.

102   **Sevareid ill and homesick:** Sevareid, *Not So Wild a Dream*, p. 178.

102   **Sevareid, "I would shuffle":** Sevareid, *Not So Wild a Dream*, p. 171.

Berlin Blues

102   **Shirer, "reduced to mouthing":** letter to Paul White, published in Shirer, *This Is Berlin*, p. 405.

102   **Shirer, "The English themselves":** Shirer, *This Is Berlin*, p. 414.

103   **Shirer offers to remain:** Shirer, *This Is Berlin*, p. 340.

103   **Brown, "the impression in Rome":** CBS broadcast, September 20, 1940.

103   **Tripartite Pact; Shirer comments:** Shirer, *Berlin Diary*, p. 532–534.

103   **Postponement of Sea Lion:** Keegan, *The Second World War*, p. 101.

103   **Shirer, "does not mean":** Shirer, *This Is Berlin*, p. 411.

103   **Murrow, "Germany has commandeered":** CBS broadcast, October 23, 1940.

103   **Keegan, "The victory of":** Keegan, *The Second World War*, p. 102.

104   **Shirer, "very skeptical":** Shirer, *Berlin Diary*, p. 558.

104   **Keitel, "an exceedingly difficult":** Taylor, *The Breaking Wave*, p. 211.

104   **Taylor, "However that might":** Taylor, *The Breaking Wave*, p. 270.

"I Was a Citizen of London"

105   **Murrow, "man to see":** Schroth, *The American Journey of Eric Sevareid*, p. 163.

105   **Ralph Ingersoll visit:** Recounted in *PM*, November 7, 1940.

105   **Murrow and RAF pilot:** *PM*, November 7, 1940.

105   **Sevareid departure:** Sevareid, *Not So Wild a Dream*, p. 180.

105   **Sevareid, "a peaceable":** Sevareid, *Not So Wild a Dream*, p. 179.

105   **Sevareid, "others will say":** Sevareid, *Not So Wild a Dream*, p. 179. Office bombing: Shirer, *Berlin Diary*, p. 603.

106   **Shirer, "We have worked":** Shirer, *Berlin Diary*, p. 604.

106 **Shirer, "We had a presentiment":** Shirer, *Berlin Diary*, p. 604.

106 **Shirer, "It's impossible to get around":** Shirer, *This Is Berlin*, p. 423.

106 **Shirer, "Most people [in Germany] thought:** CBS broadcast, December 29, 1940.

106 **Sevareid, "the most tragic year":** CBS broadcast, December 29, 1940.

106 **Murrow, "The first year":** CBS broadcast, December 29, 1940.

107 **Murrow quotes Wordsworth:** CBS broadcast, December 29, 1940.

107 **Briton, "I have not the faintest":** Letter from Lance/Corporal George Miller to Eric Sevareid, November 18, 1940, Eric Sevareid papers, Library of Congress.

107 **Sevareid, "were no longer":** Sevareid, *Not So Wild a Dream*, p. 179.

107 **Sevareid, "It is not just"..."do you think":** Eric Sevareid letter to Robert Sherwood, February 19, 1941, Sevareid papers.

107 **Collingwood at Oxford:** Barnouw, *The Golden Web*, p. 185

107 **Smith on Collingwood:** Smith, *Events Leading up to My Death*, p. 82.

108 **Collingwood and suit pressing:** *Newsweek*, April 5, 1943, p. 44.

108 **Murrow, "glanced down at":** Persico, *Edward R. Murrow*, p. 199.

109 **CHARLES COLLINGWOOD, 1917–1985:** biographical material was drawn from Cloud & Olson, *The Murrow Boys*, Sperber, *Murrow: His Life and Times*; and "Charles C. Collingwood," Michigan Journalism Hall of Fame (website: *hof.jrn.msu.edu/bios/colling.html*).

110 **Smith working with Shirer:** Smith, *Last Train from Berlin*, p. 104.

110 **Flannery hires Smith:** Smith, *Events Leading up to My Death*, p. 104

110 **Four Freedoms:** James McGregor Burns, *Roosevelt: Soldier of Freedom*, Harcourt Brace Jovanovich, New York, p. 34.

110 **Lend-Lease passage:** Keegan, *The Second World War*, p. 112.

110 **Murrow, "they will now serve":** CBS broadcast, April 9, 1941.

111 **Murrow, "The winter that is ending":** Murrow, *This Is London*, p. 231.

111 **British welcoming invasion:** Murrow, *This Is London*, p. 234.

111 **Brown, "According to":** CBS broadcast, April 8, 1941.

111 **Burdett, "the entire Greek army":** CBS broadcast, April 9, 1941.

111 **Burdett, "German armored troops":** CBS broadcast, April 12, 1941.

111 **Burdett, "Until now German":** CBS broadcast, April 12, 1941.

111 **Evacuation from Greece:** Keegan, *The Second World War*, p. 158.

111 **Evacuation from Crete:** Keegan, *The Second World War*, p. 171.

111 **Burdett assignments:** CBS broadcast logs.

112 **Burdett single broadcast:** Log for CBS broadcast, May 26, 1941.

112 **Flannery, "a cowardly and":** CBS broadcast, May 26, 1941.

112 **Murrow, "one of those nights":** CBS broadcast, April 16, 1941.

112 **Murrow, "Tonight, having been":** CBS broadcast, April 16, 1941.

112 **Murrow, "Then, a tearing":** Persico, *Edward R. Murrow*, p. 187.

112 **LeSueur, "Big Ben":** CBS broadcast, May 11, 1941.

Berlin or Washington

113   **Gallup poll results:** *Newsweek*, June 9, 1941, p. 16.
113   **Murrow, "to admit that British victory":** CBS broadcast, May 26, 1941
113   **Radio audience:** *Newsweek*, June 9, 1941; p. 13.
113   **Roosevelt, "every possible":** *Newsweek*, June 9, 1941, p. 15.
114   **Roosevelt, "stepping stones":** *Newsweek*, June 9, 1941, p. 15.
114   **Murrow, "a great speech":** CBS broadcast, May 28, 1941.
114   **Smith, "neither new nor convincing":** CBS broadcast, May 28, 1941.
114   **Editorial, "a 'gangster'":** Smith, *Last Train From Berlin,* p. 211.
114   **Reporters' phones bugged:** Smith, *Last Train from Berlin*, p. 217.
114   **Smith, "was plenty scared":** Smith, *Last Train from Berlin*, p. 219.
114   **Smith, "My heart bobbed":** Smith, *Last Train from Berlin*, p. 219
114   **Hottelet arrest:** Cloud & Olson, *Murrow's Boys*, p. 200
114   **Hottelet possible trial:** Smith, *Last Train from Berlin*, p. 225–226.
114   **Hottelet release:** Cloud & Olson, *Murrrow's Boys*, p. 200.
115   **Smith resigns UP, moves to CBS:** Smith, *Last Train from Berlin*, p. 67.
116   **Russian books unavailable:** Smith, *Events Leading up to My Death*, p. 107.
116   **Soviet non-participation, White:** "Covering a War For Radio," p. four.
116   **Sevareid, "equal time":** Schroth, *American Journey of Eric Sevareid*, p. 193.
116   **White, "It seems to me that":** Schroth, *American Journey of Eric Sevareid*, p. 193.
116   **Sevareid, "be silenced or denied"…"paralyze its action":** Six-page typescript letter from Eric Sevareid to Paul White [undated, but refers to July 5, 1941 as "last week"], p. 3.
116   **White, "I don't believe":** White letter to Sevareid, July 15, 1941, Eric Sevareid papers
116   **Smith, "On the central front":** CBS broadcast, October 12, 1941.
117   **Germans announce victory:** Smith, *Last Train from Berlin*, p. 90.
117   **Smith, "After hours of fighting":** CBS broadcast, October 12, 1941.
117   **Smith, German rationing:** Smith, *Last Train from Berlin*, p. 124
117   **Gasoline rationing:** Smith, *Last Train from Berlin*, p. 134.
117   **Barbe, "Sugar is universally":** CBS broadcast, October 12, 1941.
117   **Shirer described as "ingrate":** Smith, *Last Train from Berlin*, p. 51.
117   **Smith, "a conversation":** Smith, *Last Train from Berlin*, p. 111.
117   **German official, "You have gotten away":** Smith, *Events Leading up to My Death*, p. 111.
118   **Smith receives visa:** Smith, *Events Leading up to My Death*, p. 115.
118   **Remarks delivered at dinner:** "In Honor of a Man and an ideal," "Three Talks on Freedom, December 2, 1941, Waldorf Astoria, New York, New York; published by CBS, located in Eric Sevareid papers, Library of Congress, Washington, D.C.
118   **MacLeish, "the superstition":** Dinner remarks, p. 6
118   **"You burned the city":** Dinner remarks, p. 7.
118   **Paley, "we would not be meeting":** Dinner remarks, p. 11.

118 **Murrow's remarks, beginning, "That was":** Dinner remarks, p. 20. Murrow: "Lend-**Lease is not**": Dinner remarks, p. 23.

118 **Murrow, "If England is forced":** Dinner remarks, p. 30.

118 **Murrow, "if America comes in":** Dinner remarks, p. 25.

119 **Murrow, "Coming as I do":** Dinner remarks, p. 34.

Chapter 4: America at War

121 **Epigraph:** Franklin D. Roosevelt, address to Congress, December 8, 1941.

To Awaken a Sleeping Giant

123 **Smith told, "My dear Smith":** Smith, *Last Train from Berlin*, p. 352.

123 **Smith departure:** Smith, *Last Train to Berlin*, p. 352.

123 **Smith, "I said I":** Smith, *Last Train to Berlin*, p. 354.

124 **Sailing behind weather front:** Keegan, *The Second World War*, p. 253.

124 **Pearl Harbor attack:** Keegan, *The Second World War*, p. 255.

125 **Murrow gets news:** Persico, *Edward R. Murrow*, p. 193.

125 **Gilmore, "The Japs bombed":** Larry LeSueur, *Twelve Months That Changed the World*, Knopf, 1943, p. 74.

125 **Murrows confirm dinner invitation:** Persico, *Edward R. Murrow*, p. 193.

125 **Dinner at the White House:** Schroth, *The American Journey of Eric Sevareid*, p. 176.

125 **Murrow and FDR discuss British:** Persico, *Edward R. Murrow*, p. 194.

126 **FDR talks off the record:** Kendrick, *Prime Time*, p. 240.

126 **Sevareid broadcast on bonfire at Japanese embassy:** CBS broadcast, December 7, 1941.

126 **Murrow, "It's pretty bad":** Persico, *Edward R. Murrow*, p. 197.

126 **Murrow hears "day of infamy":** Kendrick, *Prime Time*, p. 241.

126 **Sevareid broadcast:** Schroth, *American Journey of Eric Sevareid*, p. 197.

Sinking Ships

127 **Brown, "Out towning":** Brown, *Suez to Singapore*, Random House, 1942, p. 295.

127 **Tennant, "We are off":** Brown, *Suez to Singapore*, p. 298.

127 **Brown, "stretched out across":** Brown, *Suez to Singapore*, p. 315.

127 **Tennant, "We have dodged":** Brown, *Suez to Singapore*, p. 320.

127 **Brown, "From all angles":** CBS broadcast, December 12, 1941.

127 **Sailor dives from tower:** Brown, *Suez to Singapore*, p. 324.

127 **Brown, "I cannot lie here":** Cloud & Olson, *The Murrow Boys*, p. 149.

129 **Brown jumps twenty feet:** Brown, *Suez to Singapore*, p. 327.

129 **Brown escapes from *Repulse*:** *Newsweek*, December 12, 1941, p. 18.

129 **Casualties:** Brown, *Suez to Singapore*, p. 341.

129 **Floating oil:** Brown, *Suez to Singapore*, p. 344.

129 **Brown, "I was aboard":** Cloud & Olson, *The Murrow Boys*, p. 150.

129 **White, "Overjoyed your rescue":** Brown, *Suez to Singapore*, p. 342.

129 **Cerf, "We want to publish":** Brown, *Suez to Singapore*, p. 343.

The Fall of Singapore

130 **Poor British preparation:** Keegan, *The Second World War*, p. 257.

130 **Japanese advance:** Keegan, *The Second World War*, p. 258.

130 **Brown, "The fighting thus far":** Brown, *Suez to Singapore*, p. 363.

130 **Brown, "walking death" and "by an apathy":** Brown, *Suez to Singapore*, p. 372.

130 **Brown, "To these people":** CBS broadcast, January 3, 1942.

130 **British official, "I have this day":** Brown, *Suez to Singapore*, p. 401.

130 **Bracken, "Mr. Brown's comments":** Brown, *Suez to Singapore*, p. 435.

131 CECIL BROWN, 1907–1987: biographical material was drawn from Cloud & Olson, *The Murrow Boys*; Library of America, *Reporting World War II: Part One*; and Sperber, *Murrow: His Life and Times*.

132 **Brown $1,000 bonus:** Brown, *Suez to Singapore*, p. 410.

132 **British forced to Singapore:** Keegan, *The Second World War*, p. 258.

132 **British surrender:** Keegan, *The Second World War*, p. 261.

132 **Collingwood, "as a strategic":** CBS broadcast, February 15, 1942.

132 **Brown assessment of Singapore:** CBS broadcast, February 15, 1942.

War in Russia

133 **LeSueur's frozen shaving cream:** LeSueur, *Twelve Months That Changed the World*, p. 110.

133 **LeSueur sails aboard *Temple Arch*:** LeSueur, *Twelve Months That Changed the World*, p. 3.

133 **Reports of Soviet defeat:** LeSueur, *Twelve Months That Changed the World*, p. 9–10.

133 **LeSueur, "might be a last-minute":** LeSueur, *Twelve Months That Changed the World*, p. 13.

133 **seventeen-day train journey:** LeSueur, *Twelve Months That Changed the World*, p. 28.

133 **Bathing at −15:** LeSueur, *Twelve Months That Changed the World*, p. 35.

133 **LeSueur reaches Kuibyshev:** LeSueur, *Twelve Months That Changed the World*, p. 28.

133 **German advance stalls:** Keegan, *The Second World War*, 202.

133 **Knightley, "Marooned in Kuibyshev":** Knightley, *The First Casualty*, p. 250.

134 **Cable delay; broadcast time:** LeSueur, *Twelve Months That Changed the World*, p. 56–57.

134 **"very" vs. "much":** LeSueur, *Twelve Months That Changed the World*, p. 69.

134 **LeSueur falls ill:** LeSueur, *Twelve Months That Changed the World*, p. 70.

134 **LeSueur goes to Moscow:** LeSueur, *Twelve Months That Changed the World*, p. 85.

134 **LeSueur, "grim-faced":** LeSueur, *Twelve Months That Changed the World*, p. 82.

134 **LeSueur, "The Soviet Union has":** CBS broadcast, January 9, 1942.

135   **LeSueur, "no Soviet spokesman":** LeSueur, *Twelve Months That Changed the World*, p. 268.

135   **Correspondent translates *Pravda*:** Knightley, *The First Casualty*, p. 250.

136   **LeSueur, "I have been wasting":** LeSueur, *Twelve Months That Changed the World*, p. 126–127.

136   **LeSueur, "informing me":** LeSueur, *Twelve Months That Changed the World*, p. 127.

136   **LeSueur, "They work in":** LeSueur, *Twelve Months That Changed the World*, p. 131.

136   **1,523 factories moved:** Keegan, *The Second World War*, p. 210.

136   **Iron crosses at exhibit:** LeSueur, *Twelve Months That Changed the World*, p. 147.

136   **LeSueur, "old tin hat":** LeSueur, *Twelve Months That Changed the World*, p. 155.

136   **LeSueur, "Reassured by my":** LeSueur, *Twelve Months That Changed the World*, p. 155.

137   **LARRY LeSUEUR, 1909–2003:** biographical material was drawn from Cloud & Olson, *The Murrow Boys*; Library of America, *Reporting World War II: Part One*; Sperber, *Murrow: His Life and Times*; and Associated Press, "One of WWII 'Murrow Boys'" (obituary), *Chicago Tribune*, sec. 2, p. 15.

138   **Trout, "the civilized world":** CBS broadcast, May 14, 1942.

138   **LeSueur, "According to latest":** CBS broadcast, May 14, 1942.

138   **LeSueur, "Timoshenko's actions":** CBS broadcast, May 16, 1942.

139   **LeSueur, "Naturally, there are":** CBS broadcast, May 16, 1942.

139   **LeSueur donates blood:** LeSueur, *Twelve Months That Changed the World*, p. 248.

139   **Effect of Lend-Lease:** LeSueur, *Twelve Months That Changed the World*, p. 229.

139   **Moscow joke:** LeSueur, *Twelve Months That Changed the World*, p. 276.

139   **Germans renew offensive:** Keegan, *The Second World War*, p. 237.

139   **Announcer, "Many experts":** CBS broadcast, September 9, 1942.

139   **No western correspondent:** Knightley, *The First Casualty*, p. 261.

139   **LeSueur, "The greatest threat":** CBS broadcast, September 9, 1942.

139   **LeSueur departs Soviet Union:** LeSueur, *Twelve Months That Changed the World*, p. 338.

139   **LeSueur's health declines:** Sevareid, *Not So Wild a Dream*, p. 220.

139   **LeSueur in Cairo, "I left Moscow":** CBS broadcast, November 8, 1942.

140   **Surrender at Stalingrad:** Keegan, *The Second World War*, p. 237.

The Home Front

140   **Sevareid chief Washington correspondent:** Schroth, *The American Journey of Eric Sevareid*, p. 235.

140   **Murrow, "The urgent business":** Bliss, *In Search of Light*, p. 49.

140   **Sevareid, "Our military people":** Sevareid to Murrow, July 20, 1942, letter in Eric Sevareid file, Library of Congress, Washington, D.C.

141   **Murrow, "One is almost":** Bliss, *In Search of Light*, p. 56–57.

141   **Sevareid, "can get much more":** Sevareid to Murrow, July 20, 1942.

141   **Sevareid, "If you have":** Sevareid to Murrow, July 20, 1942.

141 **Sevareid, "I think I will"**: letter to William Francis, Velva, North Dakota, July 31, 1942, in Eric Sevareid file, Library of Congress, Washington, D.C.

141 **Paley visits London**: Smith, *In His Glory*, p. 205.

141 **On Murrow, "the eloquence of his voice"**: Smith, *In His Glory*, p. 166.

141 **Murrow hosts Paley**: Smith, *In His Glory*, p. 205.

142 **Murrow, "I certainly would not"**: Murrow letter to Sevareid, August 26, 1942, on file in Eric Sevareid papers, Library of Congress, Washington, D.C.

142 **Murrow, "so long as"**: Murrow to Sevareid, August 26, 1942.

142 **Sevareid, "merely a false"**: Sevareid, *Not So Wild a Dream*, p. 225.

142 **Letter, "It is heartening"**: Letter from Ann Johnson, September 17, 1942, Eric Sevareid file, Library of Congress, Washington, D.C.

143 **Letter, "the distance from actual danger"**: Letter from Edmund Sullivan, September 20, 1942, in Eric Sevareid file, Library of Congress, Washington, D.C.

143 **Letter, "moral sabotage"**: Letter from Edith Farrar, September 1942, Eric Sevareid file, Library of Congress, Washington, D.C.

143 **Sevareid, "I have had firsthand"**: Letter by Eric Sevareid, September 22, 1942, Eric Sevareid file, Library of Congress, Washington, D.C.

143 **Sevareid, "Through someone's carelessness"**: CBS broadcast, September 7, 1942.

Victory in North Africa

143 **North African offensive**: Keegan, *The Second World War*, p. 340.

144 **1,200 mile German advance**: Keegan, *The Second World War*, p. 331.

144 **Battle of El Alamein**: Keegan, *The Second World War*, p. 337.

144 **Vichy politics**: Keegan, *The Second World War*, p. 341.

144 **Burdett background**: *Current Biography* (New York: H.W. Wilson Company, 1943), p. 88.

144 **Burdett replaces Wason**: Cloud & Olson, *The Murrow Boys*, p. 123.

144 **"who wrote in hard, bright phrases"**: Persico, *Edward R. Murrow*, p. 202.

144 **Lea Schiavi death**: Cloud & Olson, *The Murrow Boys*, p. 163–164.

144 **Burdett, "all over but the shouting"**: CBS broadcast, November 8, 1942.

144 **Burdett, "packed with German"**: CBS broadcast, November 8, 1942.

145 **WINSTON BURDETT, 1916–1993**: biographical material was drawn from Cloud & Olson, *The Murrow Boys*; Sperber, *Murrow: His Life and Times*; and Persico, *Edward R. Murrow*.

146 **Sevareid, "A great point"**: CBS broadcast, November 7, 1942.

146 **Negotiations with Darlan**: Keegan, *The Second World War*, p. 341.

146 **Murrow, "The sound was pleasant"**: Bliss, *In Search of Light*, p. 53.

146 **Burdett, "Rommel is setting"**: CBS broadcast, November 16, 1942.

147 **Burdett, "It's true they have"**: CBS broadcast, November 16, 1942.

147 **Collingwood, "Algiers...is a vast showplace"**: CBS broadcast, November 15, 1942.

147 **Collingwood, "are not treating":** CBS broadcast, November 16, 1942.

147 **Murrow Darlan broadcast, including, "There is nothing":** Bliss, *In Search of Light*, p. 55.

147 **Letter to Paley, "Every commentator":** Hal Waldo, November 21, 1942, in Eric Sevareid file, Library of Congress, Washington, D.C.

147 **Burdett, "There's a pause":** CBS broadcast, December 23, 1942.

148 **Collingwood, "When you are":** CBS broadcast, December 23, 1942.

148 **Critic, "Each day":** Barnouw, *The Golden Web*, p. 185.

149 **Darlan assassination:** Olson & Cloud, *The Murrow Boys*, p. 159–160.

149 **Execution of assassin:** *Newsweek*, February 1, 1943, p. 60.

149 **Murrow, "The Germans drove":** Bliss, *In Search of Light*, p. 58.

149 **Murrow, "A year ago":** Bliss, *In Search of Light*, p. 59.

149 **Murrow, "we have brought hope":** Bliss, *In Search of Light*, p. 60.

150 **Attack at Kassarine:** Keegan, *The Second World War*, p. 342.

150 **Collingwood, "Veteran soldiers say":** Cloud & Olson, *The Murrow Boys*, p. 164.

150 **Burdett, "Outside it stood":** Cloud & Olson, *The Murrow Boys*, p. 165.

150 **Collingwood departs:** Cloud & Olson, *The Murrow Boys*, p. 165.

150 **Murrow on Collingwood:** letter to Sevareid, January 1, 1943, in the Eric Sevareid file, Library of Congress, Washington, D.C.

150 **Collingwood receives Peabody:** *Time*, April 5, 1943, p. 43.

150 **Peabody Committee, "conveyed to us":** quoted in *Current Biography*, [1943], H.W. Wilson Company, New York, 1943, p. 138.

150 **Collingwood youngest recipient:** *Time*, April 5, 1943, p. 44.

150 **Murrow, "young boys pushing":** Bliss, *In Search of Light*, p. 60.

151 **Murrow, "The infantry moved":** Bliss, *In Search of Light*, p. 61.

151 **Murrow, "A little further along":** Bliss, *In Search of Light*, p. 62.

151 **German surrender:** Keegan, *The Second World War*, p. 343.

151 **Brown loses sponsor:** Cloud & Olson, *The Murrow Boys*, p. 169.

151 **Brown, "People are in need":** Cecil Brown broadcast script for August 8, 1943, on file with Cecil Brown Papers, Wisconsin State Historical Society, Madison, Wisconsin.

151 **Brown, "Any reasonably accurate":** Brown broadcast script of August 8, 1943.

152 **White, "would be of immense":** Cloud & Olson, *The Murrow Boys*, p. 170.

152 **CBS ad campaign:** Sperber, *Murrow: His Life and Times*, p. 226.

The War in the Air

152 **Murrow, "ought to be":** Persico, *Edward R. Murrow*, p. 197.

152 **Murrow attempts at commission:** Persico, *Edward R. Murrow*, p. 197.

152 **Murrow, "Let me ride in":** Persico, *Edward R. Murrow*, p. 209

152 **Anglo–American bombing strategy:** Keegan, *The Second World War*, p. 220.

152 **Smith describes raid:** Howard K. Smith broadcast script for May 24, 1943, in Smith papers, Wisconsin State Historical Society, Madison, Wisconsin.

152   **Bomber losses:** Persico, *Edward R. Murrow*, p. 209.

154   **Murrow offered WSC presidency:** Persico, *Edward R. Murrow*, p. 205.

154   **Murrow offered publisher's post:** Persico, *Edward R. Murrow*, p. 203.

154   **Murrow offered BBC:** Persico, *Edward R. Murrow*, p. 206.

154   **FDR suggests China mission:** Schroth, *American Journey of Eric Sevareid*, p. 207.

154   **Sevareid departure:** Schroth, *American Journey of Eric Sevareid*, p. 211.

154   **Sevareid aircraft engine failure and parachuting:** Sevareid, *Not So Wild a Dream*, p. 251–254.

154   **Plane drops note:** Sevareid, *Not So Wild a Dream*, p. 259.

154   **Sevareid, "also held wide-bladed":** Sevareid, *Not So Wild a Dream*, p. 260.

154   **Sevareid, "How!":** Sevareid, *Not So Wild a Dream*, p. 260.

154   **Message, "as they probably":** Schroth, *American Journey of Eric Sevareid*, p. 213.

155   **Davies, "Dr. Sevareid":** Sevareid, *Not So Wild a Dream*, p. 267.

155   **Sevareid, "closed his eyes":** Sevareid, *Not So Wild a Dream*, p. 268.

156   **Sevareid, "spoke in an Oxford":** Sevareid, *Not So Wild a Dream*, p. 283.

156   **Village took 106 heads:** Sevareid, *Not So Wild a Dream*, p. 283.

156   **Sevareid, "Adams took a great risk":** Sevareid, *Not So Wild a Dream*, p. 288.

156   **Return trek:** Sevareid, *Not So Wild a Dream*, p. 290.

156   **Sevareid, "Burmese jungle headhunters":** Schroth, *American Journey of Eric Sevareid*, p. 218.

156   **Sevareid, "It is staggering to realize":** CBS broadcast, September 10, 1943.

157   **Meets Stilwell:** Schroth, *American Journey of Eric Sevareid*, p. 224.

157   **Letter, "President Chiang will not":** October 1, 1943 letter, signature illegible, to Sevareid from Ministry of Information, Chungking, China.

157   **Sevareid illness and departure:** Schroth, *American Journey of Eric Sevareid*, p. 227.

157   **Sevareid essay fails censorship:** Schroth, *American Journey of Eric Sevareid*, p. 228.

157   **Pre-flight snack:** Bliss, *In Search of Light*, p. 70.

157   **Murrow, "where men must burn":** Bliss, *In Search of Light*, p. 71.

157   **Murrow, "a cigarette lighter":** Bliss, *In Search of Light*, p. 71.

157   **Murrow, "The clouds below us":** Bliss, *In Search of Light*, p. 72.

157   **Murrow, "The longest flight":** Bliss, *In Search of Light*, p. 72.

157   **Murrow, "The knees should have":** Bliss, *In Search of Light*, p.73.

158   **Murrow, "the old man reached out":** Bliss, *In Search of Light*, p. 75.

158   **Fifty aircraft shot down:** Persico, *Edward R. Murrow*, p. 216.

158   **Janet Murrow, "He sounded shaken":** Persico, *Edward R. Murrow*, p. 216.

158   **White, "I hope you are cured":** Letter from Paul White to Edward R. Murrow, December 8, 1943, from Edward R. Murrow papers, Library of Congress, Washington, D.C.

158   **Paley, "What do you":** Paley, *As It Happened*, p. 152.

158   **Sevareid, "He could be scared":** Persico, *Edward R. Murrow*, p. 221.

160   **Two dozen missions:** Persico, *Edward R. Murrow*, p. 222.

Italy

160 **Mussolini overthrow:** Keegan, *The Second World War*, p. 349.

160 **Smith report, Germans entering Italy:** Howard K. Smith broadcast script for July 27, 1943, on file with Smith Papers, Wisconsin State Historical Society, Madison, Wisconsin.

160 **Smith, "told their typesetters":** Smith script of July 27, 1943.

160 **Mussolini rescued:** Keegan, *The Second World War*, p. 351.

160 **Allied landing in Italy:** Keegan, *The Second World War*, p. 352.

160 **Stalled advance:** Keegan, *The Second World War*, p. 359.

161 **Landing at Anzio:** Keegan, *The Second World War*, p. 359.

161 **Sevareid, "You could not see":** Sevareid, *Not So Wild a Dream*, p. 367.

161 **Sevareid, "Weeks go by":** Sevareid, *Not So Wild a Dream*, p. 376.

161 **Sevareid, "Those men had a cold":** Sevareid, *Not So Wild a Dream*, p. 379.

161 **Sevareid at Anzio:** Schroth, *The American Journey of Eric Sevareid*, p. 246.

161 **Final Allied push:** Keegan, *The Second World War*, p. 360.

162 **Sevareid, "One never saw":** Sevareid, *Not So Wild a Dream*, p. 388.

162 **Sevareid, "The breakout":** CBS broadcast, May 23, 1944.

163 **Sevareid, "staring at the roof":** CBS broadcast, May 23, 1944.

163 **Sevareid May 25 scoop:** Schroth, *The American Journey of Eric Sevareid*, p. 248.

163 **Burdett, "up the swerving coast road":** CBS broadcast, May 25, 1944.

163 **Change in Allied plan:** Keegan, *The Second World War*, p. 361.

163 **Burial sergeant, "It isn't true":** Sevareid, *Not So Wild a Dream*, p. 402.

164 **Sevareid, "one of the most dramatic":** Sevareid, *Not So Wild a Dream*, p. 412.

164 **Sevareid locates transmitter:** Sevareid, *Not So Wild a Dream*, p. 415.

164 **Burdett's account from Rome:** CBS broadcast, June 5, 1944.

164 **Nation article:** *The Nation*, December 9, 1944, p. 713.

165 **Other historians agree:** Keegan, *The Second World War*, p. 362.

166 **Murrow, "The first flash":** and thereafter: CBS broadcast, June 5, 1944.

166 **Sevareid, "Eisenhower has announced":** Sevareid, *Not So Wild a Dream*, p. 417.

Chapter 5: Invasion and Liberation

167 **Epigraph:** Eisenhower, "Order of the Day," June 6, 1944.

D-Day

169 **Murrow reads Eisenhower's order:** June 6, 1944. CBS broadcast, June 6, 1944.

169 **Murrow, "complex beyond description":** Bliss, *In Search of Light*, p. 78.

169 **invasion preparation broadcast:** Kendrick, *Prime Time*, p. 265.

169 **Murrow hires Hottelet; Downs to England:** Persico, *Edward R Murrow*, p. 218.

169 **Five CBS correspondents chosen:** Persico, *Edward R. Murrow*, p. 223.

170 **use of tape recorders:** Kendrick, *Prime Time*, p. 268.

170 **Rommel appointment; German preparations:** Keegan, *The Second World War*, p. 372.

170 **Murrow receives wake-up call:** Sperber, *Murrow: His Life and Times*, p. 239.

170 **LeSueur et al, into battle:** Sperber, Murrow: *His Life and Times*, p. 241.

170 **Keegan, "The spectacle that confronted":** Keegan, *The Second World War*, p. 381.

170 **"The sky thundered":** Keegan, *The Second World War*, p. 382.

170 **Wren anecdote and "The one word":** Bliss, *In Search of Light*, p. 82–83.

170 **Hottelet broadcasts:** Sperber, *Murrow, His Life and Times*, p. 241.

170 **Collingwood difficulties with tape recorder:** Sperber, *Murrow: His Life and Times*, p. 241.

170 **LeSueur on seasickness:** Cloud & Olson, *The Murrow Boys*, p. 205.

171 RICHARD C. HOTTELET, 1917–: biographical material was drawn from Cloud & Olson, *The Murrow Boys*; Hottelet, "'Guest' of the Gestapo: Sour Food, Threats of Klieg Light Treatment, Cold, and Endless Monotony—U.S. Newsman Tells of Four Months in a Nazi Prison," *San Francisco Chronicle*, August 3, 1941; Library of America, *Reporting World War II: Part Two*; Persico, *Edward R. Murrow*; Daniel Schorr, *Staying Tuned: A Life in Journalism* (New York: Washington Square Press), 2002; and "Richard Hottelet," Speakers Agency (website: *www.speakersagency.com/ghi/ho-ri.html*).

172 **Casualties at Utah Beach:** Keegan, *The Second World War*, p. 383.

172 **German officer killed:** Cloud & Olson, *The Murrow Boys*, p. 206.

172 **Murrow reads Collingwood report:** CBS broadcast, June 6, 1944.

172 **Light opposition on four beaches:** Keegan, *The Second World War*, p. 385.

173 **Hard fight at Omaha Beach:** Keegan, *The Second World War*, p. 387.

173 **Trout relays Churchill comments:** CBS broadcast, June 6, 1944.

173 **Murrow, "Hello, New York":** CBS broadcast, June 6, 1944.

173 **Exchange between Murrow, "An elderly charwomen" and White:** "I had a young": CBS broadcast, June 6, 1944.

173 **Murrow, "We'll be here":** CBS broadcast, June 6, 1944.

174 **Eisenhower, "People of western Europe":** CBS broadcast, June 6, 1944.

174 **Stevenson, "Of course you've heard":** CBS broadcast, June 6, 1944.

174 **Murrow, "As a matter of fact":** CBS broadcast, June 6, 1944.

174 **Murrow, "Early this morning":** Bliss, *In Search of Light*, p. 81.

174 **Murrow, "You almost wanted":** Bliss, *In Search of Light*, p. 81.

175 **Murrow, "We are attempting":** Bliss, *In Search of Light*, p. 82.

175 **Rumors of LeSueur/Collingwood deaths:** Cloud & Olson, *The Murrow Boys*, p. 208.

175 **Murrow, "The latest word":** CBS broadcast, June 7, 1944.

176 **Murrow, "Those who are impatient":** CBS broadcast, June 7, 1944.

176 **Collingwood, "This beach…is still under":** CBS broadcast, June 8, 1944.

176 **Collingwood, "Yesterday, I was in France":** CBS broadcast, June 9, 1944.

176 **Collingwood, "sergeant in his foxhole":** CBS broadcast, June 9, 1944.

176 **Collingwood, "Men, with infinite tenderness":** CBS broadcast, June 9, 1944.

177 **BILL DOWNS, 1913–1978:** biographical material was drawn from Cloud & Olson, *The Murrow Boys*; and Persico, *Edward R. Murrow.*

178 **Hottelet, "Weather today has" and report on prisoners:** CBS broadcast, June 6, 1944.

178 **LeSueur, "Men are shaving again":** Cloud & Olson, *The Murrow Boys*, p. 211.

178 **LeSueur, "they know that":** Cloud & Olson, *The Murrow Boys*, p. 211.

179 **Difficulty with hedgerows:** Keegan, *The Second World War*, p. 390.

179 **Breakthrough at St. Lô:** Keegan, *The Second World War*, p. 394.

179 **Patton's breakthrough:** Keegan, *The Second World War*, p. 406.

179 **Reports from Pacific:** listed in CBS "News of the World" summaries for June 6–13, National Archives, College Park, Maryland.

Invading the South of France

179 **Sevareid lands in south of France:** Schroth, *The American Journey of Eric Sevareid*, p. 252.

179 **French and American forces:** Keegan, *The Second World War*, p. 411.

179 **Landing near Saint-Maxime:** *The American Journey of Eric Sevareid*, p. 252.

179 **Sevareid, "Nobody on board":** Sevareid, *Not So Wild a Dream*, p. 429.

179 **Sevareid, "the spectacle of power":** Sevareid, *Not So Wild a Dream*, p. 429.

179 **Few Germans in sight:** Sevareid, *Not So Wild a Dream*, p. 431.

179 **Sevareid, "Between bursts of":** Sevareid, *Not So Wild a Dream*, p. 432.

180 **Sevareid, "Where the Germans are now":** 8/15/44.

180 **Story of Sevareid in Cannes:** Sevareid, *Not So Wild a Dream*, p. 438.

180 **Sevareid, "a relatively new":** *Not So Wild a Dream*, p. 438.

180 **Burdett, "are guiding our forces":** CBS broadcast, August 19, 1944.

180 **Allies reach Grenoble:** Keegan, *The Second World War*, p. 411.

180 **Sevareid, "they would burst into":** Sevareid, *Not So Wild a Dream*, p. 442.

181 **German atrocities:** Sevareid, *Not So Wild a Dream*, p. 450.

181 **Germans executed:** Sevareid, *Not So Wild a Dream*, p. 453

181 **Sevareid, "I would like to make":** *The American Journey of Eric Sevareid*, p. 262.

181 **Sevareid surrounded:** Sevareid, *Not So Wild a Dream*, p. 445–446.

181 **Sevareid, "I felt at first":** Sevareid, *Not So Wild a Dream*, p. 445.

181 **Sevareid and the tank:** Sevareid, *Not So Wild a Dream*, p. 447.

182 **Sevareid encounters Stein:** Sevareid, *Not So Wild a Dream*, p. 459.

182 **Stein on Hitler's romanticism:** Sevareid: *Not So Wild a Dream*, p. 90.

182 **Stein on Germans:** Sevareid, *Not So Wild a Dream*, p. 459.

182 **Stein, " I can tell you that liberty":** Sevareid, *Not So Wild a Dream*, p. 462.

Liberation of Paris

182 **Collingwood/LeSueur rivalry:** Cloud & Olson, *The Murrow Boys*, p. 213; and Larry Collins & Dominique Lapierre, *Is Paris Burning?* (New York: Simon & Schuster, 1965), p. 197.

182 LeSueur, "The last signal": CBS broadcast, August 19, 1944.

183 Collingwood liberates Paris: Kendrick, *Prime Time*, p. 273.

183 Hottelet, "Columbia's Charles Collingwood reports": CBS broadcast, August 23, 1944.

184 Pons sings "The Marseillaise": Collins & Lapierre, *Is Paris Burning?*, p. 213.

184 LeSueur, "Paris has not yet been entered": CBS broadcast, August 24, 1944.

184 Censor, "was the first inkling": Bob Foster, *San Francisco Today*, September 4, 1982.

184 Reports of fighting elsewhere: listed in CBS "The World Today" summary for August 26, 1944, National Archives, College Park, MD. Hereafter: "The World Today."

184 Smiths cross border to Annecy: Smith, *Events Leading up to My Death*, p. 135–136.

185 Smiths' car ride and plane trip: Smith, *Events Leading up to My Death*, p. 142.

186 Smith, "a short, burning essay": Smith, *Events Leading up to My Death*, p. 142.

186 Smith, "rather like dead seaweed": Smith, *Events Leading up to My Death*, p. 142.

186 Collingwood greets Smith: Smith, *Events Leading up to My Death*, p. 143.

186 Collingwood and night life: Smith, *Events Leading up to My Death*, p. 144.

186 Editor, "I gave my man": Smith, *Events Leading up to My Death*, p. 144.

186 Smith, "I did not think": Smith, *Events Leading up to My Death*, p. 145.

186 Smith assigned to Ninth Army: Smith, *Events Leading up to My Death*, p. 145.

186 Murrow, "There was the memory": Bliss, *In Search of Light*, p. 86.

187 HOWARD K. SMITH, 1914–2002: biographical material was drawn from Cloud & Olson, *The Murrow Boys*; Library of America, *Reporting World War II: Part One*; ABCNews.com, "Journalist Howard K. Smith Dies" (website: abcnews.go.com/sections/us/ DailyNews/smith_obito20218.html), February 18, 2002; and Smith, *Events Leading up to My Death*.

"War Is Still War"
188 Plans for Market Garden: Keegan, *The Second World War*, p. 437.

189 Murrow, "looking out the window": Bliss, *In Search of Light*, p. 84.

189 Murrow, "You occasionally see": Bliss, *In Search of Light*, p. 84.

189 Murrow, "In just about": CBS broadcast, September 17, 1944.

189 British casualties: Keegan, *The Second World War*, p. 438.

189 Invasion of Philippines: Keegan, *The Second World War*, p. 554.

189 Correspondents at front: Cloud & Olson, *The Murrow Boys*, p. 227.

189 Smith, "carefully writing": Cloud & Olson, *The Murrow Boys*, p. 224.

189 Smith, "For fifteen": Howard K. Smith broadcast script for November 4, 1944, with Smith papers, Mass Communications History Collections, Wisconsin State Historical Society, Madison, Wisconsin. Hereafter, Smith script.

190 Smith, "didn't flutter an eyelid": Smith script for November 4, 1944.

190 Hottlelet–Smith–Calmer broadcast: Smith script for November 17, 1944.

190 Hottelet, "All of them": Smith script for November 17, 1944.

190 **Calmer, "I sure wish":** Smith script for November 17, 1944.

190 **Hottelet, "The Germans still have":** Smith script for November 17, 1944.

190 **Hottelet, "Right down below us":** Cloud & Olson, *The Murrow Boys*, p. 229.

192 **Sevareid, "Your map":** Sevareid, *Not So Wild a Dream*, p. 474.

192 **Sevareid, "We shall see":** Sevareid, *Not So Wild a Dream*, p. 474.

192 **Dunn reports Leyte Gulf:** CBS "The World Today" summary, October 25, 1944.

London

192 **Burdett, "There was a shock":** Persico, *Edward R. Murrow*, p. 240.

193 **Sevareid comments on London:** Schroth, *The American Journey of Eric Sevareid*, p. 261.

193 **V-1s and V-2s:** Keegan, *The Second World War*, p. 581–582.

193 **Murrow, "This demonstration"…"Allied nations":** Bliss, *In Search of Light*, p. 89.

193 **Murrow, "We are—we must be—less tired":** Bliss, *In Search of Light*, p. 90.

193 **Murrow returns to America:** Kendrick, *Prime Time*, p. 274.

Battle of the Bulge

194 **Smith, "The war was anticlimax":** Smith script for December 28, 1944.

194 **German Ardennes offensive:** Keegan, *The Second World War*, p. 440.

194 **To Hottelet, "For Christ's sake":** Cloud & Olson, *The Murrows Boys*, p. 230.

194 **American response:** Keegan, *The Second World War*, p. 445.

195 **Smith, "when I heard that":** Smith, *Events Leading up to My Death*, p. 154.

195 **Smith on Betty Grable's husband:** Smith, *Events Leading Up To My Death*, p. 153.

195 **CBS New York, "Today, there were":** CBS broadcast, December 23, 1944.

195 **Hottelet, "Even though it's necessary"…"They're waiting":** CBS broadcast, December 23, 1944.

196 **Smith on Allied aircraft:** Smith script of December 26, 1944.

197 **Smith, "It fell off all by":** Smith script of December 26, 1944.

197 **Report proved true:** Keegan, *The Second World War*, p. 446.

197 **Smith, "Gerd von Runstedt":** Smith script, December 12, 1944.

197 **American counteroffensive:** Smith, *Events Leading up to My Death*, p. 154.

197 **German losses:** Keegan, *The Second World War*, p. 441.

197 **Fighting on Iwo Jima:** CBS "News of the World" summary, February 23, 1945.

Crossing the Rhine

197 **Crossing the Rhine:** Keegan, *The Second World War*, p. 518.

198 **Smith report from Cologne, including "They were pale"…"elastic crime":** Smith script of March 7, 1945.

198 **Sevareid, "I'm Eric Sevareid":** Smith, *Events Leading up to My Death*, p. 162.

198 **Sevareid, "Tomorrow, the great":** Sevareid, *Not So Wild a Dream*, p. 497.

198 **Sevareid, "Seven o'clock":** Sevareid, *Not So Wild a Dream*, p. 500.

198 **Smith, "single most terrifying spectacle":** CBS broadcast, March 24, 1945.

198 **British soldier, "Come on, come on"..."Their bodies seem":** CBS broadcast, March 24, 1945.

198 **Hottelet, "eating a larger":** Cloud & Olson, *The Murrow Boys*, p. 231.

199 **Announcer, "We now resume":** CBS broadcast, March 24, 1945.

199 **Allied and German strength:** Keegan, *The Second World War*, p. 519.

200 **Burdett, "a drive due east":** CBS broadcast, March 25, 1945.

200 **Downs, "The new bridgehead":** CBS broadcast, March 25, 1945.

200 **Invasion of Okinawa reported:** CBS "News of the World" summary, April 1, 1945.

Buchenwald

200 **Murrow poker winnings:** Persico, *Edward R. Murrow*, p. 227.

201 **Murrow's descriptions of Buchenwald:** CBS broadcast, April 15, 1945.

203 **Murrow, "I could have described three pairs of those shoes":** Ben Gross in *The New York Sunday News*, June 28, 1953, as quoted in Persico, *Edward R. Murrow*, p. 230.

203 **Murrow passing out money:** Sperber, *Murrow: His Life and Times*, p. 253.

203 **Murrow in tears:** Kendrick, *Prime Time*, p. 239.

203 **Death of Roosevelt:** Kendrick, *Prime Time*, p. 278.

204 **Murrow, "I do not believe":** Sperber, *Murrow: His Life and Times*, p. 253.

Surrender

204 **Murrow, "When they began to roll":** Bliss, *In Search of Light*, p. 95–96.

205 **Hottelet, "crawled out":** CBS broadcast, April 27, 1945.

205 **Smith, "From over a ridge":** Smith, *Events Leading up to My Death*, p. 166.

205 **Hottelet to Berlin:** Smith, *Events Leading up to My Death*, p. 166.

205 **German mass surrenders:** CBS broadcast, May 5, 1945.

205 **Collingwood, "are physically too tired":** Cloud & Olson, *The Murrow Boys*, p. 238.

205 **Murrow, "Six years is a long time":** Bliss, *In Search of Light*, p. 97.

206 **Murrow, "Europe has no doubt":** Bliss, *In Search of Light*, p. 98.

206 **Douglas Edwards from the Stag Head pub:** CBS broadcast, May 8, 1945.

206 **CBS V-E Day coverage:** summary of Columbia Broadcasting System V-E Day Coverage, May 8, 1945.

206 **Murrow from Piccadilly Circus, "Believe me":** CBS broadcast, May 8, 1945.

208 **Surrender ceremony and banquet:** Smith, *Events Leading up to My Death*, p. 171–172.

208 **American officer, "You will find":** Smith, *Events Leading Up To My Death*, p. 170.

208 **Smith, "The place was not just":** Smith broadcast of May 9, 1945.

208 **Smith:** Leaving Berlin; broadcasting from Paris: Smith, *Events Leading up to My Death*, p. 174.

208 **Bennie Smith, "No matter what":** Smith, *Events Leading up to My Death*, p. 174.

Chapter 6: Murrow's Legacy

209 **Epigraph:** Murrow, in an interview with Harry Reasoner (ca. 1960), from *Edward R. Murrow: Reporting Live* (New York: Bantam Audio, 1986).

Peace

211 **German cities in ruins:** Keegan, *The Second World War*, p. 591.

211 **Murrow, "only after its downfall":** Persico, *Edward R. Murrow*, p. 231.

211 **Murrow, "used up my good luck":** Smith, *Events Leading up to My Death*, p. 176.

211 **Murrow, "I am sick":** Sperber, Murrow: *His Life and Times*, p. 256.

211 **To White, "wearing his customary":** Persico, *Edward R. Murrow*, p. 204.

211 **On Murrow, "often conveys the impression":** Charles Wertenbaker, "The World On His Back," *The New Yorker*, December 26, 1953, p. 28. Hereafter, *New Yorker*.

213 **Fighting in Greece:** Keegan, *The Second World War*, p. 588.

214 **Murrow broadcast following Hiroshima:** CBS broadcast, September 1945.

215 **Churchill, "iron curtain":** Keegan, *The Second World War*, p. 593.

215 **Labor Party official to Smith on Churchill:** Smith, *Events Leading up to My Death*, p. 200.

215 **Collingwood, "Then, as these [hopes]":** Sperber, *Murrow: His Life and Times*, p. 295.

215 **Birth of Casey Murrow:** Persico, *Edward R. Murrow*, p. 233.

216 **Murrow accept CBS vice presidency:** Sperber, *Murrow: His Life and Times*, p. 259.

216 **Murrow, "I am persuaded" and "no retreat from":** Barnouw, *The Golden Web*, p. 237.

216 **Smith, "As I heard":** Smith, *Events Leading up to My Death*, p. 237.

216 **Reporter, "When I hear a broadcast":** Smith, *Events Leading Up To My Death*, p. 146.

216 **Smith gets London post:** Cloud & Olson, *The Murrow Boys*, p. 249.

216 **Murrow, "the high privilege":** Cloud & Olson, *The Murrow Boys*, p. 240.

216 **Shirer turns down London:** Cloud & Olson, *The Murrow Boys*, p. 246.

217 **Sevareid writes in California:** Schroth, *The American Journey of Eric Sevareid*, p. 271.

217 **Smith passes up Luce offer:** Sperber, *Murrow: His Life and Times*, p. 259.

217 **Smith gets Murrow's suit:** Sperber, *Murrow: His Life and Times*, p. 260.

217 **Postwar CBS news assignments:** Cloud & Olson, *The Murrow Boys*, p. 248–250.

217 **Sevareid, "a collection of":** Cloud & Olson, *The Murrow Boys*, p. 243.

217 **LeSueur, "We not only got" and "everybody else":** Cloud & Olson, *The Murrow Boys*, p. 251.

217 **"Murrow Isn't God" club:** *The New Yorker*, December 26, 1953, p. 36.

Delivering the News

218 **Murrow and others work anthologized:** *Reporting World War II [two volumes]*, Library of America, 1995.

218 **Bate and Prince of Wales:** Sperber, *Murrow: His Life and Times*, p. 102.

218 **NBC in Europe:** Sperber, Murrow: *His Life and Times,* p. 102.

218 **Shirer kept off air:** Shirer, *Berlin Diary,* p. 102.

218 **Jordan broadcasts:** Kendrick, *Prime Time,* p. 167.

219 **Hicks's broadcast:** Barnouw, *The Golden Web,* p. 199.

219 **Chaplin broadcast:** Barnouw, *The Golden Web,* p. 200.

219 **Murrow, "The clouds below us":** Bliss, *In Search of Light,* p. 72.

219 **Landry, "than a shipful":** Robert C. Landry, *Scribner's,* December 1938, p. 8.

219 **Survey:** Barnouw, *The Golden Web,* p. 168.

219 **Murrow compared to correspondents:** Persico, *Edward R. Murrow,* p. 242.

Murrow Considered

221 **Burdett, "something sovereign":** Persico, *Edward R. Murrow,* p. 240.

221 **Smith, "the most impressive":** Smith, *Events Leading Up To My Life,* p. 145.

221 **Sevareid, "that rare thing":** Bliss, *In Search of Light,* p. 82–83.

221 **Hottelet, "His camaraderie":** Persico, *Edward R. Murrow,* p. 233.

221 **Murrow born Egbert Roscoe:** Kendrick, *Prime Time,* p. 72.

221 **Smith, "It was hard to":** Smith, *Events Leading up to My Death,* p. 145.

222 **Kendrick, "All through school":** Kendrick, *Prime Time,* p. 107.

222 **Burdett, "Accurate diction":** Persico, *Edward R. Murrow,* p. 162.

222 **Kendrick, "people who heard him":** Kendrick, *Prime Time,* p. 165.

222 **Rowse, "a certain superciliousness":** Rowse, *Appeasement,* p. 117.

222 **Shirer, "the shadow of Nazi":** Shirer, *Berlin Diary,* p. 82.

222 **Smith in prewar Germany:** Smith, *Last Train from Berlin,* p. 12.

223 **Shirer, "says I'm making myself":** Shirer, *Berlin Diary,* p. 167.

223 **Murrow, "News programs are broadcast":** Schroth, *The American Journey of Eric Sevareid,* p. 172.

224 **Sevareid, "may share the soldier's":** Schroth, *The American Journey of Eric Sevareid,* p. 265.

224 **Masaryk and Murrow:** Persico, *Edward R. Murrow,* p. 142.

224 **Smith, "inner turbulence"..."He was exhausted":** Smith, *In All His Glory,* p. 176.

225 **Shirer, "birth of the":** Shirer, *Berlin Diary,* p. 112.

225 **Barnouw, "Americans began to hear":** Barnouw, *The Golden Web,* p. 140.

226 **MacLeish, "we knew [they] were":** Remarks delivered at dinner, "In Honor of a Man and an Ideal," December 2, 1941, published by CBS, p. 7.

226 **Paley, "pleasant speaking voice":** Paley, *As It Happened,* p. 120.

226 **Murrow, "from men who spent":** Persico, *Edward R. Murrow,* p. 219.

The Future of Broadcast News

226 **Murrow at convention:** Sperber, *Murrow: His Life and Times,* p. 315.

227 **Television audience:** Barnouw, *The Golden Web,* p. 257.

227 **Murrow, "We've been here":** Sperber, *Murrow: His Life and Times,* p. 315.

227 **Radio survey:** White, "Broadcasting a War for Radio," p. 2.

227 **Nielsen survey:** Kendrick, *Prime Time*, p. 349.

227 **Numbers of televisions:** Cloud & Olson, *The Murrow Boys*, p. 288.

227 **Television replaces piano:** Lynn Spigel, *Make Room for TV* (Chicago: University of Chicago Press, 1992), p. 38.

227 **Television talent:** Cloud & Olson, *The Murrow Boys*, p. 288.

227 *Hear It Now* **moved to TV:** Smith, *Events Leading up to My Death*, p. 218.

228 **Switch and talk:** Sperber, *Murrow: His Life and Times*, p. 292.

228 *$64 Question:* Smith, *Events Leading up to My Death*, p. 221.

228 **Survey, "They just sat":** Christopher H. Sterling and John M. Kittross: *Stay Tuned: A Concise History of American Broadcasting* (Belmont, California: Wadsworth Publishing, 1978), p. 293.

228 **Personnel, "that CBS hires correspondents":** *The New Yorker*, December 26, 1953, p. 36.

229 **Paley's ownership of CBS:** Smith, *In All His Glory*, p. 147, 319.

230 **Murrow appointed to CBS board:** Sperber, Murrow: *His Life and Times*, p. 326.

230 **In the 1984 presidential campaign, CBS reporter Leslie Stahl:** James Fallows, *Breaking the News: How the Media Undermine American Democracy* (New York: Pantheon, 1996), p. 62.

231 **Murrow heads USIA:** Kendrick, *Prime Time*, p. 456.

231 **Murrow's death:** Kendrick, *Prime Time*, p. 512.

231 **Murrow to Korea, 1951:** *The New Yorker*, December 26, 1953, p. 28.

231 **Colleague, "all wound up" and "I think that":** *The New Yorker*, December 26, 1953, p. 28.

234 **Sevareid, "We were like a young band of brothers in those early radio days":** farewell commentary, *CBS Evening News*, November 10, 1977.

Bibliography

Books

Barnouw, Erik. *A Tower in Babel*. New York: Oxford University Press, 1966.

———. *The Golden Web*. New York: Oxford University Press, 1968.

Bliss, Edward Jr., ed. *In Search of Light: The Broadcasts of Edward R. Murrow, 1938–1961*. New York: Alfred A. Knopf, 1967. A valuable annotated compilation of some of Murrow's greatest broadcasts from radio and televsion.

Brown, Cecil. *From Suez to Singapore*. New York: Random House, 1942.

Cloud, Stanley and Lynne Olson. *The Murrow Boys: Pioneers on the Front Lines of Broadcast Journalism*. Houghton Mifflin, 1996. The most comprehensive text on the Murrow Boys' lives and careers from before the war to the passing of Sevareid; very readable, highly opinionated, the book's journalist-authors are very critical of the current state of broadcast journalism.

Current Biography, 1942. H.W. Wilson Company.

Current Biography, 1943. H.W. Wilson Company.

Dunning, John. *On the Air: The Encyclopedia of Old-Time Radio*. New York: Oxford University Press, 1998.

Jenkins, Roy. *Churchill: A Biography*. New York: Farrar, Straus & Giroux, 2001.

Kaltenborn, H.V. *Fifty Fabulous Years*. New York: G.P. Putnam's Sons, 1950.

Keegan, John. *The Second World War*. New York: Penguin Books, 1989.

Kendrick, Alexander. *Prime Time: The Life of Edward Murrow*. Boston: Little, Brown & Company, 1969. One of three major Murrow biographies; Kendrick was one of Murrow's boys after the war; *Prime Time* focuses on Murrow's postwar career.

Knightley, Philip. *The First Casualty*. New York: Harcourt Brace Jovanovich, 1975.

Lackmann, Ron. *The Encyclopedia of American Radio: An A–Z Guide to Radio from Jack Benny to Howard Stern*. 2nd ed. New York: Checkmark Books, 2000.

LeSueur, Larry. *Twelve Months That Changed the World*. New York: Alfred A. Knopf, 1943.

Library of America. *Reporting World War II, Part One: American Journalism 1938–1944*. New York: Literary Classics of the United States, 1995.

———. *Reporting World War II, Part Two: American Journalism 1944–1946*. New York: Literary Classics of the United States, 1995. The two volumes of *Reporting World War II* represent the best print and broadcast coverage of the war, from the Munich Conference to Hiroshima and its aftermath. Especially fine print reporting from Ernie Pyle, Dorothy Thompson, A.J. Liebling, Margaret Bourke-White, Homer Bigart, as well as Ernest Hemingway and John Steinbeck.

McKens, Joseph R., ed. *Biographical Dictionary of American Journalism*. New York: Greenwood Press, 1989.

Miller, Donald L. *The Story of World War II*. New York: Simon & Schuster, 2001.

Murrow, Edward R. *"This Is London"*. New York: Simon & Schuster, 1941. Murrow's London broadcasts through the fall of 1940.

Nachman, Gerald. *Raised on Radio*. Berkley: University of California Press, 2001.

Paley, William S. *As It Happened*. New York: Doubleday & Company, 1979.

Persico, Joseph E. *Edward R. Murrow: An American Original*. New York: McGraw-Hill, 1988. The best of the Murrow biographies. Beautifully written, with the clearest insight into Murrow the man.

Rock: William R. *Appeasement on Trial*. Archon Books, 1966.

———. *British Appeasement in the 1930s*. New York: W.W. Norton & Company, 1977.

Rowse, A.L. *Appeasement*. New York: W.W. Norton & Company, 1961.

Schorr, Daniel. *Staying Tuned: A Life in Journalism*. New York: Washington Square Press, 2002.

Schroth, Raymond A. *The American Journey of Eric Sevareid*. South Royalton, Vermont: Steerforth Press, 1995.

Sevareid, Eric *Not So Wild a Dream*: Atheneum, 1978.

Shirer, William L. *Berlin Diary: The Journal of a Foreign Correspondent, 1934–1941*. New York: Alfred A. Knopf, 1941.

———. *The Rise and Fall of the Third Reich: A History of Nazi Germany*. New York: Simon & Schuster, 1960.

———. *"This Is Berlin": Radio Broadcasts from Nazi Germany*. Woodstock, New York: The Overlook Press, 1999.

———. *Twentieth Century Journey: A Memoir of the Life and Times: The Start, 1904–1930*. Boston: Little, Brown & Company, 1976.

———. *Twentieth Century Journey: A Memoir of the Life and Times: Vol. II, The Nightmare Years, 1930–1940*. Boston: Little, Brown & Company, 1984.

Smith, Howard K. *Events Leading up to My Death*. New York: St. Martin's Press, 1996.

———. *Last Train from Berlin*. New York: Alfred A. Knopf, 1942.

Smith, Sally Bedell. *In All His Glory: The Life of William S. Paley*. New York: Simon & Schuster, 1990.

Sperber, Ann M. *Murrow: His Life and Times*. New York: Freundlich Books, 1986. An excellent biography of Murrow, with especially detailed accounts of his early career. More information, but not as accessible as the Persico biography.

Stephens, Mitchell. *The Rise of the Image the Fall of the Word*. New York: Oxford University Press, 1998.

Taylor, Telford. *The Breaking Wave*: Weidenfeld and Nicolson, 1967.

Newspapers, Magazines, and Other Publications

Brown, Cecil. "Sinkings of the Repulse and Prince of Wales: a Blow-by-Blow Account." *Newsweek*: December 22, 1941, p. 18.

"Burma Shave" *Newsweek*: August 23, 1943, p. 80. An account of Sevareid in Burma.

"Collingwood's Beats." *Newsweek*: February 1, 1943, p. 60.

"Europe's Foes Unleash Forces After Slow Start of New War." *Newsweek*: September 11, 1939, p. 11.

Foster, Bob, "How Charles and I Liberated Paris": *San Francisco Today*, South San Francisco, California, September 4, 1982.

Ingersoll, Ralph: "Bringing the War News to America." *PM*, November 27, 1940.

Jenkins, Burris Jr. "'This Is London.'" *New York Journal and American*, March 24, 1941, p. 6.

"Keynote for Americas Sounded by FDR's Atlantic Challenge." *Newsweek*: June 9, 1941, p. 13.

Landry, Robert J. "Edward R. Murrow." *Scribner's Magazine*, December 1938, p. 7.

MacLeish, Archibald, William S. Paley, and Edward R. Murrow. "In honor of a man and an ideal...Three Talks on Freedom." Publication of remarks made at the Waldorf-Astoria, December 2, 1941. Edward R. Murrow papers, Library of Congress, Washington, D.C.

"Oscars of the Air." *Time*. April 5, 1943, p. 43.

"Reporter, in Bomber, Tells What Berlin Raid Is Like." United Press. December 10, 1943.

"Sermonets and Stoicism." *Time*. August 30, 1976, p. 69. A review of Eric Sevareid's *Not So Wild a Dream*.

Sevareid, Eric: "The Price We Pay in Italy." *New Republic*, December 9, 1944, p. 713.

Shirer, William L., Thomas B. Grandin, and Edward R. Murrow. "The Censor in Three Capitals," *The Living Age*, November 1939, p. 220.

Wertenbaker, Charles: "The World on His Back." *The New Yorker*, December 26, 1953, p. 28.

Unpublished Manuscripts

Murrow, Edward R. "Edward R. Murrow in Los Angeles." Radio script, KNX. January 14, 1945. Edward R. Murrow collection, Alden Library, Ohio University, Athens, Ohio.

Patterson, Mary Marvin Breckinridge. "Broadcasting from Europe to America, 1939–1940. Talk given to the Boston University School of Journalism, Boston, 1976. Edward R. Murrow collection, Alden Library, Ohio University, Athens, Ohio.

———. "Notes for a Book [never written]." 12 pp. manuscript. Edward R. Murrow collection, Alden Library, Ohio University, Athens, Ohio.

Sevareid, Eric. (Untitled, undated radio script; subject "War aims," ca. 1943). Eric Sevareid papers, Library of Congress, Washington, D.C.

White, Paul. "Covering a War for Radio," 19 pp. report; [undated, ca. 1941]. Eric Sevareid papers, Library of Congress, Washington, D.C.

Letters

Farrar, Edith, to Sevareid. Chicago, Illinois, September 1942 (with September 22, 1942 reply from Sevareid). Eric Sevareid papers, Library of Congress, Washington, D.C.

Field, Katharine W., to Sevareid. Saranac Lake, New York, February 26, 1943. Eric Sevareid papers, Library of Congress, Washington, D.C.

Johnston, Ann, to Sevareid. Queen's Village, September 17, 1942. Eric Sevareid papers, Library of Congress, Washington, D.C.

Miller, George, to Eric Sevareid. November 18, 1940. Eric Sevareid papers, Library of Congress, Washington, D.C. On enlistment.

Murrow, Edward R., to Sevareid. August 16, 1939. Eric Sevareid papers, Library of Congress, Washington, D.C.

Murrow to Sevareid. August 26, 1942. Eric Sevareid papers, Library of Congress, Washington, D.C.

Murrow to Sevareid. January 25, 1943. Eric Sevareid papers, Library of Congress, Washington, D.C.

Pope, A.S., to Sevareid. Ventura, California, September 20, 1942. Eric Sevareid papers, Library of Congress, Washington, D.C.

Romer, Harry, to Sevareid. New York City, November 5, 1940. Eric Sevareid papers, Library of Congress, Washington, D.C. On 1940 election.

Sevareid to Robert E. Sherwood. February 19, 1941. Eric Sevareid papers, Library of Congress, Washington, D.C. About possible play.

Sevareid to Paul R. White. July 1941, 7 pp. Eric Sevareid papers, Library of Congress, Washington, D.C. Letter on broadcast time for isolationists.

Sevareid to Murrow. July 20, 1942. Eric Sevareid papers, Library of Congress, Washington, D.C.

Sevareid to William Francis. Velva, North Dakota, July 31, 1942. Eric Sevareid papers, Library of Congress, Washington, D.C.

Sullivan, Edmund, to Sevareid, East Rockaway, New York, September 20, 1942. Eric Sevareid papers, Library of Congress, Washington, D.C.

Waldo, Hal, to Sevareid. Auburn, California, November 23, 1942. Eric Sevareid papers, Library of Congress, Washington, D.C. On Darlan.

White, Paul R., to CBS European correspondents, May 25, 1941. Eric Sevareid papers, Library of Congress, Washington, D.C.

White to Sevareid. July 15, 1941. Eric Sevareid papers, Library of Congress, Washington, D.C. On censorship.

White to Murrow, December 6, 1943. Eric Sevareid papers, Library of Congress, Washington, D.C. White urging Murrow to stay out of bombers.

Credits

Photographs

Photographs on the following pages courtesy of Corbis Images: 5, 8, 15, 20, 31, 34, 41, 43, 45, 49, 52, 55, 67, 70, 76, 77, 83, 90, 93, 96, 100, 104, 108, 109, 121, 124, 131, 135, 148, 153, 155, 162, 165, 167, 175, 183, 185, 191, 195, 196, 199, 201, 207, 209, 212, 213, 214, 220, 225. Photographs courtesy of Historical Photograph Collections, Washington State University Libraries: 1, 23, 26, 63, 87, 115, 142, 159, 229, 232. Photographs courtesy of CBS: 72, 79, 82, 137, 145, 171, 177. Photographs courtesy of AP/Wide World Photos: 84, 128, 187. Photographs courtesy of the estate of Mary Marvin Breckinridge Patterson: 61, 65.

Audio

All CBS broadcasts courtesy of CBS News Archives/BBC Worldwide.

Dan Rather narration recorded at CBS studios, New York.

Archival recordings used by arrangement with the National Archives at College Park, Maryland, Motion Pictures, Sound, and Video Research Center. Digital copies of archival recordings made by Cutting Corporation and Michael Dolan. Research of the archival recordings was conducted by Alex Lubertozzi and Mark Bernstein; initial editing and restoration done by Alex Lubertozzi; final editing and engineering of archival audio and narration done by John Larson, Larson Recording, Chicago, Illinois.

Text

The texts of the CBS News broadcasts included in this book are published by permission of CBS News Archives/BBC Worldwide.

Index

Acknowledgments

THIS BOOK AND audio CD would not have been possible without the assistance, cooperation, and enthusiasm of many people. First and foremost, we wish to thank CBS for permitting us to use the actual broadcasts of Murrow, Shirer, Sevareid, Grandin, Breckinridge, LeSueur, Brown, Collingwood, Smith, Burdett, Downs, and Hottelet as an integral part of this book. We are also grateful to CBS for permitting us to use their facilities to record Dan Rather's wonderful narration. Toni Gavin at CBS News Archives, as well as Jeffrey Carroll and Nelda Gill at BBC Worldwide (who license the CBS News archive), deserve many thanks for the help they rendered to us.

We would like to thank Dan Rather for so kindly contributing his considerable talents and love of this subject to our book, and to his assistant, Eric Wybenga, and agent, Bill Adler, who helped to make it happen.

Without the help of the staff of the Motion Pictures, Sound, and Video Research Center of the National Archives at College Park, Maryland, particularly Charles De Arman, this project would not have been possible. Many thanks are due for their kind help and patience. Michael Dolan, who made recordings of many of the archival broadcasts and contributed his knowledge of these archival holdings, is also deserving of our gratitude.

For many of the letters, correspondence, and other records used in the research of the text of this book, we would like to thank the Madison Building manuscript room of the Library of Congress, Washington, D.C., and to the State Historical Society of Wisconsin in Madison.

We would also like to express our sincere thanks to Priscilla Becker, assistant to the late Mary Marvin Breckinridge Patterson; John Larson, who contributed his engineering talents to the audio CD; editors Hillel Black, Peter Lynch, and Todd Stocke; editorial interns Heidi Bell, Sarah Brittin, Emily Craighead, Bill Osterman, and John Venecek; designer Taylor Poole; Sourcebooks publisher Dominique Raccah; and everyone at Sourcebooks who helped make this book a reality.

About the Authors

MARK BERNSTEIN is a Chicago native who writes on history and biography. He is the author of *Grand Eccentrics*, a group biography of such turn-of-the-century inventors and entrepreneurs as Charles Kettering, the Wright Brothers, and NCR founder John H. Patterson; *New Bremen*, a history of a small Ohio town; and *Gentleman Amateurs*, a photo book marking the Wright Brothers' centennial of flight, for which he contributed the text. His magazine work has appeared in *Smithsonian*, *American Heritage of Invention & Technology*, and elsewhere. He was for many years a contributing editor of *OHIO* magazine. He lives in Yellow Springs, Ohio.

ALEX LUBERTOZZI was born in Chicago and educated at the University of Illinois. He has been a writer and editor for more than ten years, and is the coauthor of *The Complete War of the Worlds*, about the infamous panic broadcast and the book that inspired it. He has written articles for *Screen, Small Press*, and was a contributing editor for the twentysomething, pop-culture 'zine, *Pure*. Since 2001, he has been the editorial manager of Sourcebooks MediaFusion. He lives in Oak Park, Illinois, with his wife, Helen Martch.

About the Narrator

DAN RATHER has been anchor and managing editor of the *CBS Evening News* since 1981. Born and raised in Wharton, Texas, he grew up listening to and admiring the radio broadcasts of Edward R. Murrow, Eric Sevareid, and the other Murrow Boys. He graduated from Sam Houston State Teachers College with a degree in journalism.

In 1962, he joined CBS and has covered the civil rights movement, the wars in Vietnam, Afghanistan, the Persian Gulf, and Yugoslavia, and on November 22, 1963, in Dallas, he broke the news of the death of President John F. Kennedy. He has served as a CBS News bureau chief in London and Saigon, a correspondent for *60 Minutes, 60 Minutes II*, and *48 Hours*. On the radio, *Dan Rather Reporting* is his weekday broadcast of news and analysis, which has run on the CBS Radio Network since 1981.

Rather has received numerous Emmy Awards, the Peabody Award, and citations from critical, scholarly, professional, and charitable organizations. He is the author of *The American Dream, Deadlines & Datelines, I Remember*, and *The Camera Never Blinks*. He also writes a weekly newspaper column and speaks frequently on journalistic ethics.